"*The PTSD Workbook* is an outstanding aid to those recovering from exposure to traumatic life events and the symptoms of post-traumatic stress disorder (PTSD). For use while in psychotherapy or by itself, this workbook provides an important guideline and template for moving forward with life. Derived from considerable clinical experience and up-to-date with recent research on recovery, *The PTSD Workbook* is an invaluable addition to the growing number of clinical tools to improve resiliency and enhance healthy outcomes."

—**Terence M. Keane, PhD**, associate chief of staff for research and development at the VA Boston Healthcare System, director of the behavioral science division of the National Center for PTSD, and professor of psychiatry and assistant dean of research at the Boston University School of Medicine

"This is a treasure trove of a book filled with up-to-date information on trauma, with the best collection of self-help methods in the field. It is easy to understand, and will be a resource for all individuals who are suffering from the effects of traumatic events, as well as for professionals."

—**Atle Dyregrov, PhD**, clinical and research psychologist, and head of professional issues at the Center for Crisis Psychology in Bergen, Norway; professor of clinical psychology at the University of Bergen, Norway; author of *Disaster Psychology*, *Children in War*, *Grief in Children*, and *Supporting Traumatized Children and Teenagers*; founding member of the European Society for Traumatic Stress Studies; and chair of the Children and War Foundation

"This update of *The PTSD Workbook* nicely reflects the authors' sensitive understanding of psychological trauma and resilience. It provides individuals suffering from post-traumatic stress disorder (PTSD) and their professional helpers with an impressive compendium of self-help and therapeutic techniques. Each of its twelve chapters is full of easy-to-use exercises that allow readers to decide which techniques are most suited to their individual situation. Anyone with a personal experience of, or exposure to, traumatic events will learn something useful from an encounter with this excellent work."

—**Joseph H. Albeck, MD**, clinical associate in the department of psychiatry at McLean Hospital in Belmont, MA; Chairman (Emeritus) for the Intergenerational Transmission of Trauma and Resilience Special Interest Group of the International Society for Traumatic Stress Studies (ISTSS); and cofounder of the New England Holocaust Memorial

"This is an extremely helpful book for trauma victims and facilitators, but also for you and me, to own and look into it daily."

—**Hédi Fried**, psychologist, writer, teacher, Holocaust survivor, author of *The Road to Auschwitz*, and winner of the 2015 Public Advocacy Award from the International Society for Traumatic Stress Studies (ISTSS)

THE PTSD WORKBOOK

THIRD EDITION

Simple, Effective Techniques
for Overcoming
Traumatic Stress Symptoms

MARY BETH WILLIAMS, PhD, LCSW, CTS
SOILI POIJULA, PhD

New Harbinger Publications, Inc.

Distributed in Canada by Raincoast Books.

Elements from *The Body Remembers: The Psychophysiology of Trauma and Trauma Treatment* by Babette Rothschild. Copyright © 2000 by Babette Rothschild. Used by permission of W. W. Norton & Company, Inc.

"Assessing Your Self-Criticism," "Using Self-Compassion Phrases," and "Fostering Self-Compassion" adapted from SELF-COMPASSION: STOP BEATING YOURSELF UP AND LEAVE INSECURITY BEHIND by Kristin Neff, copyright © 2011, published by HarperCollins Publishers. Used by permission of author.

Copyright © 2016 by Mary Beth Williams and Soili Poijula
New Harbinger Publications, Inc.
5674 Shattuck Avenue
Oakland, CA 94609
www.newharbinger.com

Cover design by Amy Shoup; Edited by Brady Kahn;
Acquired by Catharine Meyers; Text design by Tracy Marie Carlson

Library of Congress Cataloging-in-Publication Data on file

Printed in the United States of America

21 20 19

10 9 8 7

One never knows the curves that life brings. In the second edition, I dedicated this book to my children, never imagining that January 2014 would bring the unexpected death of my son Cary. This revised edition is dedicated to him and his strong will to live.

—MBW

I would like to dedicate this book to my mother, Maria, a war orphan herself, and the mother of mothers.

—SP

This book is also dedicated to survivors throughout the world. It is also dedicated to all the helping professionals, members of the military, law enforcement officers, and fire, rescue, and EMT personnel who serve in spite of the challenges, danger of compassion fatigue, and certainty of impact of the work on their own lives, including potential loss of life.

—MBW and SP

Contents

Introduction

As the third edition of this workbook goes to print, subsequent anniversaries of 9/11 have come and gone. New terrorist groups, even more brutal, have come to the forefront. Security checks and rechecks continue to be a way of life: take off your shoes and put them in the container, take all metal out of your pockets, and hold up your arms over your head for the X-ray version of a strip search.

In spite of preventive efforts and best practices such as Resilience Training or Comprehensive Soldier Fitness education for those going into combat, and in spite of increased emphasis on resilience and post-traumatic growth, thousands upon thousands of young men and women have been wounded in many ways through repeated deployments, exposure to guerilla-type warfare, blasts from improvised explosive devices (IEDs) that have led to amputations and traumatic brain injuries, and other war-related traumatic events.

The US Department of Veterans Affairs (also known as the Veterans Administration, or VA) is overwhelmed with claims from veterans of past wars, particularly Vietnam veterans reaching retirement age. Now that their productive work lives are winding down, these veterans are finding that their previously effective avoidance mechanisms are no longer keeping away the memories of the past. They also are coming face-to-face with mortality as the effects of Agent Orange, dormant for decades, invade their bodies in the form of type 2 diabetes, prostate cancer, and many other VA-accepted illnesses and diseases. Add to these veterans others from Desert Storm, OEF, OIF, and other military operations, and the wait time to process an initial claim may run eighteen months or so; if veterans dispute the rating they receive, it may take another eighteen months to two years to get reconsideration.

In the years since the first edition of this book was published in 2002, tragedies and disasters have continued to plague the world. The Virginia Tech shooting in 2007 was the deadliest massacre by a single perpetrator in US history. The Aurora, Colorado, shooting on July 20, 2012, had seventy American victims, twelve of whom died. The Newtown, Connecticut, shooting on December 14, 2012, left twenty children and six adult staff members of the elementary school dead, as well as the shooter's mother and the shooter himself, who died from a self-inflicted injury. The terrorist bombing at the end of the Boston Marathon a few months later reminded Americans again that we are not totally safe in any setting.

Tragic school shootings with many victims have twice occurred in Finland and in Germany as well. Tuija Turunen's excellent doctoral dissertation (2014) focusing on the Jokela school shootings described how that community's outpouring of support for relatives and coworkers of victims could serve as a model of ongoing psychosocial support. This model ought to be adopted by American response teams and crisis intervention professionals.

Alviina Alameta was a fifteen-year-old schoolgirl in Jokela who had to hide from the bullets and run for her life. She survived, but she lost her trust in other people; in her mind, anyone could turn out to be a killer. She had nightmares; loud sounds frightened her. She was afraid that danger was around every corner. She lived in a haze for half a year. Memories from that period of time are shaky. She shared her grief with schoolmates and mental health professionals. That grief withdrew slowly.

Seven years later, as a student at a Finnish university, Alviina started to express her thoughts and feelings through the written word. Her text became a book. She wanted to understand why the shooter, a quiet boy, grabbed a weapon and did what he did. She interviewed researchers, mental health experts, the shooter's family members, relatives (of the deceased), teachers, and schoolmates. She listened to the same music and read the same literature as the shooter (Nietzsche and Plato) and contacted the shooter's Internet acquaintances. She eventually formed a different kind of picture of the shooter, a picture of a sensitive listener and a true friend. "There are many sides in all of us; no one is completely a monster," Alviina concluded.

Dutch documentarist Alexander Day learned of Alviina's book and proposed making a film on school shootings. The product of their collaborative work is *Pekka—Inside the Mind of a School Shooter*. It was presented to audiences for the first time in Finland in January 2015. Alviina's story of survival is an example of resilience, an active coping style, and also of how much energy and hard work it may take to produce something good from something evil.

In Finland's neighboring country of Norway, the worst peacetime atrocity involving children occurred in July 2011. These children were caught in the horror of Utoya Island at a children's camp when a Norwegian extremist murdered 77 and injured over 200. How did the nation react? They answered hatred with love. More than 150,000 Norwegians gathered in Oslo carrying roses to show their support for the people who were slain in the massacre. This "Rose March," the largest peacetime solidarity rally, was led by then-Norwegian prime minister Jens Stoltenberg, who said, "Evil can kill a human being but never defeat a people." Atrocities often are followed by caring: numerous interventions and research projects are instituted by various agencies, organizations, and universities to help survivors lessen the impact of traumatic events.

At the 2014 annual meeting of the International Society for Traumatic Stress Studies, psychologists Atle and Kari Dyregrov presented their work with surviving victims and family members of the deceased victims of the thirty-two-year-old man who went to the youth camp and opened fire. Social media had exposed families and friends of the victims to the horror of that July 22, 2012, day. Again, the use of extensive social support and efforts to help people cope positively with their tragedies are the core of Norway's proactive model. That model includes systematic follow-up by helpers for each family. The model also provided outreach to all victims including schoolmates and members of the wider community.

The Finnish and Norwegian events struck home for my coauthor Soili Poijula, who lives in Oulu, Finland, and is a psychologist specializing in the treatment of trauma. She got the news of the first school shooting while she was sipping coffee. As she scanned the Internet, she saw a headline announcing the Hyvinkää shooting. She wrote to me about the event, saying it occurred "after a long, dark, and cold Finnish winter, on a beautiful, sunny Saturday just one week before the summer school holiday. Again, a group of survivors and their loved ones, and the loved ones of the victims, were deeply hurt and forced to start on a path toward recovery."

She described conditions in Finland, a small country with a population of five million, afflicted with mass killings beginning in 2002, when a young man carried a self-made bomb in his backpack into the Myyrmanni shopping center, where it exploded, killing seven people and wounding many more. "Talking is silver, but silence is golden" is an old Finnish saying that typifies Finland, an entire nation silent about World War II traumas: losses of soldiers, families, and a whole nation (Karelia). Soili continued, "We still have the World War II generation of veterans, widows, orphans, war children (over 70,000 children were sent to Denmark and Sweden during the war), and Karelian immigrants. As a pioneer of psychotraumatology in Finland, I have seen how we, as a nation, have started to learn a new principle of using the talking cure for surviving trauma." Extensive international research on psychological trauma and evidence-based treatments of PTSD provides a solid ground for knowledge and a method to help survivors recover.

Healing means expressing memories of traumatic experiences and constructing a personal narrative of past, present, and future. It also means defining the biopsychosocial effects, effects which live in a survivor's present experience. A research pioneer in this field, Bessel Van der Kolk (2014), states that, in order to heal, you need to "know what you know and feel what you feel." Recovery can lead to finding a meaning and to post-traumatic growth. This is true for all of us. After all, underneath, we are all the same.

You, the reader, will also benefit from learning self-help tools and from doing the exercises in this workbook. This will not only give you more potential to recover from your wounding but also help you learn self-compassion and strengthen your personal resilience.

Most people who have experienced traumatic events or who have been personal (or professional) witnesses to the pain of others don't develop what is currently called post-traumatic stress disorder (PTSD). However, the numbers who suffer from some degree of post-traumatic stress are unknown. The worlds of neurobiology and neurocardiology, as well as research into the biological impacts of stress on the body as a whole and on the nervous system in particular, have brought new insights into the mind-body connections and the impacts of trauma on all aspects of living.

Similar to the second edition, this workbook gives you, the reader, an opportunity to do more than just read its pages. You have the chance to complete numerous exercises that will give you personal insight into your symptoms, beliefs, behaviors, feelings, relationships, and inner biological functioning. If you are a veteran, we've added some new material that will help you heal (see chapter 10). Survivors of other traumatic events will also find these exercises and suggestions to be helpful. We've also expanded on the material describing the impacts of stress on the body and mind, giving some new suggestions on how to manage that stress and how to use integrative medicine (see chapter 9).

This workbook is designed to give you, the reader, the opportunity for greater insight into your personal PTSD symptoms, your beliefs, feelings, and coping strategies, both adaptive and nonadaptive. If you have used or even just browsed through either or both of the two previous editions, you may notice some big changes in this edition. Much of the material on complex PTSD has now been incorporated into workbook chapters that support and explain the newest definition of PTSD from the *Diagnostic and Statistical Manual of Mental Disorders* (DSM-5; American Psychiatric Association 2013). The goal, as before, is to make this workbook as effective as possible. This does not mean that we must throw the baby out with the bathwater and deny the existence of complex, early, often repetitive traumatic histories that change the character (and even biological) structure of their victims, however. There may still be instances when you may be diagnosed with that condition in spite of its absence from the newest diagnostic manual.

The authors of this book have extensive experience in this field and that experience has broadened over the past decades. We also have grown in our understanding of traumatic stress. We continue to be clinicians as well as educators, devoting many hours a week to helping individuals help themselves heal and grow. We recognize that traumatic events can function like bogs that can hold you down, immobilize you, trap you, and potentially pull you under. We believe that post-traumatic growth and resilience are worthwhile goals for your journey of healing. We hope that this book will help readers who are finding it for the first time, and that it will continue to help those who discovered the first or second edition and have used it over the past few years.

—Mary Beth Williams

1

A Look at Trauma

What is trauma? What does it mean to survive it? To work through it? How many times have you thought that life was understandable and was going along smoothly when something happened to change its entire course? One morning you wake up and the sun is shining or drizzle is falling around you; you feel great. Three hours later, nothing is the same. Maybe it is because of a conversation telling you of a tragedy. Maybe a car accident has killed someone you love. Maybe a tornado swoops down and changes everything. Everything. There you are, hanging on the edge of a precipice. What do you do? Do you quit? Do you run away? Do you decide you want to just die and not face it anymore? Do you even want to go on?

Prior to the occurrence of a traumatic event or events, there are generally certain basic assumptions that guide your life. You probably believe that the world is kind, that there is meaning to your life, and that things make sense. You believe that you are good and worthy of having good things happen to you (Janoff-Bulman 1992). Then trauma strikes. It seems as though you are no longer in control of what has happened around you. You're vulnerable and your world is no longer safe and secure. Furthermore, you can't make sense of what is left over. The meaning of life that you recognized just a short time before is gone. Now life is no longer fair and just.

The first step in dealing with trauma is to recognize its impact. A traumatic event has many possible impacts. It can affect your feelings, thoughts, relationships, behaviors, attitudes, dreams, and hopes. However, it also can be a way to find a new direction and purpose in life. The title of this book was originally *Slogging Beyond Trauma*. That title evokes a journey. To start that journey, read the following description and see if you can picture it in your mind.

Trauma Stories

You have experienced something terrible. Perhaps you were in a car crash and the car is a mass of tangled metal. Perhaps you have begun to deal with your history of child abuse and feel as if you are coming out of a cave of torture and pain. Perhaps you have been a refugee and have escaped a land of hurt and loss. Now you want to get on with your life. You know that across the bog that lies in front of you is a life that is more safe and secure, peaceful and calm. You also know both that no life is ever totally safe and that the only way to gain some sense of security is to walk across the bog.

You have a backpack full of things to help you on your journey to the other side; these things include the techniques in this book. The backpack is heavy, but you can't discard anything, because you don't know what you might need. You start on your journey, and shortly you realize that the bog is actually made of tar. As the sun begins to shine, the surface gets sticky and vapors begin to swim around your head. You get dizzy. You are thirsty. Each step is like pulling a weight.

What do you do? You remember all of the things you have with you. You have a water bottle with a spray mister. You have binoculars so that you can see the other side of the bog. You have a pair of hiking boots that will prevent you from sinking and getting stuck. You have a small oxygen bottle. You have a choice: you can turn around, going back to the world of trauma, or you can go on. Your trip may take time. You may be exhausted when you get to the other side. You may sweat and smell and feel as if you can never take another step. But you can go on. The closer you get to the edge of the tar bog, the more clearly you will see the trees and waterfalls on the other side. If you use what you have and what you've learned and will learn in this workbook, you will slog through, survive, and make it.

Defining Trauma

The word "trauma" is even more familiar now than when the second edition of this book was published. You have heard it on the radio, on the TV news, in conversations. The wars in Iraq and Afghanistan brought it to the local, hometown level, as sons and daughters have been seriously wounded or killed. Post-traumatic stress disorder (PTSD) is a label given to a set of symptoms set forth in the *Diagnostic and Statistical Manual of Mental Disorders* (*DSM-5*; American Psychiatric Association 2013), the clinical manual used by treatment providers to determine diagnoses.

A recent news article in *Time Magazine* on April 6, 2015, noted that as many as 500,000 US troops who fought in Iraq or Afghanistan, or both, during the last thirteen years have been diagnosed with PTSD. In spite of allotting $3 billion yearly to treat PTSD in veterans, the government often does not have the resources to provide adequate treatment (Thompson 2015). Combine those numbers with the ever-growing population of Vietnam veterans who are reaching retirement age, and whose minds and bodies are being literally attacked by memories of the war and by the ravaging impacts of exposure to Agent Orange.

"Trauma" may describe the effects of a massive earthquake that has killed thousands, a tornado in Alabama, a plane crash, a murder down the street, or even an unexpected death. You've seen the pictures and you've heard the stories about how people feel when they've been victimized by auto accidents, hurricanes, floods, tornadoes, assaults, robberies, rapes, plane crashes, school shootings, fires, abuse, and other catastrophic events and situations. A trauma represents an injury (physical or emotional) to you or to those you love or from witnessing injuries to others.

Now it has happened to you. Or perhaps it happened to you years ago and for an extended period of time. You are either the direct victim/survivor (it happened to you) or the secondary victim/survivor (it happened in your world or you were a bystander or observer) of a traumatic event. Or you may be someone who works with the victims/survivors of traumas but has not directly experienced a traumatic event. However, your exposure to awful events has impacted you significantly and you have compassion fatigue or secondary traumatic stress yourself (Figley 1995).

Reacting to Trauma

What happens when you experience a traumatic event or series of events? There are many reactions you might have. Initially, you may feel shock, terror, or a sense that what happened is unreal or surreal. You may feel numb, as if you've left your body (a phenomenon called *dissociation*). You may not even remember all the details (or any of the details) of what just happened. If you are a survivor of lifelong traumatic events, your reactions may be different. You may feel as if you have lived in a war zone your entire life; you're always watchful, always ready to be attacked or hurt at any moment. You may not even know who you are as a person. As Tedeschi, Park, and Calhoun (1998) write, stress can have complex aftereffects resulting in an enhancement of growth. Growth may occur as an increase in self-knowledge or as a way to find meaning that leads to taking positive actions.

Many factors impact how you react to a traumatic event. Your reaction to a traumatic event can be shaped by your age (younger people often react more significantly than older people); the amount of preparation time you had prior to the event (for example, several days' notice may be possible with a hurricane, while an earthquake has no forewarning); the amount of damage done to you (physically, emotionally, and spiritually) or to your property; the amount of death and devastation you witness; or the degree of responsibility you feel for causing or not preventing the event; and these are just a few of the factors that may be involved. Your willingness to seek help, counseling, or other types of intervention also can influence your recovery. If 37 percent of military personnel develop self-diagnosed PTSD after deployment in war (Taylor 2011), more than 60 percent do not, probably because they have greater resiliency (discussed in detail in chapter 10).

In fact, three major types of factors influence the development of post-traumatic stress disorder: *pre-event factors*, *event factors*, and *post-event factors*. PTSD is the best known of the long-term consequences of trauma. (This disorder will be described in detail shortly.) About 15 percent of people exposed to a traumatic event develop PTSD at some point in time; however, the incidence can be much higher, depending on the trauma. For example, percentages are usually higher for survivors or violent rapes or intrusive sexual abuse or for veterans who have experienced multiple deployments. No matter the event or why it happened, as you deal with the aftermath, your goal is to come through on the other side in some meaningful, resilient way.

Pre-event Factors

Although there are situations in which exposure to trauma is so great that these factors are less influential (e.g., surviving a major airplane disaster in which almost everyone dies), certain pre-trauma factors often influence how a person reacts to traumatic events. Among them are the following:

- previous exposure to severe adverse life events or trauma or childhood victimization, including neglect, emotional abuse, sexual abuse, physical abuse, or witnessing abuse

- earlier depression or anxiety that is not merely situational and that impacts brain chemistry; childhood emotional problems including prior traumatic exposure and prior mental illnesses

- ineffective coping skills

- family instability, including a history of parental psychiatric disorder, numerous childhood separations, economic problems, or family violence

- family history of antisocial or criminal behavior

- early substance abuse

- trouble with authority, even in childhood, including running away from home, school suspension, academic underachievement, delinquency, fighting, or truancy

- absence of social support to help out in bad times

- multiple early losses of people, possessions, or home

- gender, with women seeming to be about twice as likely as men to develop PTSD at some time in their lives

- age, with young adults under age twenty-five being more likely to develop the disorder (Friedman 2000)

- genetics, with members of some families apparently being less able to withstand trauma than members of other families (Meichenbaum 1994), and other people whose genetic makeup allows for a greater ability to endure or thrive in the face of crises or traumas

- less functional coping strategies (Briere and Scott 2015)

- post-traumatic dissociation including derealization or depersonalization (Sugar and Ford 2012)

- hyperreactive or dysfunctional nervous system (Southwick and Charney 2012)

Event Factors

There are also factors related to the victim during the event that contribute to the possibility of developing PTSD. These may include

- geographic nearness to the event

- level of exposure to the event, with greater exposure leading to a greater likelihood of developing PTSD

- the event's meaning to the victim

- having fewer protective adults in one's life if the traumas occurred as a child

- the presence of life threat (DiGrande et al. 2010)

- witnessing death, especially if grotesque (Bills et al. 2009)

- age, with those who are younger at the time of the event being more vulnerable

- being a victim of multiple traumatic incidents

- duration of the trauma

- the existence of an ongoing threat that the trauma will continue (e.g., as in war)

- being involved in an intentional, man-made traumatic event, the closer the relationship (e.g. caretaker), the more likely the impact

- witnessing or perpetrating an atrocity—a very brutal, shocking act (e.g., purposely killing women and children)

- experiencing dissociation during the trauma and after (American Psychiatric Association 2013)

- being a veteran, particularly if a veteran of combat and/or repeated deployments

- having an occupation that provides repeated exposure to potentially traumatic events

- being a victim of rape or politically motivated genocide (American Psychiatric Association 2013)

- not having a resilient style of coping

Post-event Factors

The final category of PTSD risk factors includes those that exist after the traumatic event. On a positive note, many of these factors promote growth and resilience if presented in a positive light. These factors may include

- not having good social support and not being seen as resilient

- being male rather than female

- having a poor sense of self-esteem

- not being able to do something about what happened

- indulging in self-pity while neglecting yourself (having a victim mentality)

- being passive rather than active—letting things happen to you

- being unable to find meaning in the suffering

- developing acute stress disorder (ASD), which occurs in a certain percentage of people who experience trauma (described more fully later in this chapter)

- having an immediate reaction (during the traumatic event or shortly after) that includes physiological arousal (high blood pressure, a startle reaction) and avoidant or numbing symptoms (Friedman 2000)

To learn more about these factors, you may want to read *A Clinical Handbook/Practical Therapist Manual for Assessing and Treating Adults with Post-traumatic Stress Disorder* (Meichenbaum 1994). Tennen and Affleck (1998) and McCrae (1992) believe that there may be personality traits that help a person cope with adversity. People who are high in extraversion (they seek out others) and openness, are conscientious in working toward goals, and have a sense of agreeableness (an ability to get along) are more likely to draw strength from adversity and trauma as a way to cope with what happened.

Other important factors that might impact how you react include having an *internal locus of control* (you are able to reward yourself for behavior and you believe that control of what happens lies with you, not with sources outside you); *self-efficacy* (a sense of confidence in your own coping ability); a sense of *coherence* (the recognition that even seriously traumatic events are understandable, manageable, meaningful); and hardiness, or strength (Antonovsky 1987; Kobasa 1982). You also may do better in coping with traumatic events if you are motivated to do so, if you have an optimistic attitude, if you have an active coping style, and if you've successfully resolved other crises.

EXERCISE: My Ability to Cope with Trauma

Check those of the following statements that you believe apply to you.

_____   I have a high degree of extraversion (I like to be with people).

_____   I am open to new experiences.

_____   I am conscientious in the work I do (I follow through).

_____   I am an agreeable person.

_____   I believe that my source of personal power lies within me.

_____   I am confident in my own abilities to cope with situations.

_____   I try to find meaning in what happens to me.

_____   I try to break down bad situations into manageable parts I can handle.

_____   I am motivated to solve the problems that occur in my life.

_____   I am generally an optimistic person—I see things more positively than negatively.

_____   I take control in situations whenever possible, or at least try to take control.

_____   I like a good challenge, and I rise to the occasion.

_____   I am committed to overcoming the bad things I have experienced in life.

_____   I have a good social support network—there are people I can turn to.

_____   I understand my life's circumstances and what I can and cannot do about them.

_____   I have faith.

_____   I have a sense of humor.

_____   I have a sense of hope.

_____   I like to try new things or look at things in new ways.

_____   I am open to how others feel.

_____   I am an action-oriented person—I would rather do something than sit back and let it be done to me.

_____   I actively try to structure my own life and make plans.

What do you observe about yourself from reading these statements?

_____

_____

How many of these items did you check? Do you notice any pattern of those you did or did not check?

_____

_____

The more you checked, the more likely you are to take action and to work through the trauma that happened to you.

Before you learn more about yourself and how you respond to traumatic events, it is important for you to have more information about the numerous possible reactions to trauma. The first of these is called a *normal stress response*. In times of stress, people react in a variety of ways: they may have physical reactions—their pulse may increase, they may sweat; they may have anxiety, fear, anger, or other emotional responses; they may shut down and freeze; they may go into a rage and try to fight; or they may run from the situation. These are all normal responses. Stress that is positive is called *eustress*. It could involve lifesaving or other positive reactions to an emergency situation; a eustress reaction would allow you to rescue yourself or someone else from danger. Negative stress is called *distress*. It's debilitating and may cause you to function poorly in a dangerous situation—or one that feels dangerous. Stress can impact your body, emotions, thoughts, and relationships. This book will deal with severe, disruptive distress reactions—specifically the reactions associated with post-traumatic stress disorder.

Acute Stress Disorder

If your reactions to the event(s) developed within the first few days or weeks after the traumatic incident, you may have developed what is known as acute stress disorder. In the *DSM-5* (American Psychiatric Association 2013), acute stress disorder has the following criteria:

The definition of the stressor has changed to include exposure to actual or threatened death that is unnatural, and may include severe domestic violence, serious injury, or sexual violations in these cases:

- You directly experienced the traumatic event(s).

- You directly witnessed the event as it occurred to others.

- You learn of the violent or accidental death of a family member or close friend, whether actual or threatened.

- You have repeated or extreme exposure to really bad details of the events (such as a police officer or first responder).

This criteria for exposure does not include exposure by electronic media, pictures, or television unless exposure is work related. At least nine of the following fourteen symptoms need to be present within thirty days after the event occurred.

Intrusive Symptoms

- recurrent, involuntary, distressing memories of the event(s)

- recurrent, distressing dreams

- dissociative reactions (e.g. flashbacks)

- intense or prolonged psychological distress or marked physiological reactions in response to internal or external cues symbolizing or resembling some part of the event(s)

Negative Mood

- persistent inability to experience positive emotions

Dissociative Symptoms

- altered sense of reality of your surroundings or self

- inability to remember an important aspect of the traumatic event

Avoidance Symptoms

- efforts to avoid distressing memories, thoughts, feelings about or closely associated with the traumatic event(s)

- efforts to avoid external reminders that lead to distressing memories, thoughts, or feelings about or closely associated with the event(s)

Arousal Symptoms

- sleep disturbance (falling asleep, staying asleep, restless sleep)

- irritable behavior and angry outbursts toward people or objects

- hypervigilance

- problems with concentration

- exaggerated startle response

The disturbance symptoms last from three days to one month after the trauma exposure; they cause clinically significant distress or impairment in social, occupational, or other areas of functioning; and the reaction is not due to physiological effects of a substance or other medical conditions.

Post-traumatic Stress Disorder

Jim is an Operation Enduring Freedom (OEF) veteran who was assigned to a tower at his army base. He watched the Afghan soldiers rape young male children who were hanging out around them hoping for food or candy. He was shot at by snipers and often saw smoke in the distance and heard the booms when vehicles hit IEDs. He recognized that the explosions meant that someone he knew might have been either hurt or killed. The most traumatic events occurred in the minefield across from the tower. The local soldiers would deliberately throw candy and food into the field in front of their tents. The children described above, not knowing that the field was mined, would run to get the food. When the buried mines went off, Jim saw the carnage that was left of the children's bodies. It wasn't safe for him or others to go out and retrieve the bodies, so they would remain there for some time.

Susan is a contractor who travels to other countries with a team to perform the auditing duties of her job in a charitable organization. One day, she and her fellow workers suddenly heard shouts and gunfire. They were herded downstairs to the basement. The local women couldn't even grab their traditional covering clothing and became hysterical because they would have been shot if they had gone out without it. Everyone started trying to call out on their cell phones to tell others what was going on, until someone yelled that the phones might cause an explosion to occur if the attackers were wearing explosives. Everyone hid in the corners, and the gunfire continued for a few minutes. When the all clear sounded, Susan was still terrified that she might die. She went upstairs and saw blood on the front step and front porch of the building. She was told that two men, dressed in traditional women's clothing and each with several pounds of explosives strapped to his body, had tried to enter. However, they couldn't read English and were trying to pull open a door that said, "Push." They were killed by gunfire as they tried to enter, preventing them from carrying out their attack. When Susan returned to the United States, she started experiencing anxiety, nightmares, and intrusive thoughts. She's become extremely fearful and doesn't want to ever travel again on a job. She's furious that, at the time of the attack, she had no protective training, clothing, or weapons available to her.

Jim and Susan both suffer from PTSD, and they are not alone. PTSD is now seen to be a relatively common diagnosis. General prevalence rates for American men and women are 3.6 percent and 9.7

percent, respectively (National Comorbidity Survey 2005). Rates are generally higher after conflicts (or war). PTSD is now recognized as more than a fear-based anxiety disorder.

Symptoms of PTSD

If your reaction to traumatic events persists for a period of time over one month in duration, or if it occurs at least six months after the event occurred, you may have developed post-traumatic stress disorder.

The following description of PTSD is adapted from the *DSM-5* (American Psychiatric Association 2013). This new definition has been changed to make PTSD more about what can develop after a sudden, serious threat to your own life or from exposure to the death of others or to a serious threat to their lives; this includes the experience of EMTs, firefighters, or police.

Under the new definition, the traumatizing event has to be catastrophic or severe, involving death or threatened death, serious injury, or sexual violence, and not a nonaccidental or extended medical condition or media exposure, other than in the line of duty (see categories A and H below). To be diagnosed, you must experience at least one of the five symptoms listed in category B; among those symptoms, flashbacks are now considered to be dissociative reactions that occur on a continuum. You must experience at least one of two symptoms of avoidance in category C. And perhaps most significantly, there is a new category of symptoms, category D, described in detail below. Finally, risk taking and self-destructive behaviors have been added to the list of arousal symptoms (category E), of which two or more are needed for a diagnosis. To be diagnosed with PTSD, your symptoms have to have lasted more than a month (category F).

The new definition of PTSD now includes many symptoms that fell under the heading of complex PTSD in the two former workbooks. Complex PTSD is no longer included as a separate diagnosis in the new *DSM-5* and therefore is no longer included in this workbook, except for a very short discussion about its continued use in some facilities.

The new definition says that PTSD has significantly distressed or impaired you in social, occupational, or other important areas of functioning (category G). Functional impairment is now used as an important delineating criteria for veterans seeking service–related compensation; functioning impacts need to be significant in a clinical evaluation, impacting and often significantly disturbing personal duties, work-expected duties, or social relationships (such as parenting and intimate relationships).

Let's take a closer look at this new definition of PTSD for adults, adolescents, and children over six years of age, as adapted from the *DSM-5* (American Psychiatric Association 2013).

A. You have been exposed to actual death, threatened death, serious injury, or sexual violence through one of the following:

  - direct experience/exposure

  - witnessing the events in person

- indirect exposure, learning about events happening to a close relative or friend (if exposure involves death, it must be violent or accidental)

- repeated or extreme exposure to aversive details of traumatic events as part of your line of work (police, EMTs), not through electronic media, TV, or pictures/movies, unless work related

B. Your intrusive symptoms include one or more of the following:

- recurrent, involuntary, intrusive, and distressing memories; in children, possibly expressed through play

- recurrent and distressing dreams related to the traumatic event; in children, dream content may not be directly related to the event

- dissociative reactions (for example, flashbacks) as if events were recurring; in children possibly reenacted through play

- intense or prolonged psychological distress when exposed to internal or external cues symbolizing or resembling some part of the event

- marked physiological reactions to internal or external cues symbolizing or resembling some part of the event

C. You persistently avoid stimuli associated with the event(s) afterward, and this avoidance takes the form of one or both of the following:

- avoiding distressing memories, thoughts, or feelings about the event

- avoiding or trying to avoid external reminders that lead to distressing memories, thoughts, or feelings

D. This new category looks at repetitive alterations in cognitions (thoughts) and moods (emotions) associated with the event(s) that begin or got worse after the events occurred. You experience two or more of the following symptoms:

- inability to remember important aspect of event(s), typically due to *dissociative amnesia*, which may occur only once or multiple times. (Note: This is *not* ordinary forgetting but is generally selective for an event or events, leads to some degree of functional impairment, and is not due to physiological conditions.)

- persistent, often distorted, exaggerated negative beliefs or expectations about yourself, others, and the world

- persistent negative cognitions (thoughts) about causes or consequences of the event(s), including persistent distorted blame of yourself, others, and the world

- persistent negative trauma-related emotional states (fear, horror, anger, guilt, shame)

- markedly lowered interest or participation in pre-trauma important activities

- feelings of detachment, alienation, or estrangement from others

- persistent inability to experience positive emotions (happiness, satisfaction, love) and less outward display or expression

E. Your arousal and reactivity symptoms that are associated with the event(s) include two or more of the following:

- irritable behavior and angry outbursts (without much provocation) expressed as verbal or physical aggression to people or objects

- reckless or self-destructive behaviors

- hypervigilance

- exaggerated startle response

- problems with concentration

- difficulty falling asleep, staying asleep, or having restless sleep

F. The duration of your symptoms is more than one month.

G. The PTSD disturbance causes clinically significant distress or impairment in social, occupational, or other important areas of functioning.

H. This disturbance is not due to the physiological effects of a substance or to medical conditions.

You may also be asked if you have responded to the stressor events by depersonalizing. *Depersonalization* describes a feeling of being detached from or outside yourself, observing your thoughts or body (like being in a dream), and feeling a sense of unreality.

This symptom includes, in actuality, several parts, including unreality of the self, perceptual alteration(s) of the self, emotional and/or physical numbing, and temporal distortions (American Psychiatric Association 2013).

You may have persistent or recurrent experiences of unreality of surroundings, which is known as *derealization*. These experiences have a feeling of unreality or detachment from the world or a lack of familiarity. You may feel as if you were "in a fog, dream, or bubble, or having a glass wall between you and the world around you" (American Psychiatric Association 2013, 303). The world itself may seem to be artificial, colorless, or lifeless. Derealization often includes visual distortions (blurriness, greater acuity, altered distances, wider or narrower visual fields), which can impact both interpersonal and occupational areas of life. You may also experience decreased emotionality, difficulties with focusing, and problems retaining information.

Are There Different Types of PTSD?

Terr (1994) has written about two distinct types of trauma: type I and type II. PTSD is more likely to be a reaction to experiencing or witnessing type I traumatic events, which are single, catastrophic, unanticipated experiences. A sexual assault, a serious car crash, and a natural disaster are all type I events. These type I events also can be called *critical incidents*. If you have experienced a type I trauma, you may have a detailed, clear memory of what happened. Your memories often remain alive unless you work through them. You may find yourself frequently looking for a way to explain what happened or a way you could have prevented what happened.

Roger Solomon (2001) writes that it is possible to describe such an incident in the following way:

1. *Here comes trouble.* (You become aware of a threatening situation.)

2. *Oh, shit!* (You become aware of your vulnerability; you may feel weak and not in control.)

3. *I've got to do something.* (You realize you have to act to survive or gain control over the situation; you acknowledge the reality of the danger. You make a transition from an internal focus on vulnerability to an external focus on danger. But if you focus solely on this danger, you tend to feel even weaker and more out of control.)

4. *I have to survive.* (You focus on the danger in terms of your ability to respond to it. You consciously or instinctively come up with a plan, start to react, and begin to feel more balanced and in control. It is more important to focus on this thought than on the previous one.)

5. *Here I go.* (This is your moment of commitment: you have the resolve to act, whether instinctual or planned; you mobilize tremendous strength; your mind becomes focused and clear and you have increased awareness and control. You act, often without thinking further.)

6. *Oh, shit!* (After the event is through and you've survived, it is normal to return to feelings of "Oh, shit!" Don't let yourself get stuck here. Give yourself credit for all that you do and have done.)

Consider the above description of type I trauma as you read next about what happened to Larry. Note that many traumatic events are complex, and you may cycle through some or all of the steps more than once during the course of the event.

Larry was having breakfast at a restaurant when a waitperson ran in and yelled, "Run, run. He's got a gun!" (steps 1 and 2). Larry did not even pick up his glasses, but took off across the restaurant, out through the lobby (where he saw a dead body), and down a hall (steps 3, 4, and 5). About ten others ran ahead of him. In the middle of the hall was a woman lying face down, terrified. Everyone, including Larry, either ran over or around her. Suddenly, Larry turned and went back to try to help her (step 3). She was a large woman, a dead weight, and would not move or help Larry help her. As Larry tried to pick her up, the shooter rounded the corner and was less than six feet away from Larry (step 2). Larry instinctually thought, "I want to live." He dropped the woman's arm and ran (steps 4 and 5). He did not turn around to look at the shooter's eyes for fear that the connection between them would make him the next victim. Seconds later, Larry heard two shots. He thought one was for him, but both were for the woman—the killer shot her twice in the head. Larry kept running and escaped death by mere seconds (step 6).

You may check to see if you may have PTSD by taking the short instrument included here called the PCL-5. The PCL-5 is the first rather short self-report instrument that has been modified from the PCL-M to fit the symptoms of the new *DSM-5* definition of PTSD and the impact of those symptoms (Weathers et al. 2013).

EXERCISE: **PCL-5**

Instructions: Below is a list of problems that people sometimes have in response to a very stressful experience. Please read each problem carefully and then circle the number to the right to indicate how much you have been bothered by that problem in the last month. On this scale of 0 to 4, a 0 means not at all, 1 means a little bit, 2 means moderately, 3 means quite a bit, and 4 means extremely bothered.

In the past month how much were you bothered by:	Not at all	A little bit	Moderately	Quite a bit	Extremely
1. Repeated, disturbing, and unwanted memories of the stressful experience?	0	1	2	3	4
2. Repeated, disturbing dreams of the stressful experience?	0	1	2	3	4
3. Suddenly feeling or acting as if the stressful experience were actually happening again (*as if you were actually back there reliving it*)?	0	1	2	3	4
4. Feeling very upset when something reminded you of the stressful experience?	0	1	2	3	4
5. Having strong physical reactions when something reminded you of the stressful experience (*for example, heart pounding, trouble breathing, sweating*)?	0	1	2	3	4

	0	1	2	3	4
6. Avoiding memories, thoughts, or feelings related to the stressful experience?	0	1	2	3	4
7. Avoiding external reminders of the stressful experience (for example, people, places, conversations, activities, objects, or situations)?	0	1	2	3	4
8. Trouble remembering important parts of the stressful experience?	0	1	2	3	4
9. Having strong negative beliefs about yourself, other people, or the world (for example, having thoughts such as: I am bad, there is something seriously wrong with me, no one can be trusted, the world is completely dangerous)?	0	1	2	3	4
10. Blaming yourself or someone else for the stressful experience or what happened after it?	0	1	2	3	4
11. Having strong negative feelings such as fear, horror, anger, guilt, or shame?	0	1	2	3	4
12. Loss of interest in activities that you used to enjoy?	0	1	2	3	4
13. Feeling distant or cut off from other people?	0	1	2	3	4
14. Trouble experiencing positive feelings (for example, being unable to feel happiness or have loving feelings for people close to you)?	0	1	2	3	4
15. Irritable behavior, angry outbursts, or acting aggressively?	0	1	2	3	4
16. Taking too many risks or doing things that could cause you harm?	0	1	2	3	4
17. Being "superalert" or watchful or on guard?	0	1	2	3	4
18. Feeling jumpy or easily startled?	0	1	2	3	4
19. Having difficulty concentrating?	0	1	2	3	4
20. Trouble falling or staying asleep?	0	1	2	3	4

(adapted from Weathers et al. 2013)

Add up your score. A score of 38 or higher is indicative of PTSD. You can use this instrument for each of your significant traumatic events or groups of traumatic events.

The previous edition of this workbook included a diagnostic description that could apply to what happened to people who experienced prolonged, repeated, extensive exposure to traumatic events. Terr (1994) was one of the first people to describe some of the reactions to these types of experiences, in her discussion of type II traumatic events. This disorder, also described by Judy Herman (1992), has also been called *complex PTSD* or *disorders of extreme stress not otherwise specified* (DESNOS). Help for symptoms of complex PTSD was included in previous editions. However, the changes in diagnosis now used to identify PTSD include many of the symptom categories of complex PTSD.

Many doctors and therapists still see complex PTSD as a valuable description of one type of PTSD reaction. Some hope this description will be included in future editions of the diagnostic manual. You are more likely to experience symptoms of complex PTSD if your traumatization occurred early in your life, was prolonged, and was interpersonal.

If you have been diagnosed in the past with complex PTSD, you may have some or all of these personality issues:

- You may have problems with your ability to regulate emotions, especially anger.

- You may find it hard to "stay present" without becoming amnesic (unable to remember), dissociative (spaced out), depersonalized, or preoccupied with the trauma.

- You may not see yourself as a functioning individual who can avoid feeling helpless, shameful, guilty, stigmatized, alone, special, or full of self-blame.

- You may not have the ability to separate yourself from your abuser or perpetrator without being preoccupied with revenge, feeling gratitude, or accepting the perpetrator's introjects as true. (*Introjects* are someone else's beliefs that you take into your head as your own and then believe.)

- You may not have the ability to have positive, healthy relationships with others without being isolated, withdrawing, being extremely distrustful, failing repeatedly to protect yourself, or constantly searching for someone to rescue you (or for someone you can rescue).

- You may not have the ability to find meaning in your life and maintain faith, hopefulness, and a sense of the future, without feeling despair and hopelessness (Meichenbaum 1994).

The majority of these, with the exception of dealing with the perpetrator, are now covered in the new definition of PTSD. This short description of complex PTSD is included to show you that not everyone views traumatic reactions in the same way and that the symptoms you have may be described in different ways. Even though your diagnosis of PTSD will be limited by the new *DSM-5* definition (often as a requirement by insurance companies), complex PTSD is still another way to describe how trauma can change your entire being from the time you were a small child and had many traumatic events occur to you.

Remembering Trauma

You have various types of memory. You have *short-term memory* (items remembered quickly, such as a phone number, and then lost just as quickly), *long-term memory* (permanently stored information), *explicit* or *declarative memory* (facts, concepts, and ideas, including your ability to recall the traumatic event in a cohesive way), and *implicit* or *nondeclarative memory* (acts, descriptions, or operations based on thought and automatic internal states). The traumatic events that have happened to you or to those you know seem to be recorded more easily in implicit memory (Rothschild 2000). Implicit memory includes behavior that you learn through *conditioning*, or exposure to various stimuli. During a traumatic event, many sights, sounds, smells, or other cues get associated with that event in your mind. These cues become triggers that can lead you to have the same intense reaction to them that you had during the original event. Thus, your post-traumatic stress disorder appears to be "a disorder of memory gone awry" (Rothschild 2000, 35). Sometimes you will know how closely connected these triggers are to the trauma and what you remember about that event. At other times the connections are harder to recognize and you may have a hard time making sense of your PTSD symptoms and their triggers.

An ethical, knowledgeable trauma therapist will listen to your story without challenging it or asking leading questions or reassuring you that everything you remember happened in exactly the way you remember it. It is easier for you to reassure yourself and others that what happened was "true" when you have independent corroborating information, such as newspaper reports, medical records, personal accounts, or witnesses. Some traumatic events are indelibly burned into your mind. Others may be repressed and hidden to you, yet available to others. Still others are locked away verbally; you may have picture images and emotional outbursts in a state similar to the state you were in when the traumatic event occurred, but the actual facts are either forgotten or dissociated. Your memories are not stored like a movie on DVD, with total retrieval possible. To be sure, it may be possible to retrieve a great deal about an event, but some aspects of an event may have been lost to your mind's ability to remember.

Memory allows you to store and retrieve information about yourself, your history, and your world. Some memories just fade away over time. Others may be placed in what is called *active memory storage*; they never seem to fade away—at least, not the most significant points. Short-term memory includes information you hold while you are doing something or thinking about something. Unless you try to remember it for the long term, it will quickly disappear. A great deal of short-term memory is visual. Getting hit on the head on the front of your skull may influence your short-term memory and cause it to decrease. Short-term memory lasts between a few seconds and a minute (Michelon 2012). Anything that lasts longer is a *long-term memory*. You may be able to reach back in time to recall isolated facts or episodes, along with sensations and associated cues. Some memories are so traumatic, or occurred so early, that the brain doesn't hold them in words; instead, they may be captured in picture form, along with all the emotions that accompanied the experiences. Michelon states that "pictures are more powerful than words to help retrieve a memory" (2012, 82).

22

Psychoeducation

Learning about memories, trauma, and the impacts of traumatic events is called *psychoeducation*. Before you begin to work on what bothers you about your traumatic experiences, you should know at least some of the language trauma professionals use and have some information about trauma. The first few chapters of this book are intended to help you with your psychoeducation. You now know that the symptoms you experience in the present are related to the traumatic events you've experienced in the past. You are not going crazy, and you are not presently crazy. Many others have experienced similar events and have similar symptoms, although in different degrees or combinations. Your reactions are normal in the sense that you are experiencing the normal human response to overwhelmingly stressful events.

Why Remember?

An important reason to try to remember what happened to you is to decrease the fear associated with the traumatic events. Memories of trauma are not dangerous in and of themselves, even though they may feel dangerous. Confronting your memories in a safe environment—writing about them, describing them out loud, drawing them, or finding other ways to deal with them—helps you to work through, or *process*, your traumatic history. Processing memories helps you to integrate them into your past. Continuously avoiding memories of trauma keeps those memories in your present, with all their associated pain, fear, rage, depression, shame, and self-blame (Astin and Rothbaum 2000). Through the process of remembering, you may come to understand what happened to you. You also may become angry at the way you were violated. Remembering safely will give you a sense of control over the experience and the terror you felt.

If you choose to work on memories of trauma, talk about it in the past tense, not in the present tense. Much of the work this workbook asks you to do is on reminders of the memory rather than on the actual trauma story. If you are not willing or able to remember your traumas or if you don't want to work on your trauma narrative with a therapist or (if you are safe to do so) by yourself, do not criticize or blame yourself. This workbook can still help you control the symptoms of PTSD.

If you are willing to do some work on intrusive memories, but you doubt either their relationship to your life or their truth, answer the following questions in the spaces provided (adapted from Adams 1994).

1. Does your intuition or nonlogical insight tell you that what you remember is or was real, no matter how hard you refuse to believe it?

   _____

2. Does the memory keep returning, even after you try to forget it?

   _____

3. Does the memory fit with your habits, fears, behaviors, symptoms, health problems, or the facts of your life as you know them?

_____

4. Is your memory of certain aspects of the traumatic event clear, even if not necessarily accurate?

_____

5. Are certain aspects of the event cloudy, or is the event in picture images?

_____

6. Does your memory come in fragments or bits and pieces?

_____

7. Does remembering anything about the event bring you a sense of relief, understanding, or increased strength?

_____

8. Can you find corroboration of what you remember from other sources (people, newspaper articles, medical reports)?

_____

9. Do you get more or less distressed when you think or talk about your memory?

_____

Who Are You?

Before you look at the traumas that have impacted you, it is important for you to look at who you are. Your sense of yourself serves as the reference point for who you want to become and what you want to do with your life. Traumatic experiences can rob you of your sense of self. If you find the questions in this exercise difficult or impossible to answer, it may be that much of your self-knowledge is missing, and you may need to look to others to help you. You may need to find a therapist skilled in trauma treatment to help you do the work in this workbook and reestablish your sense of self. The following exercise is designed to help you look at what you know about your own core self—your basic identity— and whether that self is healthy, partially healthy, or unhealthy.

EXERCISE: **Am I a Healthy Person?**

Answer the following questions and complete the following statements to get a sense of yourself. (Use your journal if you need more space for your responses.)

What about me gives me a positive sense of who I am?

_____

_____

What facts describe me?

_____

_____

I feel competent about (or in control of):

_____

_____

I have value because:

_____

_____

I am able to be emotionally (and maybe even physically) close to:

_____

_____

My basic values or the truths that govern my life are:

_____

_____

I have sense of meaning to or in my life because:

_____

_____

I see myself as a real, authentic person because:

_____

_____

I make the following appropriate, reasonable demands on myself:

_____

_____

I make the following inappropriate, unreasonable demands on myself:

_____

_____

A participant in a seminar once said to Mary Beth that "shoulds are lies; don't should on me and I won't should on you!" With those comments in mind, list a few *shoulds* that govern your life and are inflexible:

I should _____

I should _____

I should _____

Which of them would you like to discard or be willing to discard?

_____

_____

Mark with an "X" where you lie on the following continuums:

Rigid _____ Flexible

Harsh _____ Gentle

Critical _____ Accepting

Inappropriate _____ Appropriate

Overcontrolling _____ Undercontrolling

What did you learn about yourself by doing this exercise?

_____

_____

Now that you have done this exercise, how would you describe your core self?

_____

_____

EXERCISE: **My Healing History**

In the next chapter you will look at how you can provide safety for yourself before and while you are doing the work in this workbook. Before beginning that work, though, it is important to look at where you believe you are in your own healing process.

The list below begins with statements of disbelief that you were traumatized and follows the steps you'll take as you work hard at healing. How many of these steps have you worked through?

☐ 1. I believe that whatever happened to me in the past was of no consequence or that nothing actually happened at all.

☐ 2. I believe something terrible happened to me and I am not just imagining it.

☐ 3. I am aware at some level that I am a trauma survivor.

☐ 4. I am aware that I am a trauma survivor and that I choose life.

☐ 5. I am aware I am a trauma survivor and I am ready to deal with my feelings of being damaged goods or unworthy of love and attention.

☐ 6. I am angry that I am a trauma survivor.

☐ 7. I feel rage toward the perpetrator of the trauma that happened to me (including God and other people or forces).

☐ 8. I have discussed my traumatic experiences with support people not in my family.

☐ 9. I have discussed my traumatic experiences with members of my family.

☐ 10. I have reexperienced at least some of what happened to me during the traumatic events and have begun to deal with my feelings.

☐ 11. I have begun to give up undeserved guilt or feelings of my personal responsibility for what happened, since it was not my fault. I have assumed appropriate guilt or personal responsibility for what happened if I was to blame to any degree.

☐ 12. I recognize that I acted appropriately, in the only way I could act at the time of the trauma; it was the traumatic event itself that was not appropriate.

☐ 13. I am beginning to understand how the traumatic events have impacted my current relationships and ways of acting.

☐ 14. I am beginning to develop some control around those aspects of myself and my life that are impacted by or connected to the traumatic events.

☐ 15. I am beginning to recognize what I want from all my relationships.

☐ 16. I have a successful intimate relationship.

☐ 17. I have a positive sense of self, and my self-esteem is consistently improving.

☐ 18. I have made a choice whether or not to forgive those who traumatized me.

☐ 19. I recognize that by forgiving, I am reclaiming my own personal power.

☐ 20. I am in touch with my anger and rage and am no longer controlled by them.

☐ 21. I have a positive, healthy sense of my own spirituality.

Given my answers to the above questions, this is how I would describe my healing history:

_____

_____

_____

Feeling Safe

As we just stated, before you look at the traumas that happened to you, it is important that you feel safe. It also is important that you are able to recognize when you need to take breaks to take care of yourself. Chapter 2 will help you with making these choices about your safety.

EXERCISE: **Committing to the Work**

If you are willing to do the work, now is the time to make an initial commitment. Where are you in regard to your desire to change? By picking up this book, you have shown that you are not denying any need to look for change. You may still have some resistance, but at least you are willing to begin to look. So, are you

- ☐ Contemplating the need to change: developing a desire to take action through seeking information?

- ☐ Preparing to move ahead in your work on trauma: beginning to focus on what you need to do?

- ☐ Taking action, with some anxiety?

- ☐ Maintaining your already developed action plan?

- ☐ Finishing up your healing process or coming back for a "booster session"?

JOURNAL EXERCISE: **Drawings of Myself and My Life**

The final exercise in this chapter is a series of drawings that will give you information about who you are. These drawings were originally designed by Spring (1993), and we will ask you to complete them now, at the beginning of the workbook, and again at the end of the workbook. Comparing them will give you an idea of the progress you have made. We suggest that you keep a separate notebook or journal to do some of the exercises in this book. The five drawings listed below should go in that journal.

Don't worry if you have no artistic ability. In drawings 1 and 5, when you draw yourself, how large are you? What facial expression do you have? What are you doing? In drawing 2, draw what is important to you in your world and how your world is to you. What symbols are present? What emotions? In drawing 3, show the ups and downs of your life in a linear way. Is your road straight, curvy, full of hills and valleys? Drawing 4 is self-explanatory.

1. **This is me; I am...** This drawing shows you what you think about yourself. It is your self-portrait.

2. **This is my space.** This drawing shows how you see your world, your position in it, and your reaction to it. Do you believe you have a space in your world? What are your relationships with significant others? Where do your fears, wishes, anger, depression, and personal strengths and weaknesses fit in? How do you tolerate your world in the present? Do you feel isolated and withdrawn or included and part of the world around you?

3. **This is my life's road.** This drawing is a visual history of your life.

4. **This is my family and me.** This drawing is a portrait of your family and your current relationships and family system. It shows how you view your family and your position in it.

5. **This is me; I am...** This second self-portrait is completed after the three intermediate drawings are done. Do you see yourself as you did before drawing the other three drawings?

What did you learn about yourself in completing these drawings?

Now it is time to look at ways to keep yourself safe and secure before you do the work of remembering and processing what happened to you. Chapter 2 has exercises to help.

2

Before Doing the Work: Safety, Security, and Intention

You have decided you want to work on at least one aspect of the traumas that have impacted you. You may choose to use this workbook as part of your therapy or you may want to work on the exercises in the workbook by yourself. No matter what your choice, it is important that you feel safe and secure as you work. This chapter helps you prepare for your work with PTSD—whether it is your first attempt or you are returning to the work. It consists of a number of exercises that you can use to relax, center, and ground yourself in the present, as well as to protect yourself.

First, imagine yourself as you would want to be if the traumas of your life were not impacting you. What type of person would you be? How would you approach life? What would your hopes and dreams be? What would make your life feel full? Where would you live? What type of relationship with a spouse or partner would you have? What would your relationship to your own body be? If you have any chronic illnesses at the present time, how would they be different? What would your relationship with any Higher Power be? What celebrations of your life would you want to have? How would you organize and structure your day-to-day life? Take some time in your journal or notebook to address these questions or others that seem appropriate.

If you get upset while doing this exercise, look at those descriptions as your goals. You are simply aiming to return to a pre-trauma existence to the greatest possible extent.

Safety

What does it mean to be safe? One definition of safety, proposed by both McCann and Pearlman (1990, 1992) and Rosenbloom and Williams (2010), is that safety is the need to feel reasonably invulnerable to harm inflicted by oneself or others. It also is the need to feel that those you value are reasonably invulnerable to harm inflicted by themselves or others. With those definitions in mind, if you are safe, you are reasonably able to prevent yourself from being hurt, or abused, or from experiencing traumatic events. As you protect yourself, you remain present and grounded in the here and now and you are able to make good decisions.

Staying Grounded

The word "grounded" means staying present in the current time, in contrast to "spacing out" or dissociating. You may have some particular ways to remain present when things come up that remind you of trauma or when you are dealing with past experiences. Trauma survivors have made many suggestions as to how to remain grounded. Some of these include:

- using all your senses to be aware of your physical environment, and then talking to others about it

- breathing to bring you back to your body in the present moment

- being aware of your physical body and how you look

- being aware of your movements in space as you walk

- exercising while being aware of what you are doing

- making a plan for the day and sharing that plan with another

- challenging yourself to a contest to increase the length of time you can remain in the present

- watching television and telling yourself or others what you saw

- doing routine activities in a different way; e.g., cleaning up the house in a different order

- asking others to help you stay connected to them

- talking to yourself about the present

- planting your feet as firmly as you can on the ground in the here and now

Types of Safety

Recognizing your beliefs about safety and what you can do to change or challenge those beliefs is important if you are to protect yourself. There are different types of safety. *Physical safety* means that your body is not in danger. Maintaining it means that if a dangerous situation presents itself to you, you can recognize the danger signals, look at possible choices, act on those choices, and remove yourself from the situation if safety does not seem possible. *Mental safety* means that you are able to choose belief systems and patterns of thinking and awareness that get you where you want or need to go. *Emotional safety* means that you are able to identify how you feel in situations, recognize what your intuition tells you, and then act on your feelings and intuition, particularly when they alert you to danger. It may be important to practice feeling your feelings in order to build your awareness of them. *Spiritual safety* occurs when you learn to identify and trust in your beliefs about a Higher Power, God, or Supreme Being and then use those beliefs as a means of protection for yourself and others.

Rosenbloom and Williams (2010) note that establishing safety is the primary goal of therapy or self-protection before any work is done on memories of or emotional issues related to trauma. What cues do you have as to whether you are physically, emotionally, mentally, or spiritually safe? Answering the following questions will help you look at your psychological need for safety. (Use your journal if you need more space.)

EXERCISE: **My Sense of Safety**

How safe is your environment? Is your home safe?

_____

_____

What makes you feel safe physically when you are alone? With others? In different situations?

_____

_____

Are those with whom you live or interact safe? If they are, what makes the setting and those people safe? If they are not, what makes them unsafe?

_____

_____

If you are not safe in your home, what can you do about it?

_____

_____

If you are not safe with or around those closest to you, what will make your situation safer?

_____

_____

How can you (and how do you) protect yourself?

_____

_____

How successful are your self-protective attempts?

_____

_____

When *are* you safest?

_____

_____

When do you *feel* safest?

_____

_____

How can you protect yourself when you are with people you do not know?

_____

_____

What do your answers to these questions tell you about you and your sense of safety?

_____

_____

_____

There are times when safety is impossible to achieve unless you change your location. If you are a victim of domestic violence in any form (verbal, physical, sexual, emotional), it is of *utmost* importance that you get professional assistance to help make you safe (and to make your children safe, if you have children), so you can get out of the situation.

EXERCISE: **Safety Assessment**

As we said earlier, it is important for you to have safety if you are doing any work on trauma-related issues. Write the answers to the following questions, expanding on your answers as much as you need to.

Will you have a safe place in which to do the work?

_____

_____

Have you set aside a specific time or day or week to do that work?

_____

_____

Will you have safe things around you when you sit down to do the exercises in this workbook?

_____

_____

Will you have things around you to ground you, to soothe you, and to make you feel good about yourself and the work you are doing?

_____

_____

If you are working with any therapists or helping people at this time in your life, what makes that work safe or unsafe?

_____

_____

How will you protect yourself from your own strong feelings and thoughts that come up when you're doing the work, particularly if those feelings and thoughts feel harmful to you?

_____

_____

It is important for you to consider your own personal safety in your beliefs and actions. Are you personally safe to yourself? Do you have any strong or life-threatening desires to harm yourself?

_____

_____

Do you have beliefs that are not safe; e.g., _I believe that I am not entitled to heal, I believe I am a bad person_, or _I believe I am responsible for the trauma that happened to me_? If so, or at any point in your work when self-harming beliefs or desires occur, stop your work and get help to prevent any harm from coming to you from yourself. You are the most important person in your life, whether you believe that or not. If you are not safe with yourself, then dealing with traumatic experiences can possibly lead you to even more unsafe behaviors.

_____

_____

What can you do to contain any harmful beliefs or actions and to prevent them from taking over and hurting you?

_____

_____

If you were to evaluate your personal safety within yourself, how would you rate that safety:

☐ I am safe within myself

☐ I am very unsafe

If you had trouble answering the previous question or rated yourself more toward the "I am very unsafe" end of the spectrum, here are some things you can do to help yourself, in addition to getting professional help:

- Write down three things you enjoy doing and then do them.

- Pick a positive feeling you want to have at the beginning of your day and then practice doing things to bring up that feeling.

- Make a list of your negative, unsafe thoughts and then write three thoughts to counter each of them.

- Notice when you begin to feel unsafe during a day, chart those times and what led to those feelings, and then consciously do something that brings safety or self-comfort.

- When you think safe thoughts, give yourself a reward with an activity or object that is healthy.

- Do something that is positive spiritually for you.

- Find your favorite soothing music and listen to it.

- Avoid music that has themes of violence or is in a minor key.

- Use earplugs to drown out excess noise, or get a white noise machine.

- Avoid watching TV shows or movies that might trigger you.

Now that you have read the list of behaviors in the previous question, which of them do you do regularly?

_____

_____

What are other things you can do to make yourself feel safe?

Creating a Safe Place

One thing that you can do is to create your own safe place. In your safe place, you may just sit and meditate or think, or you may do (or imagine doing) an activity. Generally, your safe place needs to have limited access; in other words, only you and those you totally trust or wish to protect can gain access. Your safe place needs to provide you with a sense of protection and security. It does not necessarily have to be comfortable and cozy; it can be a rocky shore along a beach or a wild landscape. What matters most is that you are safe from the dangers outside this secure location.

Before you begin the following exercises, think back over the course of your life to any and all places in which you've been safe. If you have no safe place to which you can return, think of what might make a place safe. You can find or create a safe place anywhere you choose. Would your safe place be a rocky beach or an open meadow, a castle with a moat and drawbridge or a sunny forest? As you create or remember a safe place, think of its characteristics and then add any and all items you might want to bring—weapons, furniture, equipment, items that have meaning, need protection, or make you feel safe. It is important that this place is secure for you.

EXERCISE: **My Safe Place**

This exercise (adapted from Ayalon and Flasher 1993, 73) will help you envision a safe place that you can return to mentally whenever you wish or need to do so.

If you could create a safe place in your present physical reality, and if money and time were no consideration, where would your safe place be?

_____

_____

Stay in your safe place. Look around you. What do you see? Concentrate on colors and visual elements that let the feeling of safety flow in. Then concentrate on sounds or silences that belong in your safe place, feeling that sense of safety they bring, and let it grow stronger in you. Then smell the odors of your safe place and let the good feeling flow in. Whom do you see there? Concentrate on the feelings of safety that others bring. What do you feel in your body while imagining your safe place? Concentrate on that feeling. Then open your eyes and look around you. In the space below, write down what you have just experienced.

_____

_____

_____

_____

Find a single word to describe your safe place:

_____

_____

From now on, whenever you are in distress or feel the need, you can return to your good and safe place and draw strength from it.

JOURNAL EXERCISE: **My Safe Place Collage or Drawing**

Draw or make a collage of your safe place in your journal. A collage is a group of pictures, words, and objects put on a piece of paper to represent a theme. There are no right or wrong drawings, collages, or safe places; there is only what is right for you.

Keeping Your Safe Space Safe

Before you begin to write more about your trauma, please take whatever time you need to reflect about your safe place and what makes or made it safe. You may take time to think about when you might have to use it. It is important for you to have a means to access your safe place quickly (Cohen, Barnes, and Rankin 1995).

If your safe place is in your home or in another physical location, it is important that you are able to keep that place private. It is *not* a place where children can come in and play or disturb your work. It is a place that has good energy. You may wish to clean that spot before you actually use it as a safe place. You may cleanse it with sage, cedar, sweetgrass, or incense. Make sure that it has nothing stressful or unsafe in it to jar you back to everyday reality (bills, paperwork, unfinished projects). You might put in something to give you white noise or perhaps include a miniature waterfall or fountain in the room. You may wish to find a book on feng shui and arrange the furniture in a way that seems to be healing. It is important that any energy you bring to this space is clean, new, and anger-free (Louden 1997). It also is important to bring to your safe place things that give you that kind of energy. Perhaps you have an object or picture that symbolizes who you want to be after you believe you are healed enough to continue on with a healthy life. Remember, when you create this safe place, it is important that you are able to see it, smell it, touch it, hear it, taste it, and feel it. It is a place where you can go whenever you choose, within seconds.

EXERCISE: **Getting to My Safe Space**

From now on, whenever you are in distress or feel the need to do so, you can use a symbol, phrase, or object to return to your good and safe place and draw strength from it (Ayalon and Flasher 1993).

You may use the space below to list symbols that could stand for your safe place; for example, a picture of a seashell (for a beach) or a small shell itself:

_____

_____

_____

_____

A phrase you can use to get to your safe place quickly:

_____

Getting to Your Safe Place Through Visualization

When you created your safe place in your mind, you used *visualization*. Everyone uses this technique. Every time you daydream or create a fantasy in your mind, you visualize. If you choose, you may make an audio recording that helps you get to your safe place or to create any other pleasant visualization. This recording is private and is not to be shared with those you do not trust.

Checking In with Yourself

It is important that you learn how to notice how you feel in your body and mind and how you react when you remember, work on, or deal with the traumatic experiences that have happened to you. It may take practice for you to focus on your body and your emotions and become aware of how you are reacting. The following steps, developed by Rosenbloom and Williams (2010), will help you check in with yourself:

1. Stop whatever activity you might be doing.

2. Sit quietly for a short period of time.

3. Turn your attention inward and ask your body how it feels.

4. Notice if you feel any tension anywhere in your body (e.g., in your shoulders, stomach, jaw, or back).

5. Notice if you are holding your breath.

6. Notice if you are doing any behaviors that suggest tension (e.g., biting your nails, or picking at your skin).

7. Now notice any emotions you feel, if you are able to recognize them (e.g., fearful, sad, angry, lonely, etc.).

8. Notice if you have racing thoughts or if you are able to stay focused.

9. If you've noticed any of the reactions listed above, take some time to use the deep breathing or relaxation techniques described in the next section.

Relaxation and Breathing Techniques

When you want to work in this workbook on specific areas that are problematic to you, you may want to use relaxation and breathing techniques before you do the work, during the work, or after you have completed various exercises. But why do them? If you practice relaxation for several weeks, according to Benson (1984), you will have

- reduced symptoms of anxiety

- fewer headaches and lower blood pressure

- less insomnia

- a way to prevent hyperventilation

- a way to gain more control over panic attacks

- a way to reduce stress levels

- a way to feel more at peace

- more creativity

Schiraldi (2000) notes that there are important general guidelines for you to follow when you want to use relaxation techniques. It is important that you

- practice the technique or techniques you choose regularly—at least daily

- concentrate as best you can while doing the techniques, trying to focus on the particular muscle groups and specific exercises

- combine relaxation with exercise

- trust in the power of the techniques to bring you some peace

- go to your safe place if you feel anxious while trying the technique

Before doing any relaxation techniques, it is important to have four basic elements present (Benson 1975):

- A quiet environment that has as few distractions as possible. Even background noise can be a distraction. It also is important that you will not be interrupted.

- A mental device that is a constant, e.g., a single-syllable word or sound, repeated silently or in a low, gentle tone. The repetition frees your thoughts and is your single focus. Benson suggests using the syllable "one" because it is a simple, neutral word.

- A passive attitude to help you rest and relax without forcing your response, preventing your relaxed response from occurring. Disregard any distracting thoughts that enter your mind.

- A comfortable position that is as restful as possible. This reduces muscular effort. You may support your head and arms. You may remove your shoes and prop your feet up several inches, if you choose. You also may loosen tight-fitting clothes.

EXERCISE: **Deep Breathing**

This first exercise is adapted from Davis, Eshelman, and McKay (1995, 27).

1. Lie down on a blanket or rug on the floor. Bend your knees up toward you and move your feet until they are about eight inches apart, with your toes turned slightly outward. Keep your spine as straight as possible.

2. Scan your entire body and identify any places that hold tension.

3. Put one hand on your abdomen and one on your chest.

4. Inhale slowly through your nose into your abdomen so that it pushes your hand up; your chest should move only a little bit. Hold your breath while you count to five.

5. Smile slightly and then exhale through your mouth, taking as long as possible. Make a shushing sound as you exhale.

6. Repeat this at least five times, perhaps eventually increasing the amount of time you spend deep breathing to five to ten minutes.

7. When you've finished the exercise, again scan your entire body to see if any tension remains. Once you are familiar with the technique, you also can use it while you are sitting or standing, whenever you feel tension in your body.

Progressive Relaxation

You also might want to learn to relax by tensing and relaxing various muscle groups in your body. This is done using a technique called *progressive relaxation*. This technique helps you tense and then relax your four major muscle groups:

- hands, forearms, biceps

- head, face, throat, shoulders

- chest, stomach, lower back

- buttocks, thighs, calves, feet

You may practice this technique while you are lying down or sitting in a chair. The goal is to tense each muscle group for five to seven seconds and then relax that muscle group for twenty to thirty seconds, repeating the whole procedure at least twice. If the muscle group is still tense after you've done the procedure twice, you can repeat it for that group alone up to five times. You also may talk to yourself as you tense and relax, telling yourself anything that has to do with letting go of tension. There are numerous relaxation recordings you can buy that have this procedure, or you can record the following exercise and play it back.

Another way to use progressive relaxation is to hold the tension in each of your muscle groups for about five seconds and then release the tension slowly while you say silently, "Relax and let go." Then take a deep breath and, as you breathe out slowly, silently say, "Relax and let go" again.

EXERCISE: **Basic Progressive Relaxation Sequence**

This sequence takes you from your head through your neck, shoulders, arms and hands, chest, back, stomach, hips, legs, and feet. You may choose to start in the opposite direction. The direction in which you go is not as important as following the sequence in order once you start.

If you make an audio recording of this exercise or the one that follows, allow enough time for each exercise (five to seven seconds to tense, twenty to thirty seconds to relax) on the recording, so you don't rush yourself. Also, put in two repetitions for each exercise.

1. Wrinkle your forehead.

2. Squint your eyes tightly.

3. Open your mouth wide.

4. Push your tongue against the roof of your mouth.

5. Clench your jaw tightly.

6. Push your head back into a pillow.

7. Bring your head forward to touch your chest.

8. Roll your head to your right shoulder.

9. Roll your head to your left shoulder.

10. Shrug your shoulders up as if to touch your ears.

11. Shrug your right shoulder up as if to touch your ear.

12. Shrug your left shoulder up as if to touch your ear.

13. Hold your arms out and make a fist with each hand.

14. One side at a time, push your hands down into the surface where you are practicing.

15. One side at a time, make a fist, bend your arm at the elbow, and tighten up your arm while holding the fist.

16. Take a deep breath and hold.

17. Tighten your chest muscles.

18. Arch your back.

19. Tighten your stomach area.

20. Push your stomach area out.

21. Pull your stomach area in.

22. Tighten your hips.

23. Push the heels of your feet into the surface where you are practicing.

24. Tighten your leg muscles below the knee.

25. Curl your toes under as if to touch the bottoms of your feet.

26. Bring your toes up as if to touch your knees.

EXERCISE: Quick Relaxation

Another quick way to relax is with whole muscle groups, tensing them for five to seven seconds and then relaxing them. This exercise also is adapted from Davis, Eshelman, and McKay (1995, 35–38). This exercise should be done lying down.

1. Curl both fists and tighten your biceps and forearms as if you were a weight lifter posing, and then relax.

2. Wrinkle your forehead and, at the same time, press your head as far back as is possible and roll it in a complete circle clockwise. Then reverse the roll. Then wrinkle up the muscles of your face in a frown, with squinted eyes, pursed lips, tongue pressed on the roof of your mouth, and shoulders scrunched up. Then relax.

3. Arch your back and take a deep breath into your chest. Hold it for five seconds, and then relax. Take another deep breath, pressing out your stomach. Hold it for five seconds, and then relax.

4. Pull your feet and toes back toward your face, tightening your shins. Then curl your toes and tighten your calves, thighs, and buttocks at the same time. Relax.

Successful deep muscle relaxation is a matter of practice. You may talk to yourself as you try to relax, and tell yourself to let go or relax deeper, in order to achieve a more complete relaxation. If you have muscle weakness or a muscular condition such as fibromyalgia, these exercises may not be for you. Check with your physician first.

Another Relaxation Technique

This technique is best used when you have time to try to relax as fully as you possibly can. You may wish to make an audio recording of the following instructions (adapted from Rosenbloom and Williams 2010, 21–22).

First, find a comfortable position and close your eyes. For the next few moments, concentrate on your breathing; use deep breathing. Try to see and feel your lungs, sensing how they feel as you breathe in (pause), trying to make them completely expanded (pause), and then exhaling and sensing how they feel as you release your breath. There is no right or wrong way to breathe. What is important is that you try to relax and not worry about any of the things happening in your everyday life.

Continue to concentrate on your breathing and your lungs, picturing them as you inhale, imagining them filling with strengthening oxygen, and picturing them exhaling as you relax. Now, in your mind's eye, see or hear the message that says "relax" all over, in every bone, muscle, nerve, and tissue, feeling sensations of melting into relaxation.

Next, bring your attention to your left foot and ankle and, as you inhale, gently flex your foot. As you exhale, release and relax your foot. Now bring your attention to your right foot and ankle and, as you inhale, gently flex your foot. As you exhale, release and relax your foot. Let all the cares of the day drain out through your feet. Any noise you hear will only deepen your relaxation.

Now feel the muscles of your left calf. Inhale, contracting the muscles of your left calf and exhale, letting the calf relax. Now feel the muscles of your right calf. Inhale, contracting those muscles, and exhale, letting them completely relax. Of course, adjust your breathing rhythm to what is most comfortable for you, remembering to inhale relaxation, peace, and self-love and to exhale tension, the pressures of the day, and the impacts of trauma on you. Relaxing in this way is a learning process. It is a way to learn to be at ease, to be at peace with yourself, to be at peace with your world, and to relax.

Now bring your attention to the muscles of your left thigh. Inhale and contract these muscles, then exhale and feel relaxation pour in. Next, bring your attention to the muscles of your right thigh. Inhale and contract them, then exhale, feeling release through both your legs. Now shift your focus to your buttocks, inhaling and contracting the muscles. Then exhale and let your bottom relax.

Next, shift your focus to your stomach, inhaling and contracting your stomach muscles. Then exhale, letting your stomach muscles relax, relax, relax. Now bring your attention to your chest and inhale, feeling your chest fill with oxygen and power. As you exhale, release any tightness that may be there as you release all the tensions that are bothering you. Try to feel the feeling of relaxation as a conscious process in your mind and body.

Now bring your attention to your hands. As you inhale, close both of your hands tightly, making fists. As you exhale, release the fists. As you do so, consciously try to let go of everything onto which you are grasping, and to relax. You may open your palms as you relax to receive warmth and vitalizing energy from the world around you. You also may bring your palms, cupped, closer and closer together until you feel the energy that is between them. As you do this exercise, allow the sense of relaxation and energy to move upward through your hands into your forearms, elbows, and shoulders.

Next, focus your attention on your shoulders. As you inhale, contract your shoulders. Hold them for a few seconds in this position and then, as you exhale, feel the tension they have held release outward from them. Feel the point between your shoulders and the base of your neck. Allow warm energy to melt away any built-up tension and pressure that has been stuck there. Now feel the warm energy move up through your neck, allowing your neck to release and support your head as your neck completely relaxes.

Finally, turn your attention to the muscles of your face. Gently tense the muscles of your chin, your mouth, your eyes, your cheeks, and your forehead. Then let your entire face loosen and relax. Enjoy the relaxation you feel through your entire body for a few moments. If any part of your body is not completely relaxed, turn your attention to it. Inhale, and let the last bits of tension melt out of that part of your body. If your attention drifts or if you feel drowsy, it is perfectly all right as long as you are safe, comfortable, and relaxed.

Trying Meditation for Relaxation

Some people use meditation to relax and to calm themselves as they seek heightened concentration and awareness. If you are new at meditating, thoughts may come in to distract you as you try to calm and quiet your mind. If this happens, you may try to use some imagery to focus your awareness before doing the meditation. If you are able to create clear mental images of the following scenes or things, you might then be able to direct your focus to relaxing. Try to create a clear mental image, right now, of

- your best friend's face

- a turkey waiting to be carved

- your bedroom in your present home

- a glass of cold lemonade

- a field of wildflowers

- the aroma of cooking spaghetti sauce

- riding in a race car at a racetrack

- your bare feet on a sandy beach

- the touch of velvet on your skin

- a cat meowing

Use one of these images to focus your attention and then focus on meditating. If worries keep entering, allow them to wander through your focus, noting them and allowing them to continue on without concentrating on them. It also is important to know how to do deep breathing and relax before you try to meditate. If this doesn't work, you may repeat a word or syllable (such as "one" or "om") over and over again, as Benson (1975) suggested. Try this at first for five to ten minutes, increasing it to fifteen minutes if you can.

Using Mindfulness to Help You Relax and Feel Safe

Mindfulness is a particular attitude toward experience that promises to alleviate your suffering and make your life meaningful if you practice living within your moment-to-moment experience. Mindfulness is awareness of present experience with acceptance (Siegel 2010). It can help you calm down, reduce stress, modulate your emotions, improve your performance, and learn to think more effectively, as you focus attention on what's happening in the moment: where you are, what's going on around you, how your body feels, and so on. Mindfulness teaches you how to pay attention to your inner and external worlds with kindness. It allows you to watch your own experience and the thoughts and "chatter" happening inside your head. Remember, your thoughts are not who you are. When you are not so caught up in those thoughts, your feelings won't get so intense. Some mindfulness experts state that it is a form of meditation using uninterrupted awareness of moment-by-moment happening. This includes attentive listening, seeing, and observing. In other words, according to Siegel (2010), mindfulness means noticing what you are thinking and feeling, without immediately responding, but taking the time and allowing yourself the space and the freedom not to do anything. This means you allow yourself to be in the present moment of the here and now by using your senses of sight, sound, touch, taste, and smell.

You might think of your thoughts as clouds floating over your head. You notice them, but they don't move you around or make you lose your balance as you watch them go by. Though your thoughts, feelings, and memories are moving past you, you're still grounded in the here and now. As you train yourself to be more mindful, your mind quiets itself. You can get calmer and think more clearly and gain an increased capacity to bear the intensity of painful experiences.

Mindfulness actually helps strengthen the higher parts of your brain that help balance and improve your response to stress, enhancing your immune system's ability to fight disease. People who practice mindfulness often have an enhanced ability to concentrate and even lower their own blood pressure.

You can become more mindful by engaging in deliberate mindfulness practices. A good way to begin mindfulness practice is to learn how to concentrate. Choose an object for your attention. Every time you notice that your mind has wandered from that object, gently bring it back. Informal mindfulness practice involves reminding yourself throughout the day to pay attention to whatever is happening in the moment. Notice the sensations of walking when you walk and the taste of food when you eat. Formal mindful meditation practice involves setting aside time to go to your mental "gym." Ideally, every day, you will be able to dedicate a certain period of time to sitting quietly and breathing; during that time, your only aim is to bring your attention to the sensations of your breath, gently returning when your mind starts to wander. For more information on how to practice mindfulness, check out Jon Kabat-Zinn's book *Wherever You Go, There You Are: Mindfulness Meditation in Everyday Life* (1994). Other helpful resources are available at http://www.umassmed.edu/cfm, and both http://www.mindful nesscds.com and http://www.mindfulness-solution.com have recordings of guided mindfulness practices.

Practicing mindfulness has a variety of benefits. Some studies have shown that mindfulness practice can increase the body's ability to fight off stress. Kabat-Zinn (1994) has found that practicing mindfulness can increase your positive emotions while decreasing negative ones. It can increase the amount of gray matter in the regions of the brain associated with memory, learning, and empathy.

Many of the therapeutic exercises in this workbook are forms of cognitive behavioral therapy (or CBT). "Some of the primary ingredients of mindfulness are seemingly cognitive behavioral in nature… exposure, cognitive retraining, and affect regulation" (Briere and Scott 2015, 220). Meditation may be difficult if you have continual intrusive memories; meditation is often recommended as a mindfulness technique and may not be helpful. However, learning to pay attention to the world around you, by using awareness skills of mindfulness, may help calm you when you begin to dissociate or when memories begin to intrude. In a similar light, working on your negative beliefs using a mindful, nonjudgmental approach may help to lessen negative self-judgments. In other words, mindfulness can actually help build self-compassion.

When to Take a Break from Doing Work in This Workbook

This is *not* a book to do from start to finish as quickly as possible. Choose to do only the work that applies to you. You may use techniques from only one or two chapters or sections, or you may find that many of the chapters have techniques and exercises that will be helpful to you. If any exercises that feel overwhelming to you come up, put the book away and do something else. If you notice one or more of the following signs, it is important for you to take a break from the work in this book. These signs are adapted from Rosenbloom and Williams (2010). Put the work away

- if you begin to feel that you are not present in your body or are not aware of your surroundings, or if you begin to lose your sense of time (these are symptoms of dissociation)

- if you begin to have flashbacks, or have more frequent or more intense flashbacks, of your traumatic experiences

- if unmanageable feelings begin to flood you

- if you experience anger, rage, irritability, depression, fear, anxiety, sadness, or other feelings that seem to be out of control or that seem to have no recognizable source

- if you begin to injure yourself or to injure yourself more seriously or more frequently

- if you engage in addictive, compulsive behaviors, including abuse of alcohol, drugs, eating, sex, or working

- if you begin to develop anorexia nervosa (you stop eating) or bulimia (you eat a great deal and then make yourself throw up)

- if you become completely numb and are unable to feel emotion

- if you become unaware of emotion

- if you begin to isolate yourself and avoid others

- if you have a dramatic change in any normal life pattern

If any of these signs appear, take care of yourself before you continue with your work. Should the reactions you are having become too intense, you may find that you need a few days or weeks away. Also, if you feel overwhelmed by your work and need support and guidance, seek the help of a qualified traumatologist, preferably one certified by the Association of Traumatic Stress Specialists (ATSS).

You also may choose to use any of the following strategies for self-care while you are taking that break (adapted from Pearlman and Saakvitne 1995):

- For physical self-care, you may decide to eat regular meals that are healthy and balanced, exercise, wrap yourself tightly in a blanket, sit in your favorite chair, get regular preventive medical care, get a massage, play sports, get rest and sleep, take a warm bath or shower, recycle, do housework or yard work, or take a vacation.

- For psychological self-care, you may decide you need or want to meditate, journal, listen to soothing audio recordings, decrease your everyday stress, find a certified trauma therapist, commit to doing something you want to do, read something frivolous, or say no to others' requests. To release emotion, you may also pound on a pillow or rip up a phone book.

- For emotional self-care, you may decide you need or want to spend time with family members you love and like, reconnect with people you love, watch your favorite movies or TV shows, listen to your favorite music, laugh or cry, play, or fight for a cause.

- For spiritual self-care, you may decide you need or want to go to or join a church or other spiritual group, read a spiritually oriented book, spend time in nature, spend time being thankful for who you are and what you have, pray, or do something to help better the world or the lives of animals or nature. For awe, wonder, and beauty, you may want to walk in nature, listen to music, or behold art. Awe is associated with curiosity and a desire to explore, not withdraw, from your environment and from others.

- For professional/workplace self-care, you may want or need to take your assigned breaks during your workday, see if you can use flextime on your job, try to finish assignments when (or even before) they are due, set limits, try to develop a good relationship with other workers or your boss, try to find something in your work that is rewarding to you, or balance other aspects of your life with your work.

EXERCISE: **My Safety Net**

As you work through your traumatic experiences and symptoms using this workbook, it also is important to have connections with others available when and if you need them. It is important to find others who care about you. If you don't have family members who can help you, you may build connections with others through work, church, support groups (e.g., AA, ACOA), or social organizations. You may list the phone numbers of these support people below. However, if none of them is available when you are in crisis, remember you *are* able to stay safe even when they cannot be reached. At the end of this list, you may add ways to stay safe if no one is available.

The phone numbers I need to know include

1. My best friend: _____

2. The local crisis line: _____

3. My partner or spouse: _____

4. My therapist(s): _____

5. My doctor(s): _____

6. The family member to whom I am closest: _____

7. My neighbor: _____

8. The local hospital: _____

9. My child(ren): _____

If none of these people is available and I feel unsafe, I can do the following things to remain safe until someone is available: _____

_____

Working through the following pages may make you feel more vulnerable and in need of support from others. If you feel overwhelmed at any point, remember to use the relaxation and breathing strategies included in this chapter. You have many positive techniques you can to use to comfort yourself as you work through the exercises in this book. Now you are ready to begin your hard work. As you begin, keep the following passage from the German playwright Goethe in mind: "Until one is committed, there is hesitancy... The moment one definitely commits oneself, then Providence moves too. All sorts of things occur to help one that would never otherwise have occurred... Begin it now."

3

Identifying and Writing About
What Has Happened to You

Before you work on the symptoms that are bothering you, it is important to make sure that you are aware of where your symptoms come from—in other words, what you've experienced—without overwhelming or retraumatizing yourself. Remember, at any point during this chapter or other chapters, you can refer back to the exercises in chapter 2 to help calm yourself.

Also, you may look at the work you are doing and rate yourself and the amount of distress you are feeling at that particular time by using a *subjective units of distress scale* (SUDS). Higher SUDS levels indicate a greater need to relax, ground, or take a break.

Creating Your Own SUDS

The subjective units of distress scale is one way to communicate to yourself or others how much distress you are experiencing. The scale has 11 points, from 0 to 10, from least to most distress. It is important that you assign your own measures to this scale. Sometimes, it may seem as if your distress is beyond a 10. This scale is adapted from the work of Smyth (1999).

0 = I am completely relaxed, with no distress. I may be deep in sleep.

1 = I am very relaxed. I may be awake but dozing off.

2 = I am awake but feel no tension.

3 = I feel a little bit of tension; it keeps my attention from wandering.

4 = I am feeling some mild distress, apprehension, fear, or anxiety, and body tension.

5 = My distress is somewhat unpleasant, but I can still tolerate it. (I am looking at a spiderweb with a huge spider in it, but it is several feet away and the spider can't jump that distance.)

6 = I am feeling moderate distress and unpleasant feelings. I have some worry and apprehension.

7 = My body tension now is substantial and unpleasant, though I can still tolerate it and can think clearly.

8 = I am feeling a great deal of distress with high levels of fear, anxiety, and worry. I can't tolerate this level of distress for very long.

9 = The distress is so great that it is impacting my thinking. I just can't think straight.

10 = I am in extreme distress. I am totally filled with panic and I have extreme tension throughout my body. This is the worst possible fear and anxiety I could ever imagine. It is so great that I just can't think at all.

You may use this scale at any point in time as you do the work in this book. You may decide on which SUDS rating means you should take a break from the work and return to the exercises in chapter 2 to calm you. You also may decide that getting stuck at a certain SUDS level means that you need to stop doing the work in the workbook for a period of time and consult with a therapist.

At this point in time, what is your SUDS level? _____

Why did you choose this level?

_____

_____

More About Memory and Remembering

In this chapter, we will ask you to identify what happened to you through a trauma inventory; later, you will be asked to draw a trauma time line. Both exercises ask you to remember what happened to you. But what if you can't remember? What if you have only a vague inkling that something happened to you? How sure are you that the traumatic events happened to you? Some traumatic events are easily documented (through records, newspaper articles, and so on). Others may never be fully known. Where did you place yourself on the healing continuum exercise that was given in chapter 1? You might complete this same exercise in your notebook or journal for specific traumatic events that happened to you, if you believe you need to.

You may not be able to recall your experience (Schauer, Neuner, and Elbert 2012) as a complete story with beginning, middle, and end. Your memory may be highly emotional, disorganized, or fragmentary, as you begin recalling what happened. You may wish to reconstruct a sensory perceptual representation of your memories, for example by drawing a picture or constructing a model or collage.

Your memory may be associated with a specific period of time in your life (such as childhood between ages four and nine) that is organized around a major theme of life (such as early school years). Your memories may stem from repeated lifetime events, or they may be event specific (Conway and Pleydell-Pearce 2000). However, your memory for a specific traumatic event may also be distorted in terms of your autobiographical memory. You may not be able to place the event specifically in a certain time period. It may be a *hot memory*, or a memory with particular impact.

Constructing a Trauma Inventory

Before you begin work on any of the symptoms that may be haunting you, it is important for you to have a sense of what you've experienced (both positively and negatively) in your life by listing the traumatic events in no particular order. Without going into great detail, use the following list to identify which traumas you've experienced and the age or ages at which you experienced them. After doing so, you can construct a trauma time line of those events, to the best of your ability, indicating which were long-term and which were short-term events. You also may write a very brief statement about any of the traumas you've experienced. The types of traumas you experience can impact the reactions you have about those events. They can serve as a reference point for writing a trauma narrative.

Event	Age(s)	Description
surviving a natural disaster (tornado, hurricane)		
surviving a fire		
witnessing a natural but unexpected death		
witnessing a violent death		
being in a serious automobile accident		

being in a plane crash		
surviving an assault or mugging		
surviving a robbery or burglary		
having a murder in my family		
being exposed to war		
being a combat soldier		
being a refugee exposed to suffering and death		
experiencing physical violence as a child		
experiencing life-threatening neglect as a child		
being sexually abused as a child		
being seriously emotionally abused as a child		
experiencing serious physical violence as an adult		
being raped by someone I knew		
being raped by a stranger		
being raped by more than one person at a time		
surviving cult abuse		
having some sort of involvement in pornography		
having some sort of involvement in snuff films		
working in a profession that exposed me to death, injury, and pain		
being exposed to violent death outside of my profession		
surviving torture		
surviving a holocaust or genocide		
other life-threatening event		

As you think about all the traumatic experiences you have had, remember that you survived them and that you used many positive character traits to do so (Cohen, Barnes, and Rankin 1995). The following exercise refers to some of those traits.

EXERCISE: **My Positive Traits**

Refer to the traumatic events you experienced and identify which positive traits you used during those events. In which traumatic experiences did you use them?

_____

_____

How and when did you show determination?

_____

_____

How and when did you show your will to continue to struggle and to eventually succeed?

_____

_____

How and when did your faith help you, particularly faith in yourself and your support system?

_____

_____

How and when did you show courage?

_____

_____

How and when did you take personal responsibility for meeting your needs (including your need for safety) during your traumatic experiences?

_____

_____

How and when did you exhibit your personal creativity?

_____

_____

How and when did you show your resilience?

_____

_____

How and when did you use your intuition?

_____

_____

How and when were you able to maintain any optimism?

_____

_____

How and when were you able to use any physical strength?

_____

_____

What did completing this exercise tell you about your strengths?

_____

_____

What other strengths can you identify within yourself that you used?

_____

_____

Creating a Trauma Time Line

One way to record your trauma history is to draw a trauma time line. Doing this is a big step toward being able to retell your personal trauma story. Take a roll of white paper and, beginning at the end of the roll, mark spaces for each of the years of your life on a horizontal line. This line can be a foot or many feet long. You may want to start the beginning of your life a few inches from the end of the roll so you can record any events that happened prior to its beginning. Did your mother have any serious events during her pregnancy that could have impacted you? (For example, was she battered? Did she fall? Was she in an accident? Was there a significant death during this time? Was she confined to bed?)

Put any significant events that happened to you throughout your life above the horizontal line. These can be positive or neutral events (e.g., starting school, moving to a new home, a first date), as well as traumatic events (e.g., illness, injury, abuse). Below the line, record events that happened to others who are important to you; these should be events that impacted you as an observer or witness but did not directly happen to you (deaths, births, etc.). You may use photos, magazine pictures, personal items, or drawings of yourself and others, placing them above or below the line to symbolize events, people, and places.

If you wish, you can extend your time line into the future beyond your present age and put in some of your future intentions. Some people have called this time line "the Torah of trauma." You may find that constructing a time line is too retraumatizing to do alone; seek professional help if you need to. Also, take your time. Do a year or a few years at a time and then take a break. Take time to relax, regroup, and unwind.

What did completing a trauma time line tell you about yourself or what happened to you?

_____

_____

_____

Healing by Writing: Creating Your Own Trauma Story

To move beyond trauma, you must first remember it, in all of its differing types of memory. Unfortunately, remembering traumatic experiences causes pain and suffering. Avoiding thinking and talking about what happened to you is natural. Shortly after a traumatic event occurs, avoidance can be an effective coping strategy; however, in the long run, it is both ineffective and stressful, preventing recovery and leading to development of problems and disorders.

Expressing your traumatic experiences in writing is a form of exposure therapy that will help you separate the past from the present, where you are safe. This process helps to reduce your fear and lessen your responses to sensory triggers. It also helps bring closure to traumatic memories by developing a coherent story that becomes your history so that the past is no longer reenacted in the present. Your story belongs to you alone. Your traumatic memory fragments become part of a historical narrative that makes your history sufficiently complete. You may wish to write more informally, as suggested in the next exercise, or you may want to use one of the more structured approaches set forth in the exercise that follows.

You may want to begin by describing where, when, and how the traumatic event happened. When you are ready, you may also want to describe the worst part(s) of that event or events. You may want to include losses that occurred as a result of the trauma (people, memories, physical capabilities). Your resilience is also an important part of this story, so you will want to include how you have moved forward through the events and how those traumatic experiences have helped you to grow. You may find that writing will help you to visualize your experiences or also imagine them so that they can be removed from your present and can be put into your past (Schauer, Neuner, and Elbert 2011).

JOURNAL EXERCISE: Informal Writing or Audio Recording

To get all the details of a traumatic experience into the open in an informal way, you can either write about the experience in your journal or make an audio recording. As you do so, ask yourself the following questions:

1. What happened before the traumatic event?

2. How did I first know something was wrong?

3. What happened next?

4. What did I do?

5. How was the damage done?

6. How did I know it was over?

7. What did I do afterward?

8. What did others do afterward?

9. What was the very worst moment?

JOURNAL EXERCISE: **Structured Writing for Recovery**

Writing therapy, a structured approach to writing, has proved to be effective for helping people process their trauma history (Van der Oord et al. 2010), as has more directed writing exposure (Lichtenthal and Cruess 2010). Exposure to trauma and the restructuring of trauma-related negative thoughts are crucial in this process (Kalantari et al. 2012). This exercise is adapted from the manuscript *Writing for Recovery: A Manual for Structured Writing After Disaster and War* (Yule et al. 2005, 2013). In this approach, you write for two days in a row, for fifteen minutes on the first day and for fifteen minutes at four different times on the second day. The writing is focused on six particular issues regarding your trauma experiences, as outlined below. You can write about the same event for the full fifteen minutes or about different events as they come to mind. It's important to be completely honest with yourself as you write, no matter the topic. On day 3, you write using more of an other-oriented focus (e.g. what would you share about your trauma in order to help others?).

Day 1

Write down your deepest emotions and thoughts about the trauma or traumas. How has this event touched your life? You might describe what happened, what you saw and felt, and what you remember. You also might want to tie this event to other parts of your life, such as your childhood and your relationship with your spouse or significant other, parents, family members, friends, and coworkers. How might it be related to people you love? How is it connected to who you would like to become in the future, who you have been in the past, or who you are now? You might even write about your dreams and haunting thoughts relating to the trauma, in addition to exploring your very deepest emotions.

Write about all the ways you remember the experience(s)—sights, sounds, smells, memories, thoughts, feelings, and so on. You may link the experience to other important things in your life. You may want to write about the same experience or about another aspect or event.

Day 2

Explore your thoughts and feelings about whatever emotional upheaval bothered you the most. Focus on some of the emotions that came up after the event. Did you think that you were going to die or that you were responsible for what happened? Write about what you now know: that you did not die or that you were not to blame. You also can write about the same things you wrote about yesterday, such as powerful emotions or your family, or you can write about experiences or emotions that you haven't shared with anyone.

Write the story about what happened to you and, if you want, include what you did to help yourself survive. Even though no one else may see your story, it is important that you write about all the ways you remember the trauma—sights, sounds, smells, memories, thoughts, feelings, and so on. You may link your survival to other important things in your life. You may want to write about the same subject or about another aspect of the event that you haven't covered.

Day 3

This event has affected not just you but everyone else around you. The ways you think and talk to people about it may have changed over time. However painful your experiences have been, you will have learned from them. Think of another person who has gone through a similar event. Knowing now what most helped you survive, what would you say to that other person?

Imagine that it is ten years from now and you're looking back on what happened. How will you want to think about the event(s) at that future time? What do you think you will see as the most important parts of what happened when you look back on it?

Time to Heal

Now that you have identified your traumatic experiences, it is time to begin to work on any symptoms of PTSD that you are having. Remember, this is not a start-to-finish workbook. It does not ask you to expose yourself to all the gory details of any traumas that you may have had. Choose the symptoms that bother you most, and then pick and choose among the healing strategies and exercises given for each of them. Most of the remaining chapters each treat a single symptom category, including the four major criteria for the diagnosis of PTSD. Always remember to take breaks from the work whenever you believe or feel you need to do so. Healing takes time; allow yourself that time.

4

Helping Yourself When You Reexperience a Trauma

Reexperiencing or *intrusive reactions* are among the four major types of reactions in post-traumatic stress disorder; the other three are avoidance (see chapter 5), category D symptoms (see chapters 6 and 7), and arousal symptoms (see chapter 8). This chapter gives you techniques to help you with intrusive symptoms when the following occur:

- Recurrent, involuntary, and upsetting memories or thoughts of the trauma suddenly pop into your mind.

- You dream about the trauma over and over.

- New aspects of the trauma come to you through those nightmares or thoughts.

- You have a dissociative reaction in the form of a flashback, in which the events seem to be recurring. In an extreme instance, you may even have a complete loss of awareness of your actual environment or surroundings.

- You react to triggers (internal and external cues), such as a smell, sound, date, or any stimulus associated with your original traumatic experience, with intense or prolonged psychological distress.

- You get really, really physically nervous or otherwise reactive to internal or external cues that symbolize or resemble some aspect of the trauma or are similar to the trauma. (This is dealt with in exercises relating to triggers.)

You may experience one or more of these symptoms (see category B in the definition of PTSD given in chapter 1).

Building Dual Awareness

Before you work on trauma-related dreams, nightmares, memories, flashbacks, or other aspects of the trauma, it is very important for you to accept and reassure yourself that your trauma is *not* occurring in the present time.

Having *dual awareness* helps you look at and work on the trauma while you are secure in the knowledge that you are really in the present environment. The following exercise gives you a tool to help you look at the trauma from the perspective of your observing self (now) and your experiencing self (then). You may do this exercise before you delve into your traumatic memories. It shows you the degree to which you have a capacity for dual awareness.

EXERCISE: Developing Dual Awareness

This exercise is from *The Body Remembers*, by Babette Rothschild (2000, 131).

Remember a recent mildly distressing event—something where you were slightly anxious or embarrassed. What do you notice in your body? What happens in your muscles? What happens in your gut? How does your breathing change? Does your heart rate increase or decrease? Do you become warmer or colder? If there is any change in temperature, is it uniform or variable in sectors of your body?

_____

_____

_____

Bring your awareness back into the room you are in now. Notice the color of the walls and the texture of the rug. What is the temperature of this room? What do you smell here? Does your breathing change as your focus of awareness changes?

_____

_____

Now try to keep awareness of your present surroundings while you remember that slightly distressing event. Is it possible for you to maintain awareness of where you are physically as you remember that event?

End this exercise with your awareness focused on your current surroundings.

The Rewind Technique

The British psychiatrist David Muss (1991) has developed the following technique to allow you to get rid of your unwanted, involuntary memories of a traumatic event and the emotional distress that they bring. When you try this technique, do so in a safe setting; you may wish to work on it first with a therapist. It is also known as the Muss Rewind Therapy.

1. Find a time when you can be safe and undisturbed.

2. Find a comfortable place and sit there quietly for fifteen minutes before beginning the rewind technique.

3. Begin to relax, using the techniques you learned in chapter 2. Keep your eyes closed, and tense and relax each muscle group of your body, beginning with your feet.

4. Feel the calmness that comes over you as you relax. You also might think of a pleasant place or your safe place while you do this relaxing.

5. Now allow yourself to float out of yourself so that you can watch yourself sitting in your comfortable place. Choose a memory in which you felt somewhat sick or frightened, such as just before going down the largest drop on a roller coaster. Thinking of this memory will make you feel somewhat uncomfortable. Now look at that same scene from outside the roller coaster. Float above yourself and watch yourself. Hopefully, you do not feel as bad now.

6. Now you need to experience two films. Imagine that you are sitting in the center of a totally empty movie theater with the screen in front of you and the projection room behind you. Now float out of your body and go to the projection room. See yourself sitting in the theater, watching the film. From the projection room, you can see the whole theater as well as yourself.

7. Watch the first film. The first film replays the traumatic event as you experienced it or as you remember it in your dreams, flashbacks, or nightmares. You will see yourself on the screen. It is as if someone took a video of you during the trauma and that video is now playing. When you start the film, begin it at the point just prior to the traumatic event, seeing yourself as you were before it occurred. Remember, you are sitting in the movie theater to watch the film, but you are also in the projection room watching yourself in the theater as you watch the film. Play the film at its normal speed. Stop the film when you realized you were going to survive or when your memory begins to fade.

8. Then simply watch the rewind; you will experience it on the screen, seeing it as if it were happening to you now, with all of its sounds, smells, feels, tastes, and touch sensations. You are actually in the film, reexperiencing the event. However, you see and experience it all happening in reverse, from after the traumatic event until before the event happened. This

reexperiencing takes practice and must be done rapidly. Remembering a trauma of about one minute would mean having a rewind that lasts about ten to fifteen seconds.

You may find rewinding hard to do initially. However, keep practicing until it feels right. You may find it painful to go through the first film. After you learn this process, every time you begin to remember the trauma, you can use the rewind to scramble the sequence of events and to take you quickly back to the starting point—the good image. You will be left with the preevent memory after the rewind. As time goes by, your rewind process will happen faster and faster. It is very important to include all the frightening, awful details of the trauma in your movie. As one memory gets resolved by rewinding, others may appear to take its place, memories that have been hidden under the surface of the first. These too can be addressed through this process.

If you try the rewind process with a trained therapist, use this space to describe how it worked for you.

_____

_____

_____

Containment and Traumatic Memories

Containment means using your mind to focus attention on something other than a traumatic memory, flashback, or thought. It is possible to contain reminders of the trauma and remain in the present, in spite of having strong feelings. Learning containment techniques can help you tolerate those feelings without taking negative action against yourself or others. Containment is based on choice rather than automatic response; it helps you store overwhelming, unsafe memories until you are ready to process them. However, containment does not involve indefinite avoidance or denial. In fact, learning how to contain memories means that using numbing and dissociation to deal with trauma is less necessary.

The following containment techniques were developed by a support group for people with dissociative identity disorders (formerly called multiple personality disorder) at Dominion Hospital in Falls Church, Virginia. The group noted these ways to contain traumatic intrusions (flashbacks, memory fragments, or thoughts):

- Plan ahead for potentially distressing times when you have some advance warning of them.

- Allow yourself to cry to get your emotions out.

- Record your thoughts and feelings in writing or in an audio recording.

- Perform a monotonous activity to distract yourself: play solitaire or do a puzzle.

- Ground yourself in the present time by reminding yourself that you are in the here and now (use dual awareness); grasp a favorite object and focus attention on your contact with it as a way to stay in touch with reality; or stomp your feet or push your body into a chair to remind you of where you are physically; or focus on the sensations of your own body by clapping your hands or touching your tongue to the roof of your mouth.

- Put on heavier, different shoes, such as hiking boots or steel-toed shoes that connect you to the ground.

- Put the memory into a real or imagined container outside yourself and then close the box until a more appropriate time.

- Count to yourself using your watch or pulse as a way to count.

- Get involved in an activity that involves some type of motion (walking, exercising, keyboarding, playing video games).

- Use art to express your emotions or represent the memory.

- Put on a certain color of clothing that you believe makes you invisible to others or allows you to blend in without being noticed.

- Go to a potentially traumatizing event with your camera and take photographs as a way to hide behind the camera and avoid some triggers.

Dealing with Traumatic Dreams

You may have recurrent dreams that have some aspects of the trauma. Perhaps these dreams do not scare you, or they may be nightmares that wake you and leave you feeling fearful and panicked. Sometimes dreams about traumatic events can actually give you information about what happened to you.

A woman once had dreams about a face without a body. This face appeared in her dream on many, many occasions. The face was dark complexioned and had a mustache and pockmarked skin. She had no idea if the face actually belonged to a person; she knew no one that fit its shape and appearance. After years of therapy, the woman was ready to confront her older brother about sexual abuse he had perpetrated on her. She sat him down and spoke firmly what she had practiced over and over in the therapist's office—how he had harmed her and disrupted her life. The brother began to cry. He said that he had hoped she had not remembered what he had done to her when she was under eight years of age. He begged her forgiveness and then said that he needed to "come clean and tell her about the rest of the stuff." The woman was baffled by his comment. "What do you mean?" she asked her brother. He began to tell her of taking her into an attic above a deserted store with a group of his friends. One of his friends, a dark complexioned teen with a mustache and scars from acne, raped her. Her memory of the rape only occurred in her dreams, only in the face of the rapist.

A powerful flashback-halting protocol (presented later in the chapter) can be adapted to deal with nightmares. You can do the following exercise as a ritual before sleep to prepare for any nightmares that may occur. You can also change the wording to help you gain dual-awareness during the night if you awaken from a nightmare. This exercise has been adapted from *The Body Remembers*, by Babette Rothschild (2000, 134).

EXERCISE: **Dealing with Nightmares**

Say these things to yourself, preferably aloud, before you go to bed.

I am going to awaken in the night feeling _____
(insert name of the anticipated emotion, usually fear), and in my body I will be sensing
_____(describe your anticipated
bodily sensations—name at least three) because I will be remembering _____
(identify the trauma by title only—no details). At the same time, I will look around where
I am now in _____ (the actual current year), here _____
(name the place where you are), and I will see _____
(describe some of the things that you see right now, in this place), and so I will know
_____ (identify the trauma, again by title only) is not happening
now/anymore.

If you awaken from a nightmare, be sure to try to ground yourself before you do any work on what you dreamed. As suggested previously, you can ground yourself quickly by grasping a favorite object and focusing on the contact, by using your body's contact with the bed to remind yourself of your present location, or by focusing on sensations generated by clapping your hands or pressing your tongue to the roof of your mouth.

Baker and Salston (1993) discuss ways to deal with dreams through dream preparation. In dream preparation, you follow a cognitive (thinking) procedure about your possible dreams before you go to sleep, recognizing that you may dream a distressing dream during sleep. When the dream occurs, you write it down, talk it through, and rewrite its ending as a means to take control of the dream. Then you do relaxation exercises and go back to sleep. The next exercise is adapted from Baker and Salston (1993).

EXERCISE: **Learning from and Rewriting Nightmares**

Describe your trauma-related nightmare in the space below (if you need more space, use your journal). Describe it in as much detail as possible, including the scene, any associated feelings, and as many sensory impressions as you can remember (smells, sensations on your skin, sounds, sights, tastes). If you have more than one nightmare about the trauma, download additional copies of this exercise from the website for this book, http://www.newharbinger .com/33704, and use a blank form for each.

_____

_____

_____

_____

Is your nightmare an exact reenactment of the traumatic event? Yes / No (Circle the appropriate answer.)

Now think of ways to change the nightmare's ending:

_____

_____

What new information does the nightmare give you that you can use to build an understanding of what happened to you?

_____

_____

_____

_____

How has the nightmare helped you or helped you to respond differently to your trauma?

_____

_____

EXERCISE: **Understanding the Links Between Nightmares and Trauma**

Clearly, it is very important for you to look at and try to understand the content of your nightmares. If you are in therapy, doing so can help you examine the meaning behind the nightmares and can give you a safe place to release associated emotions. Nightmares can be useful sources of information and can have both obvious and hidden messages (Daniels 2013). Dealing with your nightmares in detail may even help you reduce some of your hyper-arousal and hypervigilance by desensitizing you to their content and minimizing your attempts to avoid.

What recurring nightmares do you have?

_____

_____

_____

_____

Do they seem to have content similar to the traumas that happened to you? Are traumatic memories presented directly or in hidden forms or in disguises?

_____

_____

Are there specific triggers that occur during the day that seem to lead to your nightmares? (Triggers are explained later in this chapter.) Some of these triggers may be very subtle, such as body sensations of pain.

_____

_____

_____

_____

If your traumatic events are related to war or sexual abuse, the following questions can help you understand the impact of those events on your sleep and dreams (Daniels and McGuire 1998):

- What was your sleep like before deployment or the abuse?

- How did that sleep pattern change while you were deployed or being sexually abused?

- How often do you have nightmares?

- Do you have the same nightmare repeatedly?

- Do those nightmares depict an actual event that occurred in your military or daily life?

- Does your nightmare distort the actual event? How and in what way?

- When did you have the nightmare the first time?

- When was the most recent time you had it?

- How has it changed?

- What thoughts do you have when you first awaken after the nightmare?

- What emotions do you have when you awaken after the nightmare?

If you pay attention to your nightmares, you will reduce at least some of your distress. You also have the possibility of writing a new ending to that nightmare that gives you at least some power and control, using the techniques suggested in the previous exercise "Learning from and Rewriting Nightmares."

Dealing with Your Flashbacks as Dissociation

Matsakis defines a flashback as a "sudden, vivid recollection of the traumatic event accompanied by a strong emotion" (1994a, 33). However, a flashback is no longer viewed as merely a memory of the past that intrudes into the present and makes the past seem as if it were actually occurring in the here and now. The *DSM-5* defines a flashback as a dissociative event (American Psychiatric Association 2013). For the most part, dissociation is used as a way to avoid some part of a traumatic event. However, when you have a flashback, it is as if you have returned in time to the event and are stuck there, dissociated from the present. (Dissociation as a form of avoidance will be covered more fully in chapter 5.).

What Is Dissociation?

If you dissociate, your awareness of the world around you splits off in some way. According to Branscomb, dissociation means "the separation of things that were previously related or 'associated'" (1990, 3). Dissociation can occur at the level of physical sensation: perhaps you no longer feel parts of your body during a traumatic event. Dissociation can occur at the level of thinking: perhaps you separate out various aspects of the experience and remember only certain ones. Dissociation also can occur at the level of emotion: perhaps you get yourself into difficult situations and suddenly feel numb. It is possible to dissociate at one or at all of these levels at any point in time.

For example, say you are driving. You stop at a stop sign, look both ways, and then pull out to cross the road in front of you. Suddenly, you hear and feel the impact of another car hitting you. It has come out of nowhere. Your car spins and you end up across the road turned in the opposite direction from where you began. Your first reaction is to breathe, notice where you hurt, and then look at your body and your car from the inside. You have a few bumps, but basically you are all right. The car is crunched. You get out and see another car in the intersection. Your reaction is one of rage and anger; you go to the other driver and begin to yell. However, you are not aware of the motorcycle that's also in the intersection. This motorcycle also was coming across the intersection and its rider witnessed the entire accident. In this case, you have dissociated part of what you obviously saw during the accident, just as Rothschild writes that "amnesia of varying degrees is the most familiar kind of dissociation" (2000, 65).

Or you may dissociate your physical pain and some of your emotions. After your accident, you get out of the car and walk to the other car. You are not yet aware of the huge bruise on your leg or the significant bump on your head. The only emotion you feel is anger at the other driver; you do not yet feel relief that you are not seriously hurt or fear that the accident happened. You did not dissociate your consciousness, though, as some people might have done: you are aware that you are still in your body.

One way to look at dissociation is to use Levine's SIBAM model of dissociation (1992). SIBAM stands for sensation, image, behavior, affect, and meaning, the five elements of any experience.

Sensation means your physical reactions and body (somatic memories).

Image means the pictures that remain in your head.

Behavior means what you did during the trauma.

Affect means your emotions.

Meaning means how you make sense of it all.

One or more of these elements can become dissociated during a traumatic event rather than staying intact in a whole memory. Thus, you might have a strong alarming emotion (affect) related to your father's presence. The presence of your father means "danger" to you. You react to the danger by saying to yourself that you have to get away; in other words, your behavioral goal is to escape. You also may get a headache or goose bumps when he is near. However, as you try to make sense of your feeling of danger, you may have no visual memory (or image that tells you why your father's presence spells danger). This model does not take into account that you might merely have forgotten that aspect of the event rather than have dissociated it; however, the model does make sense in terms of the discussion in chapter 1 of the types of memory.

According to Rothschild (2000), implicit memory involves sensory images (visual memories, auditory memories), body sensations (pain, numbness, tingling), emotions, and automatic behaviors. Explicit memory involves facts, sequences of events, beliefs, and meaning. Do you have a sense that you dissociated to any degree during your traumatic event or events? Did you dissociate from what you did (how you behaved), what you felt emotionally (your affect), what you experienced in your body, your awareness that the event was even happening (your sense of time, your knowledge of the trauma), or your choices (your will) during the traumatic event? You may want to write about that dissociation in your journal or notebook.

How do you know if you are dissociating? Schiraldi (2000) provides a list of indicators of dissociation; these form the checklist below.

EXERCISE: How Do I Dissociate?

Please check off any of the following indicators of dissociation that describe what happens to you. When I dissociate, I feel or do the following:

- [ ] lie very still
- [ ] am slow to respond to others
- [ ] seem to move in slow motion
- [ ] have flat (muted) emotions
- [ ] feel no pain
- [ ] stare off blankly into space
- [ ] tune out
- [ ] am an observer of the present situation, not a participant
- [ ] have lapses in my memory
- [ ] feel as if I am on autopilot

☐ feel as if I am a stranger in my own world

☐ feel as if I am watching myself from outside my body

☐ feel as if I am in a fog

When do you feel the sensations or do the behaviors you checked?

_____

_____

What Does It Mean to Have a Flashback?

During a flashback, there is no present; instead, the reality to the person having the flashback is that of existing in the traumatic past. A flashback can occur as a slight "blip" in time or it can be a memory of an entire experience, occurring in real time just as it did in the past. This type of flashback is called an *abreaction*. The occurrence of flashbacks usually cannot be predicted. Some even occur during sleep without waking. Generally, flashbacks refer to visual and/or auditory parts of the trauma, but they also can refer to dissociated body responses (such as pain), emotions (intense anger that comes out of nowhere), and behaviors (acting in certain ways when a trigger comes up). Whenever a flashback happens, it feels as if the trauma were occurring all over again. You do not black out or lose physical consciousness during a flashback; however, you do leave the present time temporarily. A flashback that occurs during sleep can be a nightmare or even a vivid dream. Meichenbaum (1994) notes that flashbacks also can appear as intrusive thoughts or reexperiencing, or as intense feelings.

During a flashback, your traumas get replayed with great intensity; in many cases, unless you know how, you may not even be able to separate your flashback from present reality, reinforcing the impact of that trauma on you. Even young children can have flashbacks; however, they tend to act them out rather than express them in words. Sometimes children may act out upon others what was done to them; e.g., a nine-year-old boy who sexually acts out toward a younger sibling may be having a flashback rather than just acting as an offender.

Ruth, thirty, suddenly feels her uncle's body on her as she is taking a shower, and recognizes his touch. The uncle molested her twenty-five years before. Margaret, thirty-five, lives in an apartment with two other people. Their upstairs neighbors play music until late at night. When Margaret and her roommates complain to the management, the male renters upstairs retaliate by banging on the ceiling at all hours of the night and by scratching up Margaret's car and the cars of her roommates. Margaret is a date rape survivor, and these neighbors' behavior has led to flashbacks of the attack twenty years earlier. She is hypervigilant as she prepares for a potential attack.

Sometimes it is very difficult to make sense of flashbacks, particularly when there are not explicit events to use as reference points for them. Flashbacks may involve explicit memories of entire scenes of traumatic events or just parts of the events. Usually a flashback also includes some emotional and sensory aspect of the traumatic event. This means that your entire nervous system is involved when you have a flashback; your nervous system becomes hyperaroused when you are exposed to trauma triggers.

Sometimes, flashbacks occur even when it seems that the trauma has been worked through. When this happens, you might ask yourself the following questions:

- What is the flashback trying to tell me?

- Do I have more to see?

- Do I have more to feel?

- Do I have more to hear?

- Do I have more to learn or accept about what happened to me?

- Am I able to grab onto the content of the flashback after it is over, and I am no longer dissociative?

Through some of the techniques in this workbook, you can learn to deal with flashbacks in different ways.

EXERCISE: **Beginning to Deal with a Flashback**

Think of a flashback you have had in the past two weeks. Remember that the new definition of PTSD sees a flashback as a type of dissociative event, because you are not in the present when you have it but have returned to the past.

Describe the flashback and what you experienced:

_____

_____

Have you had a similar flashback in the past? If so, when and under what conditions?

_____

_____

How did the flashback smell, feel, or sound? Who was involved?

_____

_____

How did the actual traumatic experience smell, feel, or sound? Who was involved?

_____

_____

How are the flashback and the past traumatic situation different or the same?

_____

_____

What actions can you take to feel better as the flashback occurs?

_____

_____

How can you ground yourself to stay in the present when flashbacks occur?

_____

_____

How did you feel as you did this exercise? You can use it for any flashback you have.

_____

_____

The DVD Technique

Another way to deal with flashbacks is to put the content that is repeated as a shortened form on a "DVD" in your mind. Then you can play the memory in small sections using the on-and-off controls. You can even fast-forward or scan backward. These actions give you a sense of choice and control over your reexperiencing of the traumatic event. You also can add something to the beginning or end of the flashback to frame it—perhaps an alternative ending to what happened or an image of your safe place.

EXERCISE: Using the DVD Technique

Before you work on a traumatic flashback with this technique, try it with a positive memory of an event that you've experienced.

The event that I am going to use is _____

When I fast-forward through this event, I (see, feel, hear, smell, experience, etc.)

_____

When I rewind this event, I _____

When I frame this event with other pictures, I _____

If I were to use positive images to frame my flashback, I would use these:

_____

If you don't feel immediately comfortable with this technique, practice it more, until you are comfortable. Then try it with a traumatic flashback.

The flashback that I am going to use is: _____

When I fast-forward this event, and to how the flashback played out, I (see, feel, hear, smell, experience, etc.)

_____

When I rewind what I know of the flashback, I _____

When I frame the flashback with other pictures, I _____

How comfortable was this technique to use with a flashback? Was it more or less comfortable than when you used it with a positive memory?

_____

Getting Outside Your Head

One important way to deal with a flashback is to get it outside of your dissociative head and body into the present-day world around you. You can do that by writing about it, talking about it, drawing it, making a collage about it, or otherwise representing it someplace other than in your dissociated journey into your past.

The next few pages will give you more guidance about dealing with your flashbacks. If you are currently in therapy and find doing these activities to be too powerful, wait until you are in a therapy session to complete them. If you have a supportive person who is willing to listen to you as you talk about your flashbacks, then work on this section of the book in close contact with that person. Working on flashbacks can be very powerful, and it is important that you take care of yourself while doing so.

JOURNAL EXERCISE: Defusing Flashbacks

Dolan has developed a four-step approach to help defuse flashbacks (1991, 107). To use it, answer the following questions in your journal after having a flashback:

1. In what situation(s) have you felt the same way before?

2. In what ways are the current situation and the past situation similar? Is there a similar setting, time of year, sound, or other aspect? If there is a person involved, how is that person similar to one who was involved in your trauma(s) in the past?

3. How is the current situation different from the past situation into which you dissociated? What is different about your current life circumstances, support systems, or environment? How are the people around you different from those involved in your traumatic experiences?

4. What actions can you take (if any) to feel better now, particularly if you feel unsafe in your flashback? If your flashback is merely an old memory that does not cause you to be unsafe, you may merely need to give yourself a positive message that you *can* survive or work through it or do something different. However, if you truly are unsafe, it is important to be aware of the real danger and protect yourself.

Other Ways to Deal with Flashbacks

You may use any of the following techniques to help you put a flashback out of your awareness and return to the present if you actually are aware that the flashback is occurring. Some of them are designed to be quick, while others take time. Do not worry if many or most of them do not work for you. Try them out and choose those that work best.

- Repeatedly blink your eyes hard.

- Change the position of your body.

- Use deep breathing (from chapter 2).

- Use imagery to go to your safe place in your mind.

- Go to your actual safe place.

- Move vigorously around your environment.

- Name objects in your environment out loud.

- Hold on to a safe object.

- Listen to a soothing audio recording, such as one a therapist made for you if you are in counseling.

- Clap your hands.

- Stamp your feet on the floor.

- Wash your face with cold water.

- Say positive statements (affirmations) about yourself.

- In your imagination, spray the memory with a bottle of cleanser until it goes away.

- Project the flashback onto a dry erase board and then erase it; do the back and forth movements of the eraser with your hand.

- Draw the flashback on paper, then destroy or get rid of the paper (shred it, burn it, bury it).

- Put the flashback into some type of vault or container (real, on paper, or symbolically in your mind).

Using Dual Awareness to Treat Flashbacks

This flashback-halting protocol (Rothschild 2000, 133), is based on the principles of dual awareness, which was discussed earlier in this chapter. It is designed to reconcile the experiencing self with the observing self and is intended to stop a traumatic flashback quickly. Practice this technique on "old" flashbacks (those you have had, processed, and perhaps put to rest) so that you can learn it well.

And then use it later when you have a flashback that includes new aspects of traumatic events or previously unknown traumatic events or material.

EXERCISE: **Flashback-Halting Protocol**

The flashback I am using is_____.

Say to yourself (preferably aloud) the following sentences, filling in the blanks:

Right now I am feeling _____ (insert name of the current emotion, usually fear) and I am sensing in my body _____ _____ (describe your current bodily sensations—name at least three), because I dissociated into a flashback about _____ (identify the trauma by title only—no details).

At the same time, I am looking around where I am now in _____ (the actual current year), here _____ (name the place where you are), and I can see _____ (describe some of the things that you see right now, in this place), and so I know _____ (name the trauma, again by title only) is not happening now/anymore.

How did this technique work for you? What was it like to do it?

_____

_____

What else can you do to bring your dissociative flashback (more) under control?

_____

_____

Changing Negative Thoughts to Positive

An additional technique you can use when you have a flashback is to change the negative thoughts that occur after the flashback (*I'm a failure for having this flashback; I really couldn't protect myself*) into more positive thoughts. This is done through self-dialogue. Say to yourself, if you are afraid after a flashback, *This is now, not then; I did everything I could do to protect myself during the traumatic event. I survived then, and I will survive now.*

EXERCISE: **My Preferred Flashback Technique**

What have you learned about your flashbacks and how to control or deal with them through doing these exercises?

_____

_____

Which exercise(s) helped you most?

_____

Triggers: Reminders of Trauma Across the Senses

A trigger is a piece of an event that intrudes into the present and reminds you of what happened in your past. When you react to a trigger of a traumatic event, your adrenal glands get aroused and memories of the traumatic event get activated, as do emotions associated with the event. These reactions may occur even when you do not recall the exact traumatic event—the physiological reactions can get resurrected by themselves (Matsakis 1994a). Triggers may exist for nontraumatic events as well; for example, smelling brownies baking may trigger pleasant memories of childhood. However, traumatic triggers are often unpleasant or frightening. They may lead to a flashback or to feelings of anxiety, panic, fear, anger, rage, confusion, shakiness, or numbness, or to a sense of spacing out or dissociation. They can retraumatize you.

It can be helpful to develop a list of triggers that lead to flashbacks (that cause you to respond by dissociating) or to unpleasant feelings associated with trauma. Once you have identified your triggers and are aware of them, you will be better able to bring them under control, and even choose not to react to them.

In your journal, you may write about, draw, collage, or otherwise represent triggers of your traumatic event(s). In the next few pages you will also be asked to write down your reactions to those triggers when you experience them. It is important to keep some type of record of how quickly a flashback has occurred after exposure to a trigger, and of where you were, what you were doing, who was with you, and what exactly happened. Once you have identified your triggers (or at least have begun to keep a trigger list), you can then learn how to avoid or defuse them in less time. It also is important that you identify how you've previously gotten past triggered flashbacks or feelings. Identifying any small sign of returning to the present can help you control triggered reactions.

JOURNAL EXERCISE: My Trigger List

This exercise has three parts: the list, your past reaction to your triggers, and your ideas for future responses.

1. In your notebook or journal, write about or list your triggers associated with

    - what I saw

    - what I heard

    - what I smelled

    - what I touched or what touched me

    - what I tasted

    - my body (physical triggers other than sensory triggers)

    - certain places

    - nature or time (e.g., weather, seasons, time of day)

    - certain people

    If a person is a trigger, try to determine what specific behaviors, characteristics, or attitudes of the person trigger you. Then look at the specific aspects of the trauma that are triggered by this person and at how the person is related to the traumatic event. Triggers might involve the age of a particular person—for example, the person may now be at an age which you associate with a traumatic event.

2. In the next nine pages of your journal, write each category of trigger listed above at the top of a page, then write about your reactions to triggers in each category, writing about both positive and negative ways you reacted to each. How do your more recent reactions compare to reactions you've had in the past? What good things happened in those reactions? Did you experience any positive emotions or have any pleasant memories? What bad things happened? How likely do you believe it is that you will experience the trigger again?

3. Now think of ways you might deal with each of these triggers in the future to take power away from them. Write a response for each of the trigger areas on a separate page in your journal or notebook.

Managing Trigger Events

When you learn to take more control over your triggers, the trauma loses some of its power and control over you. In controlling your triggers, it is important to plan ahead and find ways to deal with them before they occur. It also is important to identify people who might help you deal with these triggers. Power (1992a) lists some ways to manage triggers that may help you plan your own strategies and techniques:

- relaxation exercises

- breathing exercises

- appropriate medication

- contact with supportive others

- establishing manageable lists of priorities

- avoiding extra stress

- structuring your life to avoid contact with certain specific triggers

As Matsakis notes, "The goal is to manage the trigger event, not…have no negative feelings or sensations about it" (1994b, 147). As you plan ways to deal with the specific triggers you named, it might be best to start by working on triggers that you believe are easiest to manage or control. Some triggers, such as seeing your perpetrator face-to-face, may take months or years to learn to overcome, if you are ever able to manage them. As you plan your strategies, think of your history with each particular trigger, the symptoms that the trigger evokes, the specific fears associated with the trigger, and the coping mechanisms you will use.

Remember, it is your choice how you deal with each and every trigger you have listed in your journal. You can never avoid everything that triggers you. Thus, as Meichenbaum (1994) notes, it is important to control your own inner experience rather than try to avoid everything that triggers your automatic responses. You can disarm a trigger when you understand how the past is not the present.

Trigger work can be very stressful. It always involves some type of processing of the feelings associated with the trauma, so you can know they can no longer hurt you. You may always turn to some of the self-soothing exercises in chapter 2 should you begin to feel overwhelmed. You also may use these calming exercises when you are aware that a trigger is about to happen. The following exercise is designed to help you with any trigger that you choose from the previous pages. If some triggers are too difficult to face alone, do not do this exercise, or do it only in the presence of your therapist or in a group situation designed to work on trauma. Please remember, too, that you cannot get rid of the power of a trigger overnight. It takes time to substitute new behaviors for old ones.

EXERCISE: **Dealing with My Trigger**

If you want to deal with more than one trigger, download additional copies of this exercise from http://www.newharbinger.com/33704 and use one copy for each trigger.

1. When you distract yourself from the power and influence of the trigger, that trigger eventually will have little or no power over your life in the present. With that in mind, please complete the following statement: I choose to distract myself from

    _____ (name the trigger) by _____ .

    List some other ways you might distract yourself (for example, listening to, singing, or whistling a favorite song as soon as the trigger starts; covering your ears or using earplugs; or talking to yourself about what is real or not real, or about the present):

    _____

    _____

2. I choose to practice staying present in the now when I experience this trigger by grounding or using other techniques I have learned.

    For example, I may ignore _____ (name the trigger). I also may _____ .

    Or, I may name five things, then four, then three, then two, then one thing, that I see, hear, or smell around me (almost as a form of mindfulness observation):

    _____

    _____

3. Now, after you have tried one or more of these ways to gain control of a trigger, write about that experience and how it felt:

    I was _____ when _____ (name the trigger) occurred.

    When I began to have a reaction to _____ (name the trigger), I chose to _____ (distract myself, ignore it, stay present) by _____ .

    When _____ (name the trigger) began to fade in its power, I felt _____ and then I _____ (describe what you did).

The Trigger Mapping Ladder

There are many ways to represent triggers. One of these, the trigger mapping ladder, was developed by one of the authors of this book as she worked with a group of people diagnosed with dissociative identity disorder. The ladder is a diagram showing that trigger events lead to an escalation of tension, which causes many different systems in a person to react and may lead to retraumatization. Thoughts and feelings, physical cues, and actions can either heat up or cool down triggers. Cooling down the trigger response involves taking away its power. It helps you make the connection between your triggers and your responses, look at your thoughts and feelings, calm yourself, and find meaning in the entire process.

This process can help you bring control into your life by separating the past from the present and changing the way you react to your trigger(s). Approach each rung of the ladder slowly and calmly, and take small steps up and down it. Some images and symbols of your triggers can lead you to more information about your traumatic experiences, serving as clues to what happened to you and why you react as you do.

EXERCISE: **Using the Trigger Mapping Ladder**

Going up the left side of the ladder, which follows (and is available for download at http://www.newharbinger.com/33704), are four phrases. Starting at the bottom, next to where it says "Trigger Event," write in the name of an internal or external trigger—a sight, sound, smell, time of year, thought, or other event or thing. Above the event or thing, write in what types of reactions you have as you become aware of your reaction to the trigger. What in your body gets tense? What emotions surface? Moving up one step to the space marked "Escalation of Tension," write in how you react. You may not have a response for each one of these sections, but write in as many as you can. Once the trigger has led to your reaction, what is that reaction? Do you have a full-blown flashback? Do you feel uneasy? Do you break into a cold sweat or begin to cry? Do you feel as if you are retraumatized?

On the right side of the ladder, going from top to bottom, are a series of phrases describing behaviors that may help you de-escalate the trigger. What might you do for each of them? What thoughts and feelings might help you take away the trigger's power? One might be *I am in the present; the trigger is from my past and it is not happening now.* Another response might be *I need to take five deep cleansing breaths.* Again, you may not have a response to each phrase, but put in whatever you can that might help you lessen the trigger's hold on you.

Here's an example of how the ladder might work for a particular situation. Let's say you are a survivor of sexual abuse. You have to go to family function, your father's birthday party, and know that your grandfather, who abused you, will be present. As you think about the party, you notice that you begin to have escalating tension both in your body and in

Trigger Mapping

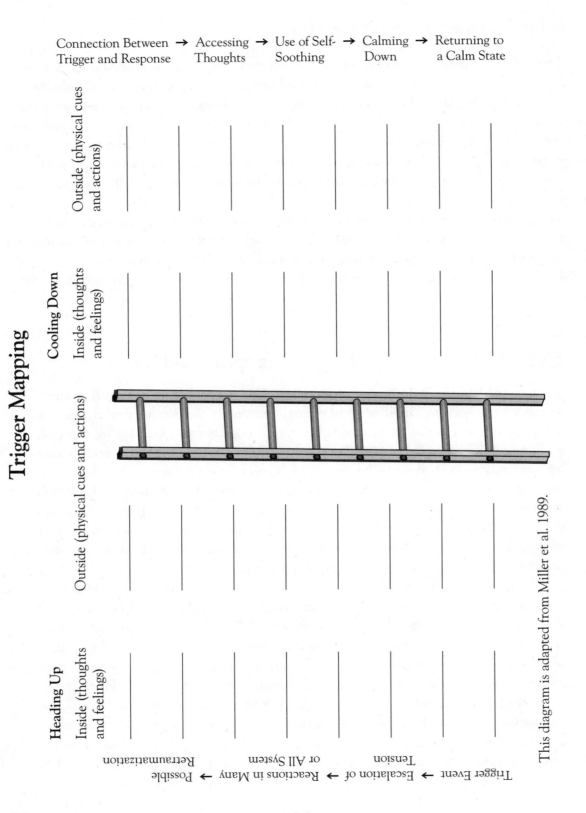

	Connection Between → Trigger and Response	Accessing → Thoughts	Use of Self- → Soothing	Calming → Down	Returning to a Calm State

Cooling Down

Outside (physical cues and actions)

Inside (thoughts and feelings)

Outside (physical cues and actions)

Heading Up

Inside (thoughts and feelings)

Trigger Event → Escalation of → Reactions in Many → Possible Tension or All System Retraumatization

This diagram is adapted from Miller et al. 1989.

your thoughts and feelings. How is your body reacting—where does the tension begin? At first, your shoulders get tight and your palms begin to sweat. Then you get a pounding head-ache and you begin to remember a specific abusive encounter, which leads to pain in your lower abdomen. At the same time, you have thoughts of wanting to escape, wanting to avoid going to the party. You feel frightened and may even begin to experience a panic attack. You may even hear some of your grandfather's words in your mind, and your thoughts about him take over.

What can you do? How can you combat all these feelings and physical symptoms? On the right side of the ladder are spaces for you to de-escalate. You may say to yourself, *This is now, that was then; I am an adult now and can protect myself; he is a little old man.* You also may recognize that the physical cues you are having reflect back to the early abuse. As you process what is going on, you might begin to look at what you can do to combat both the physical reactions and the feelings. You might set up a strategy to keep out of direct contact with him. You may ask your husband/partner to run interference. You may decide to approach him and warn him to leave you alone. You may even think of ways to avoid the party. Then you can begin to self-soothe. You may take deep breaths, go for a walk, listen to music, or write out a script to say to your abuser. While you are in this calm state, think of things that can bring you back to the here and now. When you feel calmer, look at the process and how you have helped yourself. Realize that this process is difficult and may take time (and practice) to work. Trying to do the process is the first step to overcoming major reactions to triggers!

Using Activities and Anchors to Reduce Triggers

Another way to gain some control over your traumatic triggers, dreams, nightmares, and intrusive thoughts is to participate in activities that can give you a break from reexperiencing your trauma. Helpful activities, according to Rothschild (2000), are those that need your concentration and atten-tion so that the intrusions of trauma don't take over. It is easy for intrusive thoughts to wander in while you're watching a movie or DVD. However, they do not come in as easily if you are doing some-thing that demands attention and body awareness. For example, you may iron clothes, keeping enough awareness of what you are doing that you don't burn them or yourself.

Another way to help yourself is to use an *anchor*. Rothschild describes an anchor as "a concrete, observable resource," or one that is outside your own mind (2000, 91). That resource may be a beloved person or pet, a place (e.g., your home), an object, or an activity. It helps you feel relief and well-being in your body; thinking about it can serve as a braking tool for a trigger or intrusive thought, without changing reality. Your safe place is another anchor that can provide protection for you.

What are some activities you could use to control your intrusive thought?

_____

_____

What are your own personal anchors?

_____

Exposing Yourself Safely to Your Past Traumas

You may have noticed that we have not asked you to describe your traumatic memories in great detail. Such exposure is more of a task for therapy. We do not want to retraumatize you by overwhelming you with memories unless you do the exercises with a counselor or therapist. The closest we have come to directly exposing you to the trauma has been asking you to write about what happened to you. Putting your traumatic experiences into a story with a beginning, middle, and end helps diffuse the strong emotions associated with the traumas (Meichenbaum 1994).

Direct exposure therapy, where you look at your traumatic memories in detail, needs to be done under the guidance of a professional in a course of anywhere from nine to fourteen sessions of sixty to ninety minutes each. Direct exposure therapy takes you back into your traumatic experience and asks you to discuss

- when the traumatic event happened

- how long it lasted

- the entire story, from the start of the incident to after it was over

- everything of which you are aware about the setting and the event

- any earlier incident(s) similar to the one you are describing

- your interpretation of the impact the event has on you at the present moment

All of the description is done in the present tense and in great detail. Direct exposure therapy needs a great deal of preparation in order for you, as the client, to endure the process without experiencing overwhelming anxiety, suicidal thoughts, or intense fear. The motto behind doing this work is "no pain, no gain." However, the extent of pain that can be caused by exposure therapy or overexposure to the traumatic event is too great to include it as part of the work in this workbook. This description of exposure therapy is included here strictly as information about another way to process what has happened to you.

The Flower Diagram

If you want to take a part of a memory or an entire memory and look at it in more detail, you might use the flower diagram that follows as your guide. (The diagram is also available for download at http://www.newharbinger.com/33704.) When analyzing any memory using the flower diagram, you have six separate sections to examine: sensory experiences; beliefs; body reactions; emotions; wants; and actions. Try not to allow yourself to reexperience it or to float into a dissociative state as you write in your answers; try to imagine you are looking at it on a TV or movie screen.

EXERCISE: **My Flower Diagram**

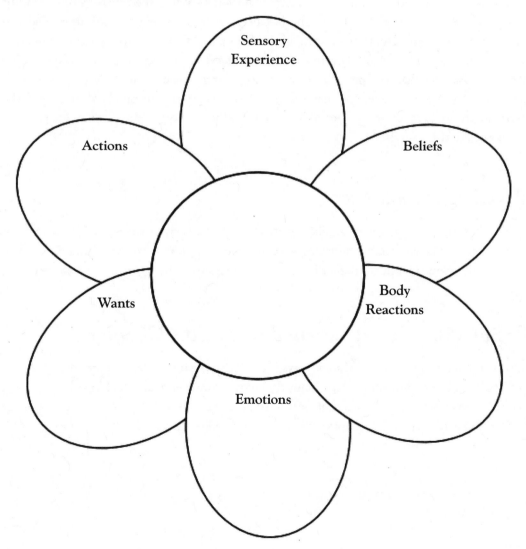

At the center of the diagram, write in the memory that you wish to examine. In the first petal of the flower, write in any sensory experiences that come to mind when you think about the memory. What smells, sights, sounds, or touch sensations come to mind? In the next petal, write in your thoughts and beliefs about the trauma. What messages were told to you before, during, and after that trauma that you have incorporated into your own mind (your introjects)? What conclusions have you reached about the trauma? (For example, *I believe it was my fault; I believe I can never be safe; I believe that I caused the event to happen; I believe that I was not to blame for anything that happened.*) In the next petal, record how your body reacted during the traumatic event. For example, did you freeze, run away, cry, or numb yourself? In the fourth petal, write down any emotions that you can remember having. Were you terrified? Embarrassed? Shocked? In the fifth petal, write down anything you wanted during the trauma. Did you want to dissociate? Did you want to just go away, or did you want to attack the perpetrator? Finally, in the last petal, record any actions you took. Did you choose to escape through dissociation? Did you fight back? Did you participate in some way? If you do not have total recall or even partial recall of any of the sections, you may have some degree of what is called traumatic amnesia, or forgetting. Just write in what you do remember. If you need more space, you may use additional pages in your notebook to record the information. Remember, try to keep a distance from the memory and the traumatic event as you complete this exercise.

Avoiding Avoidance

There are other ways to cope with traumatic events. One way is to try to avoid or deny what happened to you. Some denial is natural, but, at times, avoiding the impact on you of your traumatic events can be detrimental to you. The next chapter looks at some ways you can lessen your avoidance.

EXERCISE: **What I Learned from This Chapter**

In this chapter, you have learned some ways to deal with the intrusive, reexperiencing aspects of PTSD. These are only some of the many different techniques available. Hopefully, through practice and effort, they will work (at least to some degree) for you. Remember, you can refer back to the exercises in this chapter whenever you need to do so.

What have you learned about yourself through the work you have done in this chapter?

_____

_____

How did the techniques provided in chapter 2 help you calm yourself if you needed to do so?

_____

_____

5

Coping with Trauma with Less Avoidance

It is not unusual to want to avoid remembering or reexperiencing the traumatic event(s) that happened to you. Why on earth would you want to put yourself through it all again? Why would you want to desensitize yourself (learn to deal with all your triggers, thoughts, memories)? If you were in a hurricane at the beach and lost your home, why would you ever want to live by the ocean again? If you were on a plane that almost crashed, or that did crash, why would you ever even dream of traveling anywhere other than by car or train? If you were hurt in a certain neighborhood, why would you ever even think of going there again, even if your relatives live there or it is near your place of work?

If you refer back to the description of PTSD found in chapter 1 of this workbook, you will see the avoidance symptoms that now constitute Category C of the PTSD diagnosis. Do you avoid places, conversations, activities, objects, people, or situations that remind you of your trauma? Does that mean that you isolate yourself from others and avoid social activities? Do you try to avoid distressing memories, thoughts, or emotions to the degree that you don't let yourself feel? Do you instantaneously suppress things that in any way remind you of your traumatic experiences or of the feelings that you had during or after them? Do you use avoidance to manage symptoms of reexperiencing or arousal?

In general terms, in order to avoid memories and associated trauma symptoms, you may try to isolate yourself and avoid any triggers that remind you of what happened. This may work for some period of time, but eventually you may want or need to leave your protective cocoon and return to a world that will inevitably in some way or another trigger you.

Avoidance may have kept you from seeking treatment for PTSD. If you are at least somewhat successful in keeping the traumatic events separated from yourself, why open up the wounds? Perhaps you have put the traumas into individual boxes you have symbolically constructed in your brain. Perhaps you have manufactured ways to suppress thoughts that intrude into your daily life. Inevitably, however, the means you use or have used to avoid will no longer work. For example, as many Vietnam veterans who had long-standing careers or employment now retire, they no longer have their work as a barrier against remembering. Their memories are flooding and they are seeking treatment or at least realizing the impact that military service has had on them. If they look to PTSD treatment, they will learn that the most accepted ways of helping them deal with their pasts involve some form of reexperiencing, whether through exposure therapy, cognitive behavioral therapy, narrative therapy, or eye movement desensitization and reprocessing (see chapter 9).

Using Avoidance to Cope

Coping attempts to minimize the impacts of traumatic events are sometimes maladaptive mechanisms to protect the self from (presumed) psychological damage. This generally means you are using cognitive or behavioral ways to avoid through self-isolation and/or through emotional avoidance. These efforts may seem to help you initially, but over time, whatever is avoided tends to come back by an even more intrusive means. As Michele Rosenthal, who recently published a book based on her trauma blog, states, "Nothing in recovery happens unless you make it happen. So what will happen if you continue to avoid? Nothing" (2013, 2015). In other words, getting stuck in avoidance means getting stuck in a fear-based strategy of survival, survival that allows you to continue to function to some degree.

Briere and Scott (2015) write of other avoidance responses including

- reduced emotional reactivity to trauma triggers

- dissociative disengagement from potentially upsetting stimuli

- thought suppression through blocking or active attempts to disengage from potentially upsetting thoughts or memories

- denial, not of the events themselves but of their impact, seriousness, or threat

- use of some type of substance prior to treatment sessions that blocks anxious responses to trauma triggers but is not evident to or known to the treating professional (73).

Many times it seems as if, just as you work through some aspects of your traumas, something new shows up in its place, often something frightening that you do not want to face. Often, fear drives avoidance behaviors, emotions, and thoughts. Sometimes, in order to function, it is necessary to try to avoid facing the traumas and their impacts. Sometimes, avoidance is purposeful and shows you are not ready to do some aspect of healing work. Breaking the work into small, more manageable pieces may be the only way to slog through.

In order to move through avoidance, it is not imperative to face an entire traumatic event all at once. In fact, it makes more sense to break the trauma down into manageable pieces of your choosing and look at them one by one, not necessarily in chronological order. It is possible to block from memory, suppress, or dissociate from visual/experiential memories of the trauma. Yet verbal memories (from others' voices), physiological reactions, and emotional responses all attest to the reality of what happened. In this instance, people can spend years searching for the missing pieces that are so deeply buried or separated from the self. Recently, a presumed survivor of child sexual abuse, who has dissociative reenactments of her traumas that occur only in heightened states of adrenal reactivity, was angrily talking about her father and mother and said that it was not right for all this to happen to a seven-year-old. Later, as she had calmed herself, Mary Beth brought to her attention the comment of her being seven. It was as if a light bulb went on in her head as she began to look in a less emotional or even dissociated way at her historical past. The realization that the event had occurred about the age of seven was very significant because it allowed her to look at other events that occurred during that period of time (e.g., her mother was hospitalized) that could have allowed the events to happen.

EXERCISE: Making a Memory More Manageable by Breaking It into Smaller Parts

Choose a memory of an event that has some importance to you but is not necessarily traumatic.

The setting of the event as I remember it was

_____

_____

What is the first thing you remember about that event?

_____

_____

What were your initial thoughts about what was happening?

_____

_____

Then what happened?

_____

_____

What happened next?

_____

_____

Anything after that?

_____

_____

How did the event end?

_____

_____

What are the most important facts about the event?

_____

_____

What emotions did you have during the event?

_____

_____

What feelings do you have about it now?

_____

_____

What impact did the event have on your life, if any?

_____

_____

What have you learned about the event by doing this exercise?

_____

_____

Experiential avoidance helps to maintain PTSD over time (Thompson 2012). Suppressing thoughts about your traumatic events may lead to temporary relief, but this sense of relief is short–lived. The focus of existence for the survivor may even become how to avoid and bring back that temporary relief rather than how to heal. It is possible that more and more stimuli get associated with the trauma, leading to even more attempts to avoid. Perhaps you, the survivor, will turn to risky behaviors that can bring you harm, including the use of substances, overeating, isolation, and others (see category E). This may lead to avoidance of potentially helpful experiences, including building new friendships and being active in the world.

The Practical Function of Avoidance

If you have a positive PTSD diagnosis, it is a given that you do have some symptoms of avoidance surrounding what happened to you. As noted, it often takes a great deal of energy to avoid dealing with any traumatic memories, triggers, nightmares, or other reminders of traumatic events you may experience. You may take major steps to avoid places, people, or events that remind you of what happened to you. You may tell yourself over and over, _I'm fine; it didn't bother me at all,_ while at the same time, on the inside, you know that you are still feeling all the impacts of the trauma. You also may worry about or focus on other things to try to occupy your mind, so you don't think about the traumatic events. Pennebaker and Campbell (2000) found that people who try to suppress their intrusive thoughts, images, dreams, and memories end up having more threatening and more frequent intrusions that go beyond the actual trauma and involve thoughts of aggression, death, illness, failure, and other dreadful events.

Perhaps you do not have the words to express what happened to you. Perhaps there _are_ no words that can express your horror. Some avoidance of traumatic reminders or memories is healthy. But how do you know when avoidance is healthy and when it is not? If avoidance protects you from being traumatized further, then it is healthy. If you need to do something that is very important to you, and consciousness of the trauma would cause you to have so much pain that you could not do what you needed to do, then some degree of avoidance is healthy.

For example, George is giving a speech in his English class. He has been assigned the topic of family violence. His wife is a very verbally and physically abusive person, and he is working in therapy on controlling his angry reactions to her tirades. If he allows himself to feel all the pain he associates with this topic when he does his class presentation, he will be retraumatized. He chooses to numb out his emotions, gives his speech, gets an "A," and then talks about it with his therapist. He ends up crying because his classmates could not understand how a male could be the recipient of violence.

Dennis is nineteen. He was molested by his stepfather, as was his sister. His stepfather was a minister, and when his sister revealed her abuse, he was defrocked. He shares his abuse history with his mother and fears that something terrible will happen to him because he has told. Two days after he tells his mother, his sister is killed in a car crash. Her stepfather gets special permission from the bishop to preach at her funeral. Dennis is a pallbearer and must be there. He uses his ability to dissociate to get him through the funeral and deal with his abusive stepfather's eulogy.

You can examine your practical use of avoidance by filling in the following statement:

I have used avoidance in a protective, positive way when _____

Dissociation as an Avoidance Mechanism

Matsakis (1998) notes that many trauma survivors do all they can, including dissociate, to avoid being in triggering situations or relationships, so they won't be hyperaroused. Dissociation not only includes having flashbacks (see chapter 4) but also can function as a way to protect yourself from perceived threat and the bad emotions that are associated with what happened to you. Briere and Scott (2015) write that visible dissociative symptoms are explicit signs of avoidance, including zoning out, spacing out, or having the "thousand yard stare" (74).

Dissociation is a way to withstand an overwhelming event; it is a survival strategy to use during that event. The more severe your trauma, the more naturally you dissociate to protect yourself.

How frequently do you use dissociation now? Do you daydream, have imaginary play, or go to a fantasy world to escape? Do you watch TV for hours without remembering anything you watched? Do you play computer or video games for hours on end?

EXERCISE: When Do I Dissociate?

List up to five situations that lead you to space out or dissociate at the present time:

1. _____

2. _____

3. _____

4. _____

5. _____

What Can You Do About Dissociating?

The first thing to do about dissociating is to realize when you dissociate and why. Building awareness of triggers that might lead to dissociation can help you prepare yourself for the dissociative experience or can help prevent it from occurring. Grounding techniques, such as those discussed in chapter 2, also can help you prevent dissociation or cut it short.

The following technique for dealing with dissociation comes from the field of neurolinguistic programming (NLP); it was developed by Bandler (1985):

1. If you find that you have dissociated some aspect of a traumatic event, allow yourself to put the event on a movie screen and then sit in the audience (much as was done with the rewind technique in chapter 4).

2. Now go to your safe place to anchor yourself (see chapter 2 for information and exercises about your safe place).

3. Now freeze what you saw, heard, or otherwise experienced (mentally put it in a container on ice, or compartmentalize it in some other way) and move back into your body.

4. Spend time comforting both your present self and the younger self who experienced the trauma. Tell that younger you that she or he is going to be okay and that she or he was not responsible for what happened. Explain to your younger self all the details of the trauma that you observed.

5. Use grounding techniques, such as those in chapter 2, to return to the present time.

There are many other ways to deal with dissociation. One excellent resource is the Sidran Institute for traumatic stress education and advocacy.

CONSEQUENCES OF DISSOCIATION

Among the consequences of dissociating are

- blunted emotional and physical pain, pleasure, and responsiveness; loss of interest in the world and things that previously brought pleasure to you

- inability to discriminate between pain and pleasure (when you do not feel emotions, it is easier for you to be revictimized)

- errors of thinking

- lack of emotional responsiveness, leading to feelings of shame and the belief that one is shameful

- retreating from life

- feeling detached from others

- having no interest in sex; having sexual dysfunction (behaviors)

- having no energy; feeling apathetic (not caring) and lethargic (being tired all the time)

- experiencing mental sluggishness

- being unable to feel physical pain.

Do any of these happen to you?

Returning to our previous example of the automobile accident, you may ask yourself the following questions: Have you previously ever been involved in an automobile accident? Have you ever experienced a broken bone and not felt the pain? Perhaps, after the automobile accident, you got out of the car and walked to the other car that was involved. You were not yet aware of the huge bruise on your leg or the significant bump on your head. Your only emotion was the anger you felt toward the other driver who hit you. You felt no relief that you were not seriously injured. You were still in your body but felt no pain. You may want to write in your journal or notebook about any experiences with this type of dissociation of pain.

The following exercise lists a number of ways to shut down, so you do not feel or do not face the traumatic events that happened to you. If you use any of these methods other than using them to protect yourself in a constructive way, consider seeking support and help from others, such as a professional trauma therapist, supportive family members, understanding friends, and fellow survivors. This exercise can then be something you share with those supportive others, particularly a therapist.

EXERCISE: **What I Do to Avoid My Traumatic Past**

Put a check mark by every one of the ways you avoid facing your traumas through different types of dissociative responses:

☐ separate myself from my body

☐ become out of touch with my surroundings

☐ stare off into space blankly for more than a minute

☐ become an observer of my present situation rather than a participant in that situation

☐ escape into fantasy or daydreaming

☐ use magical thinking excessively (thinking you can control with your thoughts events unrelated to you)

☐ act like a robot; being on autopilot

☐ feel as if I am watching myself from outside my body

Put a check mark by any of the arousal responses you've had. Arousal responses are those in which you might find that you are:

☐ unable to concentrate

☐ unaware of potential dangers in my environment

☐ participating in high-risk activities or play (list which ones)

☐ falling asleep even when I'm around others

☐ exhibiting compulsive behaviors, including workaholism

☐ compulsively or addictively using drugs or alcohol

☐ acting much younger than I am

☐ seeing shadowy black figures or ghostlike figures, particularly when I am falling asleep or just waking

☐ being confused much of the time

☐ taking risks of all kinds to create excitement and counteract the dead feeling inside

☐ rocking back and forth to soothe myself

Describe when, where, why, and how you use these ways to avoid or dissociate.

_____

_____

_____

What do your answers tell you about yourself and how you avoid your traumatic experiences or memories of your traumas?

_____

_____

Reducing Dissociation as Avoidance

It is important that you focus more on personal self-care and safety than on exploring the memories of your traumatic events if you find that you are frequently dissociating or avoiding them. You may even want to ask yourself regularly, "Where am I now (in reality)?" rather than "Where did I go?" if you dissociate when you avoid. This will help you return to the present time and remind you where you are in the physical world. It also is important for you to identify the triggers that lead you to avoiding, as well as the functions the avoidance serves by your dissociating.

Remember, your dissociative responses to trauma were adaptive at the time that the trauma happened. That is, they were behaviors that helped you survive. They may continue to be adaptive if you still feel that need. However, it is up to you to decide when and where that occurs and, if dissociating appears to be maladaptive (harming rather than helping you), it is also up to you to decide whether or not you want to implement exercises in this workbook that may reveal if they are helpful or not.

Here are some strategies to reduce avoidance. After each strategy, in the space provided, write about how (if) you used this strategy and how (if) it has been helpful to you.

1. A first step in reducing avoidance is to identify the feared memory or trigger. You can do this without going into great detail.

    How I do this: _____

    _____

2. The next step is to set some goals for engaging in safe, positive activities.

    How I do this: _____

    _____

3. You can use mindfulness to help you relax and feel safe (see chapter 2).

    How I do this: _____

    _____

4. You can also get help in exposure therapy with a trained professional in a safe setting, who can help you break the trauma down into manageable pieces or segments of your trauma story. Take it slowly.

    How I do this: _____

    _____

EXERCISE: **What I Learned About Dissociation**

What have you learned about yourself by completing the exercises on dissociation? Are there parts of what happened to you that are totally gone from any type of memory (body, emotional, or cognitive memory)? Do you dissociate frequently? Are you more able to identify the triggers for that dissociation?

_____

_____

Working to Reduce Other Types of Avoidance

If you avoid because you are afraid of feeling the emotions associated with what happened to you, then it is important that you begin to allow yourself to feel in little doses. If you are extremely anxious, you may want to take medication to help reduce your anxiety. Emotional over- or under-responsiveness is covered in the next chapter.

There are many ways you can reduce your attempts to avoid . First, allow yourself to look at what happened to you without going into the whole memory. You may use the writing techniques in chapter 3 to help you. You also may want to develop an outline or short version of your trauma as a beginning, using the following exercise. If you are a victim of long-lasting traumatic events, please do not try to do this exercise for all of them. You have had too many bad things happen to you to look at them one by one. Start with the least destructive traumatic experience.

EXERCISE: **A Short Outline of My Trauma**

Before the trauma, I felt _____.

Then, suddenly, _____ (name the trauma) happened.

The pieces (parts) of that trauma included a beginning, middle, and end, listed here:

_____

_____

During _____ (name the trauma) I (did or was) _____.

I also felt _____.

I was able to control _____.

I was unable to control _____.

When _____ (name the trauma) stopped,

I was _____.

Again, sometimes avoiding is necessary as a way to protect yourself from being absolutely overwhelmed by all of the bad things that happened to you. If you feel helpless in the face of your memories and therefore want to avoid them, use the following exercise to think of ways that you can take some control over your life in other areas.

EXERCISE: **Where I Experienced Losses Because I Chose to Avoid**

There are times when using avoidance as a coping mechanism may bring you pain or harm, may undermine achieving your goals, or may otherwise hurt. Looking back at your life, are there times when using avoidance behaviors got in the way of your success? Did you use avoidance and have negative results

☐ at work (if so, how and when?): _____

_____

_____

☐ at home (if so, how and when?): _____

_____

_____

☐ with children (if so, how and when?): _____

_____

_____

☐ with pets (if so, how and when?): _____

_____

_____

☐ at play (if so, how and when?): _____

_____

_____

☐ when doing spiritual practices (if so, how and when?): _____

_____

_____

Keeping Safe as You Try to Lessen Avoidance

If you do not feel safe enough to work on any of your memories, please turn back to chapter 2 and work on modifying and challenging your present beliefs about safety. Other areas of belief are addressed in chapter 6.

If you are going to face your traumas at all, it is important that you learn to look at yourself in a realistic way and learn how to respond to threats in an accurate, realistic manner. What do you believe will happen if you begin to look at your traumas? Do you believe that someone will come and get you, if you tell? Do you believe that someone will still punish you if you talk about what happened? Do you believe that there are people out there who still have control over your life and who can hurt you, if you deal with your traumas?

Beginning at age four, Annette was abused by her father. She continued to be molested until she was eighteen years of age and married. She told her mother about her abuse when she was twelve and her mother beat her. Annette finally confronted her father about the abuse in a therapy session with her therapist present. She had made an audio recording of what she remembered and had played it over and over with her therapist. They had talked about her memories, worked on what she would say, and practiced her confrontation. Her mother came with her father to the session. Her father admitted what he had done, and Annette recorded his response. Still, she continued to fear his retaliation and what the confrontation would mean. She became suicidal and ended up in a hospital. She has now taken the recording to the police, and the police want to prosecute her father. Still, she fears what he will do to her and that she will lose any contact with her mother and siblings because she told.

Tolerating Your Fears

Learning to deal with what happened to you means learning to tolerate painful emotions without needing to hurt yourself or trying to avoid them totally. Some of the emotions that get associated with trauma are grief, guilt, anger, shame, and fear. Probably the hardest emotion to deal with is trigger-based fear. Again, identifying your triggers and then working on ways to take away their power is a very important way to give you a sense of control. If you have not done this already, go back to chapter 4 and use the journal exercise "My Trigger List" to identify your triggers.

EXERCISE: **Triggers**

List the five triggers which you try to avoid the most, due to associated fear or pain, beginning with the worst. You may seek to develop ways to desensitize yourself from them, to get some distance away from them, or otherwise gain a sense of power over them.

1. _____

2. _____

3. _____

4. _____

5. _____

In the next exercise, you will choose three things you can do for each of these triggers to cause less pain or a desire to avoid them. For example, if you are triggered by the smell of a particular cologne that your abuser wore, you might

- Go to a perfume store and smell different colognes; include the one you fear as one of those you put on a tester strip. Take the strip and rip it up or stomp on it after you are done.

- Buy a bottle of the cologne and smash it.

- Take the cologne and spray it on something you really like to change your association with the cologne.

EXERCISE: **Dealing with Triggers That Lead to Avoidance**

Choose three actions to help you control each of your five triggers.

Trigger 1: _____

    a. _____

    b. _____

    c. _____

Trigger 2: _____

    a. _____

    b. _____

    c. _____

Trigger 3: _____

    a. _____

    b. _____

    c. _____

Trigger 4: _____

    a. _____

    b. _____

    c. _____

Trigger 5: _____

    a. _____

    b. _____

    c. _____

Now that you have listed what you can do, choose one or two triggers to work on, beginning at the bottom of your list with trigger five—the least terrible trigger. Do what you have said would work.

Write what happened when you did the three things.

_____

_____

What has this exercise taught you about your triggers and the power they can have over you?

_____

_____

Another way to deal with triggers that lead to avoidance is to learn new activities that you will enjoy, and combine some part of a trigger in the activity, making the trigger become something positive. These techniques take time. Do not expect a trigger to lose its power overnight.

If looking at your triggers is painful, you might find ways to look at your fears indirectly, including writing (letters, journals, poetry), doing art projects (drawing, photo journaling, making a collage), dancing or participating in other types of creative movement, playing or listening to music, and constructing (objects, structures, rituals). What activities might you do to help you express your traumatic experiences indirectly?

Other Ways to Reduce Avoidance

Trauma experts, such as Wilson (Wilson, Friedman, and Lindy 2001) and Courtois (1988), give us other ways to lessen avoidance behaviors:

- Lessen your efforts to try to avoid memories of the trauma.

- Increase your contact with others; join some type of social organization.

- Lessen your use of self-medication of any kind.

- Work on your belief systems, perhaps using a workbook such as *Life After Trauma: A Workbook for Healing* (Rosenbloom and Williams 2010).

- Learn to use your head, not your emotions, to appraise the threat in situations.

- Look at the losses trauma has caused you and develop a plan to work through them. What have you lost: people, possessions, home, etc.?

- Learn to stay more present in your safe place.

- Participate in activities that lead to positive emotions.

- To separate the past trauma from the present, use the grounding techniques you have learned.

- Learn to pace yourself and how you deal with your trauma; set up a certain time period during a day or week to work on your traumas; journal or do a trauma-inspired craft.

- Develop a flower diagram about a part of the trauma that bothers you most and that you most want to avoid (use the flower diagram from chapter 4, available online, or make a copy in your journal or notebook).

- Begin doing some form of exposure therapy.

EXERCISE: **What I Learned from This Chapter**

How have the exercises in this chapter helped you face more of what happened to you?

_____

_____

_____

_____

_____

6

Dealing with Category D Symptoms: Part I

Category D is a newly introduced category of symptoms for inclusion in the PTSD diagnosis and requires two or more of those symptoms to be diagnostically present. It incorporates many of the symptoms that in past editions of this workbook were included in chapters describing complex PTSD. There is so much material associated with these symptoms that this edition will divide category D into two separate chapters. This chapter will cover three category D symptoms. The first one is dissociative amnesia, or memory loss. The second one is long-lasting and exaggerated negative beliefs about yourself, others, and the world. The third category D symptom covered here is persistent, long-lasting, distorted thoughts about the cause or consequences of the traumatic event, which can lead to blaming yourself or others.

Trauma changes the self in many ways. Sometimes, memories of what happened are challenged if not apparently lost. While it may appear somewhat strange to lump dissociative amnesia with the impact of trauma on your belief system and on how you view yourself and others, authors of the *DSM-5* have done so. This workbook is following the latest format.

Dissociative Amnesia

Dolan describes traumatic amnesia as the "complete repression of memories associated with a traumatic event" and notes that it is "an extreme defense reaction to inescapable trauma" (1991, 141). It is not normal to forget parts of your life, particularly very early parts (Boon, Steele, and Van der Hart 2011). Some professionals consider it to be a situation-specific amnesia, also known as *repressed memory syndrome*. Freud wrote that dissociative amnesia is a way to preserve the self from extreme anxiety or memories of a traumatic event or events. These repressed memories may suddenly come to the forefront of consciousness or even appear in dreams years after the event occurred. Traumatic amnesia is much more than forgetting.

It seems strange that creators of the new definition included this symptom here rather than as another type of avoidance mechanism. The belief that lies behind this symptom is one of total separation from the memory. Even though others may know that an event happened and share that knowledge with the victim, that victim cannot wrap thoughts around its possible occurrence. See chapter 5 for a more detailed discussion of dissociation in all its forms.

Negative Beliefs About Self, Others, and the World

Human beings hold certain beliefs or expectations about themselves, others, and their personal worlds, which are also known as *schemas*. Beliefs are *knowings*—what you perceive to be true or think is true. Your beliefs and how you think about yourself, others, and the world can impact how you behave and the choices that you make. The next exercise looks at various beliefs that may be the result of exposure to traumatic events, beliefs that are frequently related to your five basic psychological needs: for safety, trust, power, esteem, and intimacy. Recognizing that these beliefs have possibly been changed because of what you endured is one way to identify the impact of trauma on your life and to get information about which of these new beliefs you may choose to challenge or change.

EXERCISE: What Are My Trauma-Related Beliefs?

Check the beliefs that apply to you and then write about a situation (or situations) in which that belief was created or in which it determined your actions or decisions. Try to be specific when describing what happened. Is it trauma-related?

Belief 1:

☐ I believe I am a victim and that my troubles are the fault of others.

Situation(s) in which this belief determines my actions:

_____

_____

Belief 2:

☐ I believe that I can't do things—that I am physically or emotionally incapable of doing them. (By the way, be aware that "I can't" generally means "I won't" or "I don't want to." "I can't" is really a statement of refusal.)

Situation(s) in which this belief determines my actions:

_____

_____

Belief 3:

☐ I believe that my actions don't impact others. My actions won't bring injury or harm to them or cause them emotional pain.

Situation(s) in which this belief determines my actions:

_____

_____

Belief 4:

☐ I believe I am unable or unwilling to put myself in others' places.

Situation(s) in which this belief determines my actions:

_____

_____

Belief 5:

☐ I believe I am unwilling to do something that is disagreeable to me.

Situation(s) in which this belief determines my actions:

_____

_____

Belief 6:

☐ I believe I have no money, time, etc., to spare when others ask me to do things.

Situation(s) in which this belief determines my actions:

_____

_____

Belief 7:

☐ I believe that I develop aches and pains in order to avoid doing things I don't want to do.

Situation(s) in which this belief determines my actions:

_____

_____

Belief 8:

☐ I believe I often don't have energy to do things—particularly when I don't want to do them.

Situation(s) in which this belief determines my actions:

_____

_____

Belief 9:

☐ I believe that I don't have to live up to obligations—that it's okay to say, "I forgot" or to just ignore my responsibilities.

Situation(s) in which this belief determines my actions:

_____

_____

Belief 10:

☐ I believe that I frequently expect others to do what I want them to do, even if they do not understand my reasoning.

Situation(s) in which this belief determines my actions:

_____

_____

Belief 11:

☐ I believe I am entitled to use others' property as if it were my own, and to borrow things without permission.

Situation(s) in which this belief determines my actions:

_____

_____

Belief 12:

☐ I believe that my wants are really my rights.

Situation(s) in which this belief determines my actions:

_____

_____

Belief 13:

☐ I believe that others betray my trust regularly and therefore cannot be trusted at all.

Situation(s) in which this belief determines my actions:

_____

_____

Belief 14:

☐ I believe that things will happen because I think they will.

Situation(s) in which this belief determines my actions:

_____

_____

Belief 15:

☐ I believe that I can make decisions without finding out the facts.

Situation(s) in which this belief determines my actions:

_____

_____

Belief 16:

☐ I believe that I am right and that my point of view is right, even when evidence says that it's wrong.

Situation(s) in which this belief determines my actions:

_____

_____

Belief 17:

☐ Even when I am proved wrong, I believe I must cling to my original position.

Situation(s) in which this belief determines my actions:

_____

_____

Belief 18:

☐   I believe that thinking or planning ahead is unnecessary or not useful.

Situation(s) in which this belief determines my actions:

_____

_____

Belief 19:

☐   I believe that I am always supposed to win and that failure is not an option.

Situation(s) in which this belief determines my actions:

_____

_____

Belief 20:

☐   I believe that fear is a weakness, so I deny that I am afraid even when I am.

Situation(s) in which this belief determines my actions:

_____

_____

Belief 21:

☐   I believe that expressions of anger, like direct threats, intimidation, sarcasm, or passive-aggressiveness, are good ways to get what I want from people.

Situation(s) in which this belief determines my actions:

_____

_____

Belief 22:

☐ If something doesn't turn out the way I expect it to, I believe I will be criticized and found wanting.

Situation(s) in which this belief determines my actions:

_____

_____

Belief 23:

☐ I believe I will be let down by others.

Situation(s) in which this belief determines my actions:

_____

_____

Belief 24:

☐ I believe that I will win in any struggle. I have power.

Situation(s) in which this belief determines my actions:

_____

_____

Belief 25:

☐ I enjoy a debate in and of itself.

Situation(s) in which this belief determines my actions:

_____

_____

Have you learned anything new about yourself by completing this exercise? Has it confirmed anything you knew previously? What does it say about how your traumatic experiences have impacted you? (Use your journal to write more if you need to.)

_____

_____

_____

_____

How can you work on changing or challenging these beliefs that have a negative impact on your life? One way is to use cognitive processing therapy (CPT). This is an adaptation of several other therapies including cognitive behavioral therapy and constructivist self-development theory, which was initially developed by McCann and Pearlman (1990, 1992) and modified by Rosenbloom and Williams (2010). The theory has been developed into a structured format that can be used with individuals or groups. The goal of CPT is to help you understand and, if necessary, modify, address, challenge, or change beliefs that have been affected by traumatic events. With CPT, you are also taught to identify what are called stuck points, or the problematic beliefs that can get in the way of recovery. In the following pages, you will be introduced to some CPT techniques that will help you to challenge and possibly even change your problematic beliefs (Resick and Schnicke 1993).

EXERCISE: **My Stuck Points or Problematic Beliefs**

If you hold any of the following common distorted beliefs, they may be getting in the way of your healing process. The beliefs listed below generally reinforce negative thinking or negative emotions. Please check each one you use and note whether it reinforces your thoughts and/or emotions. You may also write in your notebook or journal about when you use these distortions.

☐ 1. I focus on negatives and filter out positives about a situation.

☐ 2. I use black-and-white thinking; there are no shades of gray. This kind of *all-or-nothing thinking* oversimplifies things.

☐ 3. I overgeneralize and make a conclusion based on a single piece of information or a single incident and then expect the same conclusion to happen again, no matter what, or once something bad has happened to me, I expect a similar situation to always have similar bad results.

119

☐ 4. I *catastrophize* and think a disaster is always about to happen. Things will end badly no matter what I do.

☐ 5. I jump to a conclusion about how people feel toward me; this is a form of *mind reading*. It is also known as making premature conclusions without having evidence to back them up.

☐ 6. I believe that everything others do or say is really about me; I take everything personally and may even believe that I am the cause of everything bad that happens.

☐ 7. I judge situations by my own standards of fairness, and I resent others who do not agree with my judgments; this is called the *fallacy of fairness*.

☐ 8. I blame others for what happens to me.

☐ 9. I use the word "should" to describe what might happen and feel guilty if it doesn't happen. If others do not follow my *should statements*, by doing what I think should happen, I get angry.

☐ 10. I feel that I am externally controlled by others and am a helpless victim; this is known as the *fallacy of control*.

☐ 11. I use *emotional reasoning* and believe what I feel about something must be true.

☐ 12. I believe my feelings are all-powerful, and they determine my reality.

☐ 13. Because of their power, my feelings prove that that's the way it is (Schiraldi 2011).

☐ 14. I believe I have the power to make other people change to suit me and do what I want them to do.

☐ 15. I make global judgments based on limited information; I put labels on people or situations. This is called *overgeneralizing*.

☐ 16. I believe I am always right; being wrong is not an option for me. I use all-or-nothing thinking here as well.

☐ 17. I believe I will be rewarded in the end for all my sacrifices and am bitter if that reward doesn't come.

☐ 18. I believe that I am able to know what another person is thinking or feeling; this is called *mind reading* (already mentioned above).

☐ 19. I blow any mistakes I make out of proportion; this is called *magnifying*.

☐ 20. I believe anything I do is never good enough or is not right.

☐ 21. I believe I am worthless or defective, that I have no value.

☐ 22. I make excuses when things don't go my way to protect myself from being hurt. This is called *rationalizing*.

Which of these beliefs did you check? Are they helpful or harmful to you? Are they based on facts? How do you know they are true?

_____

_____

Have you ever tried to challenge any of these beliefs by looking at evidence for or against them? Have you ever considered that there might be positive features of experiences that you are looking at only negatively? Do others agree with your conclusions, or are they willing to offer alternatives to you? Is there any logical sense to your beliefs?

_____

_____

If you want to look at how you use cognitive errors of belief in more detail, choose which (if any) you use and, in your notebook or on separate pieces of paper, write one or more examples of when you used these beliefs and if the decisions you made based on these errors in thinking helped or hindered you and how. If your beliefs have hindered you, can you also think of how you can challenge those beliefs?

_____

_____

Where Beliefs About the Self Come From

Repeated instances of overwhelming trauma can impact all parts of yourself: the way you see yourself (your identity), your body image (and body sensations), your internalized images of others, your values, and your sense of purpose and meaning. Loss of your sense of you, as a person, as a self, may lead you to believe that you are not really a person. Instead, you view yourself as some type of worthless piece of garbage, or as evil. If your traumas began very early and were quite severe, you may have developed a fragmentation of yourself called *dissociative identity disorder* (previously called multiple personality disorder). This permanent damage to your sense of self can never be totally overcome. However, it can be modified. We will discuss ways to modify and deal with feelings of guilt and shame in chapter 7. You may find it helpful to refer to that chapter and its exercises as you work through this chapter.

The traumatic experiences you had may have led you to believe that nobody can ever possibly understand what you went through and what happened to you. Not only can others not understand the traumas themselves but they cannot understand why you react as you do and why you think so poorly about yourself. McKay and Rogers (2000) discuss how triggers that bring back various aspects of the trauma (emotions, thoughts, memories, etc.) can lead to negative perceptions of yourself in relation to others. When you perceive that you have been harmed and victimized deliberately and intentionally, as well as that you were totally helpless and powerless to do anything about what happened to you, you can develop feelings of helplessness.

In many instances, your beliefs have been gathered from others (including medical professionals) and are introjects, or the beliefs of others that you have incorporated into your belief system. You have a choice to accept or deny those beliefs. In this chapter we will give you strategies to challenge them.

Your schemas are your beliefs and expectations about yourself, others, and your world. Schemas guide and organize how you process information and how you understand your life's experience. Your schemas become your basic rules of life; if they are based on distorted or incorrect information, they can lead to negative ways of viewing yourself, others, and the world. Your strongest schemas are those that have been the most powerfully reinforced. You may develop new schemas to serve old functions; you also may try to apply old schemas to new situations. Negative beliefs about yourself are central to maintenance of PTSD (Ehlers and Clark 2000). Do you view your world as an unsafe place to live or yourself as incompetent?

Five basic psychological needs motivate behavior, according to McCann and Pearlman (1990, 1992). We have previously discussed the basic need for safety (see chapter 2). The other needs are trust, power, esteem, and intimacy. It is your *ego resources* that allow you to meet your psychological needs. Your ego resources are your intelligence, your sense of humor, your willpower, your ability to look inside yourself (be introspective), your awareness of and ability to set boundaries, and your ability to make self-protective judgments. Adequate ego resources allow you to keep yourself stable as an individual. They help you tolerate and regulate your emotions, moderate self-hate, and be alone without being lonely.

Trauma disrupts your psychological experience of the world and distorts your schemas about safety, trust, power, esteem, and intimacy. You develop new schemas that the world is dangerous and that you are powerless. Your beliefs may become negative and disrupt your identity, your emotional life, and your ability to meet your psychological needs. Sometimes these schemas can keep you chronically anxious and hypervigilant. Continuously seeing the world as dangerous and threatening will lead to feelings of fear, anxiety, and panic. If your trauma history prevents you from trusting, you will be suspicious and guarded, and your life will involve feelings of abandonment, disappointment, reluctance to ask for help and support, self-doubt, disappointment, betrayal, and bitterness. You will be led to make bad judgments about others and will put yourself in difficult, risky positions, and you may avoid close relationships. Many soldiers believe that their government has betrayed them or that others want to harm them (Scurfield 2011).

Challenging Core Beliefs

Any negative beliefs you have may be challenged and modified if you choose to do so. This process is not always easy and may require a great deal of persistent effort.

If you want to challenge or dispute core beliefs, you have several options:

- You may look for evidence or proof that your belief is valid.

- You may find others and debate your belief with them.

- You may try to use imagery and visualization to change certain aspects of the belief.

You also may ask yourself the following questions to challenge your belief (partially adapted from Resick 1994):

- What is the evidence for and against the belief?

- Is the belief a habit or a fact?

- Is my interpretation of the situation accurate or not part of reality?

- Am I thinking in black-and-white or all-or-nothing ways?

- Are the words and phrases I am using extreme and exaggerated (such as "always," "forever," "must," "should," "ought," and "have to")?

- Am I making excuses?

- Is the source of information for my belief reliable?

- Am I thinking in terms of probabilities (shades of gray) or certainties (black and white)?

- Are my judgments based on feelings, not facts? Do I consider a feeling to be a fact?

- Is this belief my own, or does it come from or belong to someone else?

- Does it fit in with my priorities, values, and judgments?

- Does it make me feel bad?

- Is it hurtful to me?

- Is it hurtful to others?

- Is it appropriate in the demands it makes on me?

- Is it appropriate in the demands it makes on others?

- Is it considerate of me?

Beliefs about safety of self, others, and the world and how trauma may impact them have been discussed in chapter 2, so this chapter will focus on beliefs related to the other four basic psychological needs.

Challenging Beliefs About Trust and Betrayal

Traumatic event exposure can result in an inability to trust. Enduring and surviving those events can lead to problems with attachment, intimacy, and interpersonal relationships that were not present before the trauma (Wilson, Friedman, and Lindy 2001). Among the problems that may occur are

- feelings of alienation from others in social, emotional, and personal areas of life

- mistrust and guardedness

- detachment, isolation, and withdrawal

- a loss of pleasure in life and of your capacity to feel joy

- a loss of the ability to feel sensual and sexual or have sexual feelings

- a loss of your capacity to have healthy connectedness to others

- repetitive self-destructive relationships

- discontent with self-comfort and an inability to receive nurturing (and even touch) from others and yourself

- problems with setting or maintaining boundaries

- problems with communicating your wants, needs, and feelings

- feelings of abandonment and loss that may or may not be based on fact

If you have identified with any of the problems listed above, the exercises found in this chapter may help you build trust and, eventually, may help you establish some level of intimacy in relationships. Trust and intimacy are two of your five basic psychological needs.

In many instances, trauma survivors find it difficult to trust others, the world, and themselves after a traumatic event has occurred. This is particularly true if their traumas were because of human intention or error. Over time, these survivors can become isolated and alone.

A betrayal in the past may lead you to have difficulties with trust in the present. In the past, have people in close relationships with you ever betrayed you? If so, you may complete the following exercise modified from Matsakis's work (1998, 62).

JOURNAL EXERCISE: People Who Have Betrayed Me

For each person who was in a close relationship with you and betrayed you, complete the following sentences (do the first one here, and the others in your journal):

I was betrayed by _____.

As a result, I _____.

One example might be *I was betrayed by my father, who molested me. As a result, I have very few memories of my childhood and have never been able to trust men.*

According to constructivist self-development theory (McCann and Pearlman 1990, 1992), trust involves your need to feel confident about your own perceptions and judgments about yourself, others, and the world, and to be able to depend on others to help meet your emotional, physical, and psychological needs. It is important for you to examine your own beliefs about trust if you are going to be able to set boundaries, communicate effectively, and know when and how to rely on yourself and others. One way to find and challenge your beliefs about trust is to complete the following two exercises.

JOURNAL EXERCISE: My Beliefs About Trust

Ask yourself the following questions and record your answers in your journal or notebook:

1. What does it mean to me to be able to trust?

2. In what situations do I trust my own thoughts?

3. In what situations do I trust my own judgments or conclusions about a person?

4. In what situations do I trust my own judgments or conclusions about a situation?

5. How do I define the word "intuition"? Is it nonlogical insight?

6. When do I feel that my intuition speaks to me? When do I notice my intuition?

7. How else do I become aware of my feelings, impressions, and beliefs about others or situations?

8. Am I a trustworthy person?

9. When do I keep promises? When do I not keep them?

10. Do I develop trust in someone gradually or all at once?

11. What people or groups do I trust? Which do I distrust?

12. How do I feel when I have to depend on another person?

13. When do I ask others for help with tasks?

14. When do I ask others for help with my emotional needs?

EXERCISE: Identifying and Challenging My Core Beliefs About Trust

Choose one answer from the questions in the preceding exercise, and answer the following questions about it.

The answer from the preceding exercise:

_____

1. What does that answer say about me?

_____

_____

2. Now what does *that* answer say about me?

_____

_____

3. And what does *that* answer say about me?

_____

_____

The answer to the third question gives you your core belief. What is it?

_____

_____

In order to challenge or examine that belief, you can ask yourself the following questions:

Does this belief belong to me or to someone else? _____

Does this belief fit with my priorities and goals? _____

Does this belief fit with my values and judgments? _____

Does this belief make me feel better or worse (about myself or others)? _____

Is this belief hurtful to me in any way? _____

Does this belief put appropriate demands on me (at home, work, or play)?_____

CHALLENGING BELIEFS ABOUT POWER AND CONTROL

A basic need of life, according to McCann and Pearlman (1990, 1992) and Rosenbloom and Williams (2010), is to have power and influence over what happens to you and over what happens to others. However, a life of traumatic experiences can lead you to believe that you are helpless to control forces outside yourself. You may feel trapped and see no way out of your situation. You may believe that you must try to dominate others to avoid being dominated yourself or that you must give way to others' demands rather than face the world assertively with personal power.

JOURNAL EXERCISE: My Beliefs About Power and Control

If you are interested in exploring your own beliefs about power and control, you might ask yourself the following questions, answering them in your journal or notebook.

1.   What does personal power mean to me?

2. In what situations in my life right now do I have to share power with others? Who are those others?

3. In my past, when was I forced to give up my personal power?

4. When do I try to control others?

5. Where is my locus (place) of control—is it inside me or outside of me?

6. Over what aspects of my life do I have control?

7. Do I get into power struggles? With whom? How do they get resolved?

8. How do I react to maladaptive expressions of power in others—threats, manipulations, suicide gestures, etc.?

9. Where does my own sense of power come from? Is it from my job? My size? My gender? My culture? My accomplishments?

10. When my power is threatened, do I try to dominate another person or am I appropriately assertive?

11. What are my fantasies about power?

12. Do I see myself as an independent person? Where? When?

13. Can I rely on myself or must I always rely on others?

EXERCISE: Identifying My Core Beliefs About Power and Control

The answers you gave to the questions in the preceding exercise are the first step toward identifying your beliefs about power and control. Now, choose one of your answers and ask yourself the following questions:

1. What does that belief say about me?

_____

_____

2.   Now what does *that* statement say about me?

_____

_____

3.   And what does *that* statement say about me?

_____

_____

The third question gives you your core belief—the deep belief that underlies the others.

EXERCISE: **Challenging Negative Beliefs About Power and Control**

Use the technique given in the exercise "Identifying My Core Beliefs," above, to identify two additional core beliefs. (You may use your journal or notebook to repeat the exercise.) Fill in the three core beliefs where indicated in the spaces that follow. Then use the list of questions under the section titled "Challenging Core Beliefs" above to challenge each core belief (e.g., What is the evidence for and against the belief?), and write your responses in the spaces below. Use your journal, as well, if you need more space to answer.

Core belief 1: _____

Answers to the questions challenging this belief:

_____

_____

_____

_____

_____

_____

_____

_____

Core belief 2: _____

Answers to the questions challenging this belief:

_____

_____

_____

_____

_____

_____

_____

Core belief 3: _____

Answers to the questions challenging this belief:

_____

_____

_____

_____

_____

_____

What have you learned about your beliefs about power and control?

_____

_____

In April 2012, Mary Beth and her three teenage children participated in a mission trip sponsored by the Warrenton United Methodist Church under the guidance and direction of Puentes de Esperanza (Bridges of Hope), located in Matagalpa, Nicaragua. The twenty-member team spent a week in a small, impoverished village of about eight hundred people building two houses. It was Mary Beth's blessing to have the opportunity to work with about thirty adults from the local Pentecostal church, teaching them about their basic psychological needs, particularly their need for safety, power, control, and a cohesive life narrative. Almost all of these adults were illiterate with the exception of the pastor and a few male deacons. To watch them use this next exercise to draw their life stories, safe places, and power shields was truly amazing. The experience was very meaningful to them, and seeing this brought Mary Beth an immense sense of awe and gratitude.

JOURNAL EXERCISE: **My Power Shield**

One way to develop your personal power is to draw it in the form of a power shield. You may draw a shield in your journal or notebook in any shape that suits you. Divide the shield into six parts and, in each section, draw, write, or attach something that is a symbol of the power you have or of potential sources of your power. You might use words or pictures to symbolize your skills, abilities, resources, accomplishments, or support systems. If you have problems filling in all six sections using your present reality, think of yourself as you would like to be one year from now, after doing all the work in this workbook, and then draw a shield based on that vision. You may draw both a shield based on your present and one based on your hopes for the future. Some sources of your personal power might be:

- a symbol of your life's motto (e.g., *It can be done*; *Live life to its fullest.*)

- a symbol of your knowledge

- a symbol of your ability to communicate

- a symbol of those you love or who love you, care for you, and accept you

- a symbol of things for which you have passion and commitment

- a symbol of things over which you have some control

- a symbol of your life

- a symbol of the energy from which you draw strength and find your will to survive

- a symbol of your personal resources

- symbols of those to whom you owe allegiance

- symbols of those who are your mentors

- a symbol of a promise to yourself

- a symbol of a promise to others

- symbols of life experiences that have given you strength

- symbols of beliefs that protect you

- a symbol of your support network

- a symbol of your safe place

- a symbol of your ability to change situations

- symbols of your self-care strategies

What does your power shield say about you? Do you have any sources of power that are more important than others?

Challenging Beliefs About Self-Esteem

If you are going to overcome at least some of the negative impacts of the traumas that happened to you, it is important for you to learn to nurture yourself and to develop a positive sense of who you are, what you like about yourself, and what you see as your strengths. Trauma can challenge your good feelings and beliefs about yourself and lead to negative thoughts and feelings of unworthiness, contempt, and disillusionment. You may believe that you are flawed, bad, or damaged. You also may think that you will contaminate others or will doom them to a life of pain, just by your presence. A poor sense of self-esteem is associated with feelings of self-loathing, despair, cynicism, and general withdrawal from others.

Your sense of self-worth is the core of your identity. If you see yourself as having worth as a person, you have good self-esteem. A part of good self-esteem is self-respect. If you see yourself as capable and competent, you will be more able to cope with stress and respond to crisis as a challenge. Doing something well leads to higher self-esteem. A higher sense of self-esteem and of being able to do things leads to accomplishments. In other words, these three things (activity, a sense of being able to do something, and having high self-esteem) are related (Schiraldi 1999). The major way to build self-esteem is to picture and develop high self-esteem affirmations. An affirmation is a positive self-statement. Affirmations will be discussed in more detail later in the chapter.

When you develop high self-esteem affirmations, it is important for you to begin the exercise with relaxation (see chapter 2). Once you have relaxed your body, visualize a success that you have had—or a problem or crisis you resolved in a way you felt good about. Experience those good feelings as you remember them.

Ways to Raise Your Self-Esteem

There are other ways you can raise your self-esteem. You may want to improve your communication skills, find a hobby that you can do, or do something for others. You also may want to look at the beliefs you have about self-esteem. It is important that the beliefs you hold about yourself are realistic, accurate, and honest (Schiraldi 1999). Self-esteem is built on feelings of unconditional worth and unconditional love for yourself, which is really self-acceptance.

JOURNAL EXERCISE: Understanding My Self-Esteem

In your journal or notebook, answer the following questions as fully as you like:

1. What do I like or value about myself?

2. What do I do to take care of my physical self (my body)?

3. How do I take care of myself emotionally?

4. What do I do (if anything) to reward myself, and when and how do I do it?

5. When and how do I devalue myself or cut myself down?

6. What are my hopes and dreams?

7. What are my realistic expectations for myself?

8. What are my unrealistic expectations for myself?

9. In what situations do I have a sense of humor?

10. When and how do I show love and affection?

11. Where do I find hope?

12. Under what circumstances am I open and honest about my feelings?

13. Do I help others feel good about themselves even when I feel bad about myself?

EXERCISE: Identifying Core Beliefs About Self-Esteem

Choose one of your answers in the previous exercise and ask yourself the following questions:

1. What does that belief say about me?

_____

_____

2. Now what does *that* statement say about me?

_____

_____

3. And what does *that* statement say about me?

_____

_____

The third question gives you your core belief—the deep belief that underlies the others.

JOURNAL EXERCISE: Challenging My Core Beliefs About Self-Esteem

Use the previous exercise to identify two more core beliefs (writing in your journal or notebook). Then use the list of questions under "Challenging Core Beliefs" to challenge each core belief (e.g., What is the evidence for and against the belief?).

What does completing this exercise teach you about yourself?

_____

_____

By recognizing which of your beliefs you want to challenge (and perhaps even change), you begin to improve self-esteem. Other ways to improve your self-esteem include the ability to

- Be aware of your negative thoughts.

- Stop your negative thoughts by using the thought-stopping technique (introduced in chapter 8).

- Practice your affirmations.

- Set realistic goals you can achieve.

- Develop a variety of interests and participate in related activities.

- Maintain a high level of energy while pacing yourself.

- Take appropriate risks.

- Trust in yourself and the decisions you make.

- Stay who you are rather than change to fit a situation or another person's ideas of you.

- Live in the present while being aware of your past history and having realistic future goals.

- Turn any mistakes into lessons.

EXERCISE: **My Self-Esteem Affirmations**

Choose four or five self-affirmations. Relax your body, and then state your first self-esteem affirmation out loud or to yourself while visualizing it in detail, as if it were totally true. Some affirmations you might use include:

- I have worth.

- I like myself for myself, without comparing myself to others.

- I can do good work at my job.

- I do my best.

- I care about others.

- I make a difference in my own life.

- I make a difference in the lives of others.

- I am worthy of love from myself.

- I am worthy of respect from myself.

- I am worthy of love from others.

- I am worthy of respect from others.

- I respect my own and others' boundaries.

- I am lovable and capable.

- I love myself unconditionally.

- I am capable of changing and growing.

- I am willing to accept love.

- I am proud of my body.

- I am no longer a helpless child.

How does this exercise work for you?

_____

_____

Challenging Beliefs About Intimacy

Intimacy is the capacity to feel connected to yourself and to others. Enduring trauma may lead to disconnects between you and others or within yourself. The aim of this section is to help you learn ways to set boundaries, communicate with others, and build healthy attachments that do not make you feel vulnerable, that do not repeat trauma-related patterns of interaction, and that are based on new or modified belief systems. These beliefs include beliefs of empowerment and self-acceptance. The following questions may help you identify a belief or beliefs about intimacy that you might want to examine or challenge.

EXERCISE: **My Beliefs About Intimacy**

Answer the following questions or complete the following thoughts (use your journal or notebook if you need more room).

Do I feel connected to others? If so, to whom? _____

_____

To me, an intimate relationship means I _____

_____

At this moment in time, I have an intimate relationship with _____

I believe that the word "love" means _____

I am able to express love safely with _____

From whom and where do I get support? _____

From whom and where do I get love? _____

Do I feel more distant from others now, after the trauma (or after I have begun to work on the trauma)?

_____

How do I express love and caring to others? To myself? _____

Am I able to have an intimate sexual relationship with another? _____

Which of the following statements describe you? Check all that apply.

☐ I stay away from people.

☐ I avoid certain social activities (such as _____).

☐ I want to spend my time alone.

☐ I am afraid to talk to others.

☐ I am afraid to be physically close to another.

☐ I try to force others to have physical contact with me.

☐ I say no to any suggestion of sexual contact with someone I love or for whom I have loving feelings.

☐ I overdo taking care of others.

☐ I have no one to take care of me.

☐ I am generally hostile toward others.

☐ I feel afraid to depend on others.

☐ I believe others will always let me down.

☐ I fear touch of any kind.

☐ I am unable to play.

☐ I am unable to make friends.

☐ I am unable to keep friends.

☐ I have no friends.

☐ I am unable to disclose my real self to others.

☐ I am unable to go out to meet others.

☐ I do not trust that I am okay.

☐ I am unlovable and undeserving of love.

☐ I don't believe anything nice that others say about me.

☐ I cannot make decisions.

☐ I continue to get in disastrous relationships (modified from Leehan and Wilson 1985).

The more statements you checked, the more you need to look at ways to challenge and change your beliefs about intimacy and trust. You also need to look at your boundaries and communication skills (see chapter 7).

EXERCISE: Identifying Core Beliefs About Intimacy

Choose one of your answers in the previous exercise and ask yourself the following questions:

1. What does that belief say about me?

   _____

   _____

2. Now what does *that* statement say about me?

   _____

   _____

3. And what does *that* statement say about me?

   _____

   _____

The third question gives you your core belief—the deep belief that underlies the others.

JOURNAL EXERCISE: Challenging My Core Beliefs About Intimacy

Use the previous exercise to identify two more core beliefs (writing in your journal or notebook). Then use the list of questions under "Challenging Core Beliefs" from earlier in the chapter to challenge each core belief (e.g., What is the evidence for and against the belief?).

What does completing this exercise teach you about yourself?

_____

_____

_____

_____

Blaming Yourself or Others for the Trauma

You may have persistent, long-lasting distorted thoughts about the cause or consequences of the traumatic event, which can lead you to blame yourself or others for the trauma. This is the third symptom listed under category D.

Looking at Blame

Blaming yourself for the traumas you have experienced, if you truly are not to blame, is a cognitive distortion. The flip side of that belief is to blame others, including God or another higher power, for what you have experienced. The following exercise will help you look at how you may blame yourself or others.

EXERCISE: **Whom Do I Blame?**

The following process (adapted from Boon, Steele, and Van der Hart 2011) allows you to begin to look at distorted beliefs about blame and the consequences of having those beliefs.

When _____ (name the trauma)

happened, I blamed _____

_____ (myself, others).

Describe the situation leading to the appearance of the belief:

_____

_____

My thoughts about this belief include:

_____

_____

My emotional responses to this belief include:

_____

_____

The physical sensations that are a result of the belief include:

_____

_____

Any decisions that I might make and actions I might take because of this belief include:

_____

_____

EXERCISE: **Examining Negative Beliefs**

The following way to examine negative beliefs was developed by Mary Beth in her private practice and has not been published elsewhere. She used this with clients who were victimized early in life and carry with them beliefs related to shame, humiliation, and negative self-perceived worthlessness and blame. An example is included. Space is left after each step of the exercise for you to put in your own example.

Step 1. What event led to this belief?

Example: *I am being denigrated by colleagues who believe I am doing a very poor job and have been ordered to create my personal remediation plan.*

My event: _____

_____

Step 2. What disempowering beliefs (about my lack of power and negative responsibility for what has happened) do I have?

Examples:

I am disrespected and am being laughed at and humiliated.

I am angry about having to do this plan after being a veteran teacher.

I am bad.

I have no value.

I don't belong here.

I have no power.

I am being disgraced.

My beliefs: _____

_____

Step 3. What proof is there that this belief (these beliefs) is (are) true?

Examples:

I have been exposed to similar attacks since I was a small child.

I have incorporated these negative beliefs into my character structure.

I hear in my head what people in my past said.

My personal proofs for my negative beliefs are _____

_____

Step 4. What defense can I offer to counter the belief(s)?

Examples:

I filmed myself at work and watched the videos. I also had trusted colleagues watch them. The videos show that I am good at what I do.

I have been a target of others all my life. I seem to have a bull's-eye on my back that attracts abusers to me.

I have been singled out for standing up for truth and ethical behavior.

It is time for me to assert myself.

I have never had a negative job evaluation before.

My friends stand up for me.

What defenses can I offer, either statements or beliefs? _____

_____

Step 5. What can I do now that I understand that the negative self-criticism and beliefs are not true?

Examples:

I can act assertively.

I can develop a plan that speaks to my strengths.

I can seek legal counsel and bring suit for a hostile work environment.

I can decide it is time to move on and get an advanced degree or look for a better-paying position that honors my talents.

And what about my new behaviors? _____

_____

Step 6. Create an alternative less blaming belief to explain what happened, and write it here.

_____

_____

Challenging your beliefs about blame, looking at the evidence for it or against it, and asking others how they thought or felt about it are other ways to help create an alternative, less blaming belief (Burns 1989). However, you don't want to dwell on self-blame. It is also important to consider how you might develop self-compassion and self-forgiveness.

Self-Compassion

Symptoms of PTSD can disrupt many areas of your life. You may start to have negative thoughts about yourself. You may feel injured or worthless or view yourself as a failure. A lack of self-compassion combined with self-criticism may increase your feelings of helplessness and hopelessness, as well as feelings of shame and guilt (see chapter 7). Self-criticism also has a negative effect on your body. When the amygdala detects a threat in the environment, it triggers a flight-or-flight response that increases blood pressure and the secretion of adrenaline and cortisol and also mobilizes the strength and energy you need to confront or avoid the threat, whether it's physical or emotional, and whether it has an external or internal source. Therefore, self-criticism can actually trigger a stress response. Kindness toward yourself, on the other hand, is associated with the area of the brain that creates positive emotions and compassion. When you experience warm and tender feelings toward yourself, you alter both your mind and your body. Self-kindness allows you to feel safer so that you don't operate from a place of fear when painful experiences occur.

When you give yourself compassion, you replace negative self-judgment with peaceful, connected acceptance. In the view of Kristin Neff (2003, 2009), a leading researcher in this field, a key feature of self-compassion is lack of self-criticism, especially during suffering. Self-compassion provides a larger perspective on problems and is associated with greater wisdom and emotional intelligence, and it also bolsters positive states of being. Self-compassionate people tend to experience more happiness, optimism, curiosity, and positive affect than those who lack self-compassion (Neff, Rude, and Kirkpatrick 2007). For more detailed information on self-compassion and a test to determine how self-compassionate you are, consult Neff's website, http://www.self-compassion.org.

Neff's approach to self-compassion involves three main components: self-kindness, common humanity, and mindfulness (2011).

SELF-KINDNESS

Self-kindness means being warm and understanding toward yourself when you suffer, fail, or feel inadequate, rather than degrading or punishing yourself with self-criticism, causing stress and frustration (which is particularly likely when you can't get what you want or be what you want to be). Experiencing life's difficulties is inevitable; however, with self-kindness you can soothe, help, and nurture yourself when confronting your pain, rather than get angry. Self-kindness also involves active, not passive, self-comforting, responding just as you would to a dear friend in need. If you allow yourself to be emotionally moved by your own pain, you might consider how you can comfort yourself in that difficult moment and then offer warmth and gentleness to yourself.

COMMON HUMANITY

Harsh self-judgment tends to make you feel isolated. When you notice something about yourself that you don't like, you may feel everyone else is perfect and only you are inadequate. This irrational self-centeredness gives you distorted tunnel vision with a focus on your worthless self. Self-compassion does not mean self-pity ("Why me?"); it recognizes that life challenges and personal failures are part of the human condition—something we all experience. Self-compassion helps you feel less desolate and isolated when you are in pain.

MINDFULNESS

Mindfulness (introduced in chapter 2) is a nonjudgmental, receptive mind state in which thoughts and feelings are observed as they are, without pushing them away or denying them. Mindfulness teaches you to notice and be aware of difficult thoughts and emotions in the moment, so you can look at and experience them with kindness, acceptance, and nonjudgment. Being mindful means accepting yourself, whether or not the thoughts you have about yourself are right or wrong. Mindfulness fosters compassion. You can't ignore your pain and feel compassion for yourself at the same time. In order to comfort yourself, you need to face your difficulty.

The following exercises on self-compassion are modified from Neff's recent work (2011).

EXERCISE: Assessing Your Self-Criticism

What types of things do you typically judge and criticize yourself about (appearance, career, relationships, parenting, etc.)?

_____

_____

What type of language do you use with yourself when you notice some flaw or mistake (insulting or kind and understanding)?

_____

_____

How does self-criticism make you feel inside?

_____

_____

How do you typically react to life's difficulties?

_____

_____

How do you treat yourself when you run into challenges or when adverse life events happen? Do you tend to ignore your suffering and focus on fixing the problem or do you stop, give yourself care and comfort, and then proceed?

_____

_____

Do you tend to make a bigger deal out of a difficult situation (worrying and constantly thinking about it), or do you try to keep things balanced between good and bad outcomes?

_____

_____

Do you tend to feel cut off from others when things go wrong? Do you believe that everyone else is having a better/easier time in life than you are? Do you try to remember that all people experience hardships in their lives?

_____

_____

EXERCISE: Using Self-Compassion Phrases

When you're feeling emotional pain, it's helpful to have memorized a few phrases that can aid you in remembering to be compassionate to yourself in the moment. In those difficult times, take a deep breath, put your hand over your heart or gently hug yourself, and repeat the following phrases, which capture the three components of self-compassion:

This is a moment of suffering.

Suffering is a part of life.

May I be kind to myself.

May I give myself the compassion I need.

JOURNAL EXERCISE: **Fostering Self-Compassion**

Try keeping a daily self-compassion journal for one week. At some point toward the end of each day, review the day's events. Write down anything about which you felt badly, anything for which you judged yourself, or any difficult experience that caused you pain. For each event, use mindfulness, a sense of common humanity, and kindness to process the event in a self-compassionate way.

What About Forgiveness?

Many trauma specialists have written about the trauma victim's need to forgive his or her abuser. Forgiveness supposedly is a way to release the rage and hatred you have toward your perpetrator, as well as a way to release your desire for revenge. But many offenders do not deserve unconditional forgiveness. Many also do not even admit that they have done wrong; therefore, they don't seek or want forgiveness.

If your trauma was perpetrated by a person, you may choose to forgive that perpetrator. Your forgiveness of that person does not mean that what she or he did was right or acceptable or that your trauma has had no negative impacts on your life. It does not mean that you are now to forget what happened to you, as some people may say you are to do (Schiraldi 2000).

According to Enright and Fitzgibbons (2000) forgiveness is the willful abandonment of resentment and the willingness to respond toward your perpetrator with compassion, generosity, beneficence, and moral love. Big words, but what do they mean? This definition does not mean you are to go back into a relationship with an abuser, or that you will trust or reconcile with that person. It does not mean you condone or excuse what was done to you or what happened in your world. It does mean a change in your own internal response. If you forgive, you do a willful act that is for your benefit alone. Enright and Fitzgibbons say that forgiveness has degrees that range from slight to complete, surface to deep. In addition, forgiveness often develops over time as you sort out what happened to you and as you consider whether or not you are willing to forgive.

You may forgive on a variety of levels. You may forgive emotionally (you feel compassion for the perpetrator), cognitively (in your statements or thoughts), or spiritually (by turning to a Higher Power or God to help you with the act of forgiving). A focus on forgiving is a coping strategy that may help you improve your psychological functioning, these authors say.

They also say what forgiveness is not. Forgiveness is not just having the perpetrator apologize and then accepting that apology. Forgiveness does not restore your situation to what it was prior to the traumatic event or offense. An apology says that the perpetrator has regret; it also may mean that you still have limitations to the amount of healing you have done, because accepting a quick, superficial, or even emotionless apology as an end point does not allow for later expression of sadness or anger. Instead, if other emotions arise after an apology is accepted and forgiveness is given, you may blame yourself for being uncaring. Forgiveness by you also does not depend upon the existence of remorse in your perpetrator. Forgiveness is not about granting your perpetrator pardon, leniency, or mercy; it does not mean you excuse the trauma, forget the offense, or abandon resentment. If you quickly tell your perpetrator, "I forgive you," without a great deal of thought, the perpetrator may believe that he or she is off the hook with a quick fix and can then move on, while you may still continue to be stuck in your trauma.

Self-Forgiveness

Forgiving your perpetrator may allow you to let go of your anger and rage to some degree. However, it is more important that you forgive yourself for any perceived complicity in what happened, whether through something you did or something you did not do. You need to forgive yourself if you lost control, feel guilty for what happened, were unable to fight back, or were unable to stop what happened. Forgiving yourself also can help you let go of your rage and thoughts of revenge; it can help you decrease your fears, lessen the amount of obsessive thoughts you have about your perpetrator, and help you access additional memories of what happened to you. Letting go of anger through forgiveness also can help you let go of at least some of the power your offender has had over you.

EXERCISE: Forgiveness

How much anger do you still hold against yourself for what happened?

_____

What do you need to do for yourself if you are to forgive yourself?

_____

_____

How do you think forgiving yourself can help you heal?

_____

_____

Do you also want to forgive those who hurt/betrayed/abused you? _____

If so, what will you do?

_____

_____

EXERCISE: Lessons About Forgiveness

What have you learned about self-forgiveness? What have you learned about yourself?

_____

_____

_____

_____

_____

Challenging and Modifying Your Beliefs Through Affirmations

An additional way to help modify beliefs is to challenge them through the use of repetitive affirmations. To repeat, an _affirmation_ is a positive thought you say to yourself over and over in order to combat, challenge, or even change negative thoughts and a negative self-image. Affirmations are statements in the present tense that represent what you want to bring into your life or how you want to see yourself (Zampelli 2000). Affirmations are a form of positive self-talk that can state how you really want to see yourself and your body. Thus you are the best person to create your own affirmations. Although others may say positive statements to you about your body, if you do not buy into those statements, you will have a hard time believing them and won't make similar statements to yourself.

Regular use of affirmations can change your beliefs about yourself and your emotions and actions based on those beliefs. This kind of real change has six stages, and it does not happen overnight. Here's an outline of these stages, along with an example of typical thinking at each stage:

Precontemplation: *My negative beliefs about myself are right; I don't need to change them.*

Contemplation: *Well, maybe I do need to make some changes.*

Preparation: *I guess I can begin to focus on what I need to do and what affirmations I might write or say.*

Action: *I will do and am doing this; I am saying or writing the affirmations on a daily basis.*

Maintenance: *I am beginning to believe the affirmations. I don't need to say them as often, and I sort of believe them; I am beginning to see things in a different way and feel better about me.*

Termination (the ideal end): *Wow, I actually am okay and don't need to see myself so negatively. Sometimes I forget that I am okay, but I recover quickly. The affirmations really are acceptable ways to describe myself—they work even when I am in crisis. I am able to do what is best for me.*

An affirmation begins in a personal way with the word "I" ("I weigh the right amount for my frame") or the word "my" ("My ability to finish a job is excellent"). In addition, affirmations occur in now time, not in future time. An affirmation is "I do a good job," not "I will do a good job." Affirmations also can be statements designed to counteract your trauma-related fears ("I am able to walk to work alone"; "I can drive my car by myself after the accident"). Affirmations are stated in your own personal language, which fits you and your personal style of relating to the world. If you do not believe the affirmation you create is totally true, then write it with a conditional word or words that imply positive movement: "I am becoming a more capable person" or "I am constantly trying to do my best." The most effective affirmations are realistic and include hope, and may even be based on faith.

Affirmations do not take the place of hard work. However, they are one way to change your beliefs about yourself and your way of dealing with the world ("I can relate to others without getting angry"; "I can do _____ without being afraid") and lead to the ability to change any self-harming behaviors that are based on those beliefs. Affirmations are not meant to help you avoid your emotions or to control events or others. If your affirmations are to work, you need to repeat them over and over and over to yourself until you actually begin to believe them. When you believe them, you will begin to see your world from a different perspective.

Begin by writing several of your affirmations down in this workbook, five times each, to start getting them into your mind. If you find that you have trouble saying an affirmation to yourself at least twenty times a day, then take some notebook paper and write the affirmation at the top of the page. Before you go to bed, fill that entire page with the affirmation, saying it out loud each time you write it. You also may rewrite it numerous times before you begin your day in the morning.

Writing affirmations uses more than one of your body's means of expression: it involves eye/hand coordination to write, language to say the affirmation out loud and put it on paper, and thought to start the entire process. Writing helps an affirmation to become a habit of thought, a new self-message that you have incorporated into yourself and made a part of your belief system.

If you do not want to write the affirmation over and over again, you may choose to write the affirmation down once and then say it to yourself over and over again. Repeating the affirmation over and over will also help you eventually believe it and feel as if it belongs to you. Repetition also will help you see that the affirmation is a more acceptable way to describe yourself. It is particularly helpful if you have positive, action-oriented affirmations available to say to yourself when you are in a state of crisis, to help you get through the situation, e.g., "I am able to do what is best for me" or "I am able to be assertive in this situation."

EXERCISE: **My Affirmations**

The affirmations I have chosen to use:

1. _____

2. _____

3. _____

Now write each one five times in the space below (if you need more room, use a page in your journal or notebook):

1. _____

_____

_____

_____

_____

2. _____

_____

_____

_____

_____

3. _____

_____

_____

_____

_____

EXERCISE: **What I Learned from This Chapter**

Do you believe that you have any of the symptoms we discussed in this chapter? If so, what have you learned about you?

_____

_____

_____

_____

_____

_____

_____

7

Dealing with Category D
Symptoms: Part 2

Chapter 6 examined the first three symptoms included in category D of the *DSM-5*. This chapter will look at the remaining four symptoms in that category: persistent negative trauma-related emotional states; markedly lowered interest in pre-trauma activities; feelings of detachment, alienation, or estrangement from others; and the persistent inability to experience positive emotions and less outward display of emotions.

It is important to recognize that chapters 6 and 7 together cover the symptoms included in category D and that two or more of these symptoms must be present for a diagnosis of PTSD. Therefore, you may need to consider the symptoms in both chapters to understand how two (or more) have contributed to a PTSD diagnosis.

Long-Lasting Negative Emotions

This section of the workbook looks at long-lasting negative emotions that are impacted or changed by trauma or become a part of the post-traumatic self and that are negative in nature. Some of these emotions are related to others and may be lesser or more serious versions. The major emotions included in this chapter are fear, anger and rage, depression, guilt, survivor guilt, shame, helplessness, sadness, and grief and loss. Anger will also be covered in chapter 8, which deals with arousal symptoms. The major emotions examined in this chapter are not the only ones impacted by trauma. You may think of others that have impacted your life.

First, ask yourself the following questions: Are you unable to experience life because you feel empty inside or have only negative emotions? Do you let these negative emotions guide your life?

Emotions as Messengers of Information

Linda Kohanov, creator of the Epona method of on-the-ground experiential therapy using horses, utilizing the work of Karla McLaren (2001), notes that emotions are messages that carry information. The ability to use emotions as information and, hence, discover the message behind the emotion, is called *emotional agility*. Capacchione (2001) writes that emotions are both responses to experience and shapers of experiences. They are a form of energy that we hold in our bodies. If you have difficulty identifying emotions, look to your body as their source.

What emotions do you feel? Are there many or only a few? Do you recognize the existence of many emotions or are you "stuck" and feel only one or two, such as rage and sorrow? Emotions are shown in a multitude of ways, through words, sounds, body language, body reactions, and physical manifestations (tears, clenching of fists, grinding of teeth, and others), and sometimes are the opposite to what is being expressed verbally (your words say one thing, but your body says another). Feelings may flow outward from the self or flow inward to cause illness, blockages, and even self-destructive behaviors. When emotions are expressed authentically, they may lead to motivating change. In order to heal from traumatic events, it is important to recognize what emotions have been impacted, changed, or buried and then act to modify or change them. First you need to examine the origin of negative emotions that lead to negative emotional states, and then you can accept these emotions as valid and helpful or as destructive and needing to be modified or changed. Capacchione (2001) also writes that emotions are indicators of health or unhealth. Your emotions are also a part of your body and are carried in molecules called neuropeptides and are created by the head brain, heart, and gut (Pert 1999).

In this chapter, you will take a closer look at several negative emotions that can persist with PTSD, and you will be asked some questions about how each of these emotions can give information to you in your life:

- What is the message this emotion is giving to you?

- What questions do you want to ask of this emotion?

- If you allow this emotion to continue, what might it intensify into?

- What is a positive way to feel this emotion without allowing it to take over your life?

We may also ask you to express your feelings in a number of other ways, such as by drawing them, writing about them, or using movement.

Capacchione (2001) believes that there are five families of negative feelings expressed as general categories: sadness, anger, fear, confusion, and depression. Anger leads to rage, at its most destructive state, and to irritation and anger, at its lesser state. Fear leads to panic, terror, and horror at the most severe level, and leads to shakiness, nervousness, and anxiety at the less extreme level. Sadness leads to hurt, loneliness, and grief, on the one hand, and to gloom, melancholy, and discouragement, on the other. An emotionally healthy person can look at emotions and answer the above questions without self-doubt, self-criticism, or self-punishment. Many trauma survivors, however, cannot accept or deal with negative emotions, or they try to change or substitute more positive emotions for those that cause intense pain or conflict. Can you self-soothe when emotions threaten to overwhelm you? When you experience negative emotions, can you still make good decisions? Are you trying to act in a congruent fashion with words and actions matching? How and when are you able to tolerate emotional pain?

Bloom (2000) writes that people start with a normal potential to grow. You started life with the potential to be a healthy, happy human being, within the context of certain genetic and bodily predispositions. However, if you were traumatized early in life, the effects of trauma soon interfered with your physical, psychological, social, and moral development. If you were repeatedly traumatized, you may have developed *learned helplessness* in order to endure abusive situations; that is, you learned that it was useless to try to get away. Later, even if you could have escaped, you may not have done so, or you went from one abusive situation into another (e.g., from a violent family situation to a harmful dating or marriage relationship). If you continued to have positive feelings toward an abuser, you also may have experienced what is known as *traumatic bonding* (you have a deep bond with the person who abused you).

Exposure to repeated trauma, type II trauma, may prevent you from attaching in a healthy way to others. It may cause you to be unable to control your emotional arousal. In a matter of milliseconds, you might go from being okay to being in a rage. You also may find that you do not have enough trust in others or yourself to allow yourself to develop a stable relationship. Instead, you may become aggressive toward others (either outwardly or in a more subtle, passive form), as well as toward yourself, when things don't go your way.

Your capacity to regulate your own internal emotional states, your body sense, and your response to external stress helps to define who you are (Cole and Putnam 1992). If you were a victim of type II trauma, you may lack a predictable sense of yourself, have a poor sense of separateness from others, have a disturbed body image, have poor impulse control, and become suspicious and distrusting in social situations.

Does this description sound familiar to you? Are you able to be emotionally upset without hurting yourself? Are you able to be emotionally upset without becoming aggressive? Are you able to stay present when you are emotionally upset, without dissociating? Are you able to find words to identify bodily sensations that occur when you are upset? Are you able to find words to name emotional states; that is, are you able to name how you feel, and do those feelings match the situation?

Feelings generally can be associated with joy or with pain. Each feeling of pain has an opposite feeling associated with joy. For example, the opposite of fear is hope; of sadness, joy; of hate, love. Painful feelings that result from exposure to trauma frequently are denied and avoided. Many trauma survivors have a hard time keeping their feelings under control. Many times, people with severe PTSD are also not aware of the range of feelings that exist and have only limited emotional responses to most situations. Having feelings or recognizing having certain feelings may make you want to hurt yourself. Examples of feelings that may lead to self-hurt include anger, sadness, shame, emptiness, guilt, and betrayal. But if you do not know what many different feelings are like, you also cannot use them either positively or negatively.

EXERCISE: **Recognizing My Emotions**

Which of the following emotional states do you personally know, and which have you felt in the past two weeks? Please circle those you have felt in the past two weeks and underline all those about which you can say that you know how they feel.

abandoned	dependent	humiliated	shy
accepted	deserted	hurt	sorry
aching	desirable	impatient	stimulated
affectionate	desperate	inadequate	stunned
alone	devastated	incompetent	stupid
aloof	different	innocent	sweet
amused	disappointed	insecure	sympathetic
angry	discouraged	interested	tense
annoyed	distressed	irate	terrified
anxious	dominated	irked	thrilled
apologetic	doomed	irritated	tired
at peace	eager	isolated	tolerant
aware	easygoing	jealous	tortured
betrayed	ecstatic	joyful	trapped in time
bitter	elated	loyal	troubled
bored	embarrassed	lucky	trusted
brave	enraged	mad	ugly
calm	excited	mean	unappreciated
capable	exposed	miserable	unaware
caring	foolish	patient	understood
cautious	frantic	peaceful	unfriendly
cheerful	friendly	pleased	unhappy
composed	fulfilled	powerless	upset
confident	full	preoccupied	useless
conflicted	furious	proud	valued
connected	giving	regretful	victimized
content	glad	rejected	violated
courageous	grateful	remorseful	vulnerable
cranky	grouchy	responsible	warm
crazy	grumpy	revengeful	weary
crushed	guilty	safe	whipped
curious	happy	screwed	wiped out
defeated	helpless	serene	withdrawn
dejected	hopeful	shamed	wonderful
delighted	hopeless	shocked	worthwhile

This is only a small proportion of the words that are associated with feelings. Were you able to identify and imagine or remember having most of them? What has completing this exercise taught you about yourself?

Looking at Emotions That May Persist Negatively

The first long-lasting negative emotion that we will look at is fear.

Fear

Fear involves developing an awareness of something that is an actual threat or danger to one or more aspects of your life (physical, emotional, spiritual, or mental). Fear is a very basic emotion and a natural warning system that has the ability, on the one hand, to protect life and, on the other, to destroy it. According to Kearney et al. (2014) and the broaden-and-build theory of positive emotions, fear is a hallmark emotion associated with PTSD. Fear may be huge and lead to terror, or it may be small and lead to worry. Worry is a needless expenditure of energy that prevents happiness. It will be addressed later in this chapter when we discuss the symptom category of absence of positive emotion. If a situation truly is fearful, it's important to figure out or seek counsel from others about how to get out of that situation, while staying in your body and not dissociating. According to McLaren, fear includes the emotions of anxiety and worry (2001).

Fear is a common trauma-based emotion that can greatly impact the body. It is quite possible that you were very afraid during and after the traumatic event or events that occurred. If you have been a victim of lifelong trauma, you may not even know what it is like to live without fear. How many times a day or week do you feel jumpy or nervous? Do you shake, tremble, or hide? How often do you look around in a state of panic, waiting for the other shoe to drop? Do your muscles tense up and ache? Do you get bouts of diarrhea, stomach pain, or headaches when any reminder of the trauma intrudes? Do you find that you cry, whimper, or become speechless if you believe you are about to be retraumatized? If you answered yes to yourself as you read this paragraph, it is likely that you are experiencing trauma-related fear. Often an awareness of fear becomes intuitive.

EXERCISE: **Examining My Fear**

Answering these questions will help you gain a better understanding of your fear.

What is the message that fear is giving to me?

_____

_____

What questions do I want to ask of my fear?

_____

_____

If I allow my fear to continue, what might it intensify into?

_____

_____

What is a positive way to feel my fear without allowing it to take over my life?

_____

_____

You may use the space below or a page in your journal to draw a picture of your fear or fears. Drawing a picture is a way to gain more control over an emotion by externalizing it.

If fear from a threat is ignored, emotions such as worry, anxiety, panic, and terror may develop. Have you experienced a panic attack due to your traumatic experiences? If you had a panic attack during the trauma or if you experience panic attacks now, there are books and other materials available to help you. This workbook is not designed to repeat what those books say, but it is important that you recognize that panic reactions occur suddenly and involve feelings of fear and terror, doom and danger (Meichenbaum 1994). You may use your ability to dissociate and avoid, to limit your susceptibility to panic attacks and fear responses. Panic attacks include body reactions and sensations, feelings of fear and anxiety, thoughts (expecting a panic attack to occur, predicting it will occur), and behaviors (avoidance, hyperventilation).

When you were being traumatized, your body recognized danger and responded by fleeing, freezing, or fighting. However, after the trauma, if you continue to be hypervigilant and hypersensitive to such a great degree that you respond with panic when there is no objective sign of danger, you may end up relating to the world as if it were a constant war zone. You may even diagnose yourself with a serious medical condition (e.g., a heart attack or nervous breakdown) when you are feeling anxious and panicked. You may start to hyperventilate and have tingling sensations in your hands and feet. You may tremble or even faint.

A panic attack is not a sign of imminent death. Panic attacks do not just come out of the blue without any trigger, even though they may seem to do so. If you begin to recognize what is truly dangerous to you, or if you reduce your inaccurate perception of danger and if you control your thoughts about danger, your panic attacks will begin to decrease.

How can you control your panic attacks and master the fear of arousal that they cause? Meichenbaum lists six steps (1994, 43):

1. Recognize when you have the physical sensations that indicate a panic attack is coming— face your symptoms (Weekes 1986).

2. Note how you misinterpret body signs that something serious is wrong.

3. Catch yourself beginning to hyperventilate and control your breathing; accept your symptoms.

4. Interrupt the panic attack and identify the trigger that began it and the feelings that accompany it (helplessness, hopelessness, sadness, loss); begin to try to relax.

5. Use various coping strategies, such as changing what you are doing, grounding yourself, doing something fun, or calling someone. Realize that your panic attack will subside naturally within about five to ten minutes and that you are not dying.

6. Take charge of your behavior and, when you have interrupted the panic attack, take credit for what you have done.

Other means of controlling, limiting, or recovering from a panic attack include using the skills you learned in chapter 2 to relax, float, breathe gently, and decrease your arousal. If you fight and overtense, the attack will last longer. It also helps to recognize the memories that led to the attack so that you can work on them (perhaps using techniques from chapter 4). Let your body readjust itself chemically. Get good sleep, eat properly, and exercise well. Also, list your strengths and the sources of your resilience (you may use the final chapter of this workbook to do so).

EXERCISE: Listing Negative Thoughts

It may be helpful to you to list negative thoughts that automatically fill your mind and are connected to body reactions; it is common to find tens to hundreds of such thoughts, often starting with minor worries and ending with a fear of death. Externalizing them in a list here will help you start to diffuse their energy and separate them from unreality.

_____

_____

_____

_____

_____

_____

_____

_____

Fear may also lie behind any avoidance mechanisms you use—your fears about remembering, your fears about facing the future, and/or the fear of facing your feelings.

Anger and Rage

As a trauma survivor, you may also experience anger or rage. Irritability and outbursts of anger are symptoms of increased arousal that many trauma survivors face. Anger and rage are often by-products of trauma; in other words, people who have experienced traumatic events often focus their emotions onto other people, events, or circumstances. When a traumatic event has knocked your socks off, and there is no explanation that makes sense as to why the event happened, your anger may erupt, over-shadowing your emotions of fear, grief, sadness, shame, or guilt. Your anger may be directed at the perpetrator of the traumatic event, if you know that individual. If the perpetrator is a person who was supposed to protect, love, and honor you, your anger may become rage. Your anger may be directed at those who seem to have survived a similar event undamaged. Your anger may be directed at "the system" for its continued hurts, if you have to deal with law enforcement, the criminal justice system, attorneys, insurance companies, and even therapists. Your anger may erupt at the normal events of life that frustrate you rather than at the true sources of your anger. Your anger also may erupt toward yourself and your own body, particularly if you blame yourself for what happened to you or to the others who were impacted by the event. On the positive side, your anger also may motivate you to make changes in yourself or to work for a cause. As Cohen, Barnes, and Rankin note, anger can become a "typical response to the injustice of traumatization" (1995, 58).

There are many different levels and types of anger. However, trauma survivors often lump all of them together in one big pot. When anger is trauma-based, there may be many reasons for feeling angry. Matsakis (1994a) says that you may be angry at

- people (whether individuals or members of groups or organizations) you blame for what happened to you

- symptoms that keep sneaking up on you and smacking you in the face

- physical limitations or disabilities that were caused by the traumatic events

- the behaviors you have used to try to avoid the traumas, including addictions to substances, gambling, spending, work, or other things

- the lack of understanding of those around you

- an inability to get financial compensation for what happened from insurance companies, your perpetrator, or responsible institutions or organizations

- society for subsequently traumatizing you, e.g., through a legal system that doesn't seem able to punish those responsible

- yourself for not acting to protect yourself or to prevent the trauma from happening

Do any of these reasons for anger apply to you?

_____

_____

EXPRESSING ANGER

You may be angry about what happened to you, your life, or those you love. You may want to lash out at someone, something, somewhere, somehow. Perhaps you have a specific perpetrator in mind as the target of your rage or anger. Or you may wish it were possible to lash out at nature itself for sending the tornado that destroyed your home. When it is impossible to focus anger on whoever or whatever deserves it, you may turn that anger onto others, including those you love. If any statements in the following are true for you, you may be using inappropriate ways of expressing anger.

EXERCISE: **How I Express Anger**

Check any items that apply to you.

☐ I am the authority and force my opinion on others, even if means my showing anger to do so.

☐ I time my angry attacks well. I strike out when the other person is vulnerable, tired, involved in something, or has her or his guard down.

☐ I have a way of arguing that is unbeatable. I monopolize the conversation, ignore the feelings of the other person, refuse to listen to the other person, or talk so much that the other person gives up.

☐ I never forget a sin or slight against me and let my anger build and build until I explode.

☐ When I am angry, I shout, scream, throw things, hit, or become violent.

☐ I don't get mad; I get even by getting revenge.

☐ I walk out or refuse to talk after I have become angry. Then the other person has no chance to participate, discuss, or fight back.

☐ I use sarcasm or say things that are hurtful to others when I am angry.

☐ I play people against one another.

☐ I play a martyr role; I put guilt on others.

☐ I never accept an apology; I hold a grudge for years, if necessary.

☐ I throw everything into a fight, including the kitchen sink; I bring up everything that has ever made me angry, even from years in the past.

☐ I secretly gather ammunition for my next fight. I go through e-mail messages, wallets, or pockets, or listen in on phone conversations, so I can use that information later against the other person.

☐ I refuse to talk about my anger; talking would be a waste of time.

☐ When I think bad thoughts, I make bad things happen.

☐ I say things when angry that are hurtful and irreversible.

☐ If I get angry with _____, she or he will get angry back and will be aggressive toward me. I know this will happen, but I do it anyway.

☐ If I share the reasons for my anger with _____, it will devastate him or her to know the truth.

☐ If I allow myself to be angry, I will reveal who and what I really am and will be even more vulnerable.

☐ My anger is ugly; if I express it, others will think negatively of me.

☐ I must avoid making others angry at me or at other people or things at all costs.

☐ I must avoid showing my own anger at all costs.

☐ If others are angry at me, I must fix it or fix them to make everything right.

The more statements you checked in this exercise, the more unhealthy your way of expressing anger is, and the more you need to work on learning different ways to express it. Before looking at some of the ways to get anger out in a healthier manner (see chapter 8), let's look at what anger is.

Anger as a Warning

Anger warns you of a threat to your well-being or of actual danger. What you do with your anger involves making choices. If you make inappropriate choices when you express your anger, that anger can lead to self-harm, depression, feelings of helplessness, risk-taking, and explosive outbursts. Expression of anger exists on a continuum and ranges from annoyance and irritation to fury and rage. When anger is associated with trauma, angry outbursts can be out of proportion to what provokes them. These outbursts can be quick and explosive and can bring about physical symptoms including high blood pressure, headaches, and body aches and pains. There are times when anger becomes rage;

rage is anger accompanied by helplessness. It occurs when you believe you have no control over a situation, person, or event. When you have experienced a trauma, anger may become the central emotion that you feel after enduring a traumatic event. Angry thoughts about revenge may consume you. According to Enright and Fitzgibbons (2000), your anger is more destructive if you focus it on another person or people; it is intense, even in the short term; it leads to a learned pattern of annoyance, irritation, or frustration with others who are not the source of your anger; it is extremely passive; it is extremely hostile; or it is developmentally appropriate for someone much younger than your actual age (e.g., you act like a two-year-old and have a temper tantrum).

EXERCISE: How Anger Has Hurt Me

Think of any ways anger has caused you problems. What are they, and when did the situations in which anger hurt occur?

The ways that my anger hurt me (and those around me) are

1. _____

2. _____

3. _____

What do your answers tell you about how you may want or need to change the way your anger hurts you?

EXERCISE: A Situation Where I Expressed Anger Inappropriately

Think of a time when you were being hurt and had angry thoughts and emotions that you may have expressed inappropriately. Describe that situation and your emotions below.

The situation in which I was harmed and victimized was _____.

I believed that _____ (name someone who hurt you) harmed me deliberately because _____.

I believe that _____ (the person who hurt you) should have done something different. This could have been to _____.

I got angry because _____.

I expressed anger this way: _____.

Perhaps I could not have done things differently because _____.

However, if there was something I could have done to express anger appropriately, I could have

_____.

What has this exercise and the one before it said about you and your anger?

_____

_____

When you keep your anger bottled up inside your body, it can lead to illness. However, as Capacchione (2001) indicates, anger can also be expressed appropriately and thereby accepted. If you choose to express anger appropriately, after examining the situation, ask yourself the following questions about your anger:

- What message did that anger give to me? Were my boundaries violated?

- What questions do I need to ask of my anger? What am I trying to protect or restore?

- When has my anger become stuck?

- When has my anger intensified into rageful explosions?

Kohanov (2013) notes that anger may not lift until you learn to take specific actions to protect yourself. Women may cry when angry, and men may express anger to mask sadness because they do not want to feel vulnerable. Anger may also turn to shame and guilt when you become angry at yourself for violating others' boundaries. Sometimes when anger is turned inward, it can be expressed as sadness and/or depression.

When has your anger actually been frustration, which is a result of being ineffective? Frustration can also build to a point of rage.

Answering the following questions may help you to deal with frustration:

- What is the message your frustration is sending?

- What can you do differently to resolve the frustration?

- Whom can you turn to for ideas and/or assistance?

Frustration occurs when you use the same methods over and over again to achieve a different result to change or influence some aspect of your life, work, or relationships. This is a definition of insanity—doing the same thing over and over again and expecting different results.

For more exercises dealing with ways to modify or limit anger, look at chapter 8 on arousal.

Depression

The next negative emotion is depression. Kohanov (2013) notes that depression can be seen as the "stop sign of the soul." She writes that depression frequently follows periods of sadness, fear, anger, or grief, when you have not listened to the messages of these emotions or asked what these emotions are saying to you. Depression prevents you from moving forward and, in some ways, may protect you from getting yourself into dangerous situations. In that way, it acts as an emergency brake.

Think of a time recently when you felt depressed.

- What was the situation?

- What was the message behind that depression?

- What questions do you want to ask of your depression? For example, what was its origin?

- Do you feel as if you have any energy? If your energy is depleted, where might you find a new source?

When depression intensifies, it can have disastrous consequences including suicidal thoughts or even attempts (see an "Aside About Suicide" in chapter 8). It can also lead to deep sadness and grief (discussed later in this chapter). The common definition of depression is anger turned inward. Learning how to deal with anger, especially when turned on yourself, can help with depression.

The next group of long-lasting negative emotions is guilt/survivor guilt, and shame.

Guilt

If you feel at all responsible for the traumatic event or events you have experienced, there is a good possibility that you have some feelings of guilt. Guilt occurs when you feel bad about your behavior: what you did or did not do before, during, and after the traumatic event. Guilt can be a positive emotion if you really were responsible for what occurred. For example, if you were driving drunk, lost control of your car, and killed someone, you are guilty and have good reason to feel guilty. If you were using illegal drugs and provided those drugs to someone else, and that person went into cardiac arrest, you are guilty. If you perpetrated violence against another person in any circumstances other than self-defense, you have every reason to feel guilt.

EXERCISE: **My Feelings of Guilt**

Do you feel any deserved guilt about the trauma or traumas that happened to you or in which you participated? List what you did and why you deserve to feel the guilt.

I feel guilty because

1. _____

2. _____

3. _____

4. _____

5. _____

Now look at the circumstances of the trauma. What did you do or not do to cause the trauma or traumas to happen? Think of yourself as a reporter looking at the event and writing a factual story. Ask yourself the following questions (adapted from Figley 1989) and write your replies in the space provided.

What happened?

_____

_____

Why did it happen?

_____

_____

Why did it happen to me?

_____

_____

Why did I act the way I did during the event or events?

_____

_____

Why have I acted as I have since the event or events occurred? How have I changed?

_____

_____

If the event or events happened again, how would I act? Would I want to do anything differently? Would I be able to do anything differently?

_____

_____

What did this exercise teach you about your actions?

_____

_____

Now it is time to look at the actual level of responsibility you had for the event. You may have a distorted sense of your responsibility. For example, Susan was a victim of sexual abuse when she was six years of age. She blames herself for what happened. In fact, her perpetrator was a coach, thirty-five years old, left in charge of her while her single-parent mother was away on a business trip. Looking at this situation, what degree of responsibility did that coach have for the abuse? What percentage of responsibility did her mother have? And Susan? In this situation, does anyone else (society, for example) have any responsibility? How much?

The exercise that follows helps determine the percentage of responsibility that you have for the trauma or traumas you experienced; it was developed by Scurfield (1994).

EXERCISE: **My Responsibility**

1. Reviewing what you wrote in the previous exercise, what are the central details of the traumatic event or events as you remember it or them? Use the first person ("I") to answer this question.

_____

_____

_____

2. Now, what percentage of the responsibility, at this point in time, do you believe you have (had) for the event? *I am _____ percent responsible for what happened.* Are you sure this is your percentage of responsibility? (Answer yes or no.) Could it be more or less? Examine your responsibility in detail, including both irrational and rational statements, factual statements, and your feelings (Matsakis 1994a). (You may need to use extra paper.) You may use these questions as prompts: Do you believe that the event and its consequences were the result of your innocent mistake? Your inability to make a decision that was appropriate? Your competence or incompetence? Your abilities and knowledge, or your stupidity? Your thoughtfulness or thoughtlessness? Your carefulness or carelessness? Your impulsivity or immaturity? Your lack of skill? Your lack of morality and, thus, your sin? Your lack of character? To what degree and in what ways do you blame yourself for the occurrence of the traumatic event? How responsible are you for the injuries or damages to others during and after the event?

_____

_____

_____

3. Now look back at the level of responsibility you assigned to yourself in step 1. Could you now convince someone that you truly are responsible to this degree, based on what you have just written? How would you now revise your percentage of responsibility?

_____

_____

4. Now think about anyone else who was involved in the trauma. What was each person's role? Assign a percentage of responsibility to each person involved.

_____

_____

5. If others have some degree of responsibility, what happens to the responsibility you have assigned to yourself? Look again at what you did or did not do during the trauma or traumas and what you could and could not have done, and assess your level of responsibility. My total responsibility is _____ percent, because _____.

    In what ways do you still feel responsible? (For example, if you did not tell, why not? Were you threatened? Were you ever taught to tell?)

    _____

    _____

6. If there is any part of the event or events for which you still feel responsible, might you consider that you have already been punished enough by your own beliefs or actions? How much more must you suffer? Self-forgiveness may be a very long process for you, depending on your actual responsibility for what happened. Still, it is important that you ask yourself exactly what it would take for you to be able to forgive yourself for any involvement and responsibility you had. Take the space below to write your answers to some or all of these questions: What would you need to do to be able to forgive yourself? If you have not done this act or these actions, what is stopping you? Do you need to get more information about the event before you can forgive yourself? Is there something missing in your explanation of what happened that might lead to your forgiveness? If you are unable to forgive yourself, are you at least able to accept who you are and what you did?

    _____

    _____

    _____

    _____

7. If you still believe you need to pay for your responsibility in the traumatic event or events, think of some non-self-destructive ways in which that might occur.

    _____

    _____

To summarize the preceding exercise, the steps are as follows:

1. Verbalize what happened using "I," the first person.

2. Ask yourself, "What percentage am I responsible for? Am I sure? Is it possible my responsibility is more or less than that?"

3. Convince yourself and others that you are and deserve to be this percent responsible.

4. Challenge that level of responsibility by looking at who else is responsible, and then state anyone else's percentage of responsibility.

5. Recalculate any responsibility to make a total of 100 percent while looking at what you did and did not do.

6. Describe the level of suffering you have had for the percentage of responsibility you gave yourself and decide if that suffering is or is not enough, and if it fits or does not fit with your actual percentage of responsibility (Schiraldi 2000).

7. Figure out ways for making amends, if appropriate, and then commit to moving on with life.

JOURNAL EXERCISE: What I Learned from the "My Responsibility" Exercise

What did this exercise teach you about the trauma or traumas that happened? What did it teach you about yourself and your responsibility? Did what you learned show you that there was any way you could have prevented what happened?

_____

_____

_____

_____

As Schiraldi notes, "Guilt affirms morality" (2000, 182). The successful resolution of guilt involves a series of stages of denial, processing, and resolution. When you process guilt, you assess any harm that you did and your responsibility for that harm. If you find that you are guilty to any degree, then it is appropriate for you to express how sorry you are and make appropriate amends.

Many beliefs that get associated with guilt include *shoulds* and *ought tos*. If these beliefs are inaccurate, it is important to challenge them by asking yourself what each of the beliefs says about you and then by looking for evidence, both pro and con, to dispute or support the belief.

If you continue to feel guilty for any part you played in the trauma, ask yourself what your guilt can do for you. Does it provide a way for you to atone (in part or totally) for what you did or the part you played? Does your guilt motivate you to change your behavior?

_____

_____

Are you still saying "If only…" to yourself after answering these questions? When you say "if only," you may be placing blame on yourself that you do not deserve. The guilt you feel now may be due to the messages others instilled in you at an earlier time, perhaps during the trauma itself. One way to combat guilt, particularly if the trauma happened when you were a child, is to gather photos of yourself at the time the trauma occurred or look at children now who are the same age you were then. Does this help you see yourself as small and helpless, perhaps in contrast to a large adult perpetrator? Recognizing that a small child can do little in self-defense against an adult perpetrator will help you realize that a child is *never* responsible for any abuse perpetrated against him or her. You also can look at any real choices you had the chance to make during the traumatic situation, if you were given any, as well as evidence that shows how you made and acted on those choices.

Schiraldi suggests that you answer the following questions about your reactions during a traumatic situation in order to put them in perspective (2000, 195–196):

- Were you able to think coolly at the time of the trauma?

- Were you aware of all of your options at that time?

- Were you able to make choices?

- Were any of those choices positive or good ones?

- Was this situation familiar to you, or was it new and different?

- Did you have any way to know, for sure, which option was best?

- Did you have a clear awareness of all possible outcomes of all your options?

- Did anyone or anything take away any of your options?

- Were you missing important information that would have helped you make good choices?

- Did you have time to weigh all the options and make good choices?

- Did other things get in the way of your making choices (fatigue, hunger, confusion, panic)?

- What outcome did you intend?

- Did you try to harm someone on purpose?

- Did you make an honest mistake that led to your harming someone?

- Did you make a reasonable decision under the circumstances, even if it wasn't the right decision?

- Did you accomplish any initial goals you had when the traumatic event began?

- What other coping strategies could you have used?

- Did you avert a worse traumatic situation?

- What else could you have done, in an ideal world, to deal with the trauma?

- If your best friend reacted the way you did, would you understand those actions? What would you say to that person? Could you forgive him or her?

It's important that you remember, as Schiraldi says, "Guilt can be adaptive [healthy] if it is realistic and if it leads to improvements in…behavior and character" (2000, 27).

Survivor Guilt

Matsakis (1999) writes about survivor guilt, the guilt that comes from the belief that your actions or nonactions during a traumatic event may have caused or could have prevented the death, injury, or mistreatment of others. Survivor guilt also occurs if you believe you should have experienced death, injury, or mistreatment yourself, but somehow escaped your fate. You may try to keep this aspect of guilt secret because you fear others would condemn you if they learned what you did or did not do.

For example, say you are a war veteran. During the war, you were leading your platoon across an open field. You told two of your men to assume certain positions as they walked beside you. Both of them were killed; you lived. Your guilt says that it should have been you who died, because one of the men switched places with you and had you been walking where he was walking, you would have been dead. Since that time, you keep seeking direct or indirect ways to kill yourself to "take his place." His ghost comes to you in nightmares, and you think that you owe him your life. Your guilt over his death has grown and grown and grown, even though in reality you are not responsible for it. Had you known that death lay in that path, you would not have sent him to walk there. You would not have walked there either. But you did not know. Naturally, you wish that things had turned out differently and that no one had died in battle. Your pain about the losses of your friends is deep, and your sadness does not go away.

You may experience similar guilt if you were involved in a car wreck that was your fault and some friends riding with you were killed. You may choose to harm yourself because you do not believe you deserve to be happy or successful. However, you did not have the power to stop their deaths, no matter if you caused them to die through your acts of commission (doing something) or omission (not doing anything). Your survivor guilt may be a way to honor the dead and not forget them, without grieving them or putting their deaths to rest. If you truly were responsible for the deaths, your survival guilt may be particularly strong. If you believe that you suffer from survival guilt, the following exercise may help you identify its existence (Matsakis 1999).

EXERCISE: My Survivor Guilt

Fill in the blanks of any statement that applies to you.

I made it out alive from _____ when _____ did not.

I made it out less damaged or injured than _____.

I escaped the emotional pain and distress when _____ happened.

I escaped social disgrace and humiliation when _____ happened, and _____ did not.

I wish I could die to join _____.

I should have died when _____ happened, and _____ should have lived.

If _____ had lived and I had died, _____ would have had a better life than I have had or been a better person than me.

_____ is luckier than I am because she or he has no more pain or suffering and I am stuck here with all this pain.

I dream of _____. In my dreams _____ happens. At times, _____'s ghost haunts me.

I fantasize that I could relive _____ and change the outcome to _____.

I have never talked about _____ and/or _____ because of my involvement, which was _____.

I am so guilty that I believe I have lost my soul because _____.

I wish that I had the courage to kill myself but am afraid of what will happen to me after death, because I did _____.

I will be punished if I ever talk about _____.

I no longer have religious faith or a sense of spirituality because _____.

When I have periods of intense grieving about _____, I _____.

When I have periods of intense rage about _____, I _____.

I use substances because I try to numb what happened. I use _____ when _____.

If I watch movies or documentaries about _____ or similar events, I become very depressed and emotional, and I _____.

I cannot live for myself; the reason I stay alive is for _____.

I am living for someone who died named _____.

I don't deserve to live. If I had my way, I would _____.

I should have died on (date) _____ when _____ because _____.

I believe _____ would have had a better life than I have had and/or would have had more to live for, had she or he lived.

I now sabotage my personal relationships with _____ by _____.

I sabotage my professional relationships with _____ by _____.

My guilt is there because I was negligent during or after the traumatic event and I

_____.

In hindsight, I know that I could have prevented what occurred by _____.

I also know that I must deal with the fact that I participated in the following amoral actions:

_____.

I feel that doing _____ has made me lose my faith.

I have tried to escape my guilt by _____.

What did you learn about yourself through completing this exercise?

_____

_____

_____

If completing this exercise has triggered old memories or brought up new memories, list those memories here and then go back to some of the exercises in chapters 3 and 4 to work on them.

_____

_____

_____

HEALING FROM SURVIVOR GUILT

Matsakis (1999) says that healing from survivor guilt does not mean that you are to forget what you did or forget those who were hurt or who died. It also does not mean that you will never have regret or guilt again. It does mean that you will look at your responsibility in the events realistically and honestly and will let go of at least some of the destructive ways you use to punish yourself. Part of healing from survivor guilt is to grieve the losses. Ways to deal with loss are found later in this chapter.

Another way to deal with survivor guilt is to find restorative experiences that are economic, vocational, political, or interpersonal and that allow you to help others or somehow atone for what happened before. Matsakis describes seven stages of healing from survivor guilt (1999, 164–165). You can refer to this seven-step process as you complete many exercises in this book:

1. remembering what happened

2. separating survivor guilt from other emotions

3. examining your role in what happened before, during, and after the trauma; looking at your errors in thinking and your irrational emotions, perhaps by using the exercise "My Responsibility" found earlier in this chapter

4. countering self-blame and irrational guilt through newly constructed statements about the self that are based on true responsibility

5. accepting guilt for what you did do

6. examining the personal consequences of your guilt to your own self-esteem, self-care, physical health, emotional health, job performance, life contributions, and life

7. making a commitment to being honest about the guilt and to taking action toward putting that guilt to positive use

Now take some time to identify a guilt-producing event that you want to describe in detail here. This activity may trigger your traumatic reactions. It also may bring new information to you. Remember to refer back to some of the exercises in chapter 2 to calm yourself when you need to do so.

EXERCISE: Events That Caused My Survivor Guilt

What event or events caused you to have survivor guilt? Describe the event or events here, and use your notebook or journal if you need more space.

_____

_____

_____

It also is very important for you to look at any beliefs or thinking errors you have that are getting in the way of your healing or at least lessening your guilt. Answering these questions about each of your chosen traumatic events can identify some of your beliefs and help you decide which (if any) of them you want to challenge.

Do you make wrong conclusions about your degree of
responsibility for the event? Do you assume too much or too
little responsibility?   _____

Do you believe you could have prevented the event from
occurring?   _____

Do you come up with the wrong conclusions about why you
made the decisions you did?   _____

Do you believe what you did was ethical?   _____

Do you have full information about the event to judge the decisions you made? If not, where
can you get that information?

_____

_____

Do you judge yourself against some ideal picture of what might
have happened?   _____

Do you have good intentions to make up for what happened? What are they?

_____

_____

Will you follow through on one of those intentions? Which one?

_____

_____

Are you using only your emotions to judge yourself in relation to
the event?   _____

Do you still believe you were totally responsible for what
happened, even after completing the "My Responsibility"
exercise above?   _____

Could you really have prevented the event?   _____

Did you really have the power to stop the event?   _____

Could you really have reacted differently?   _____

Do you really believe that if you had died during the event,   _____
another person would have survived?

Another way to deal with survivor guilt is to try new ways of self-talk and new ways to think about what happened. Whenever you have an irrational thought about your guilt, try to counter it with something more positive and realistic.

EXERCISE: Substituting Positive Thoughts

Look at the previous exercise. Identify five irrational thoughts about your participation in and responsibility for the event:

1. _____

2. _____

3. _____

4. _____

5. _____

Now what positive thoughts might you substitute for each of these negative thoughts?

1. _____

2. _____

3. _____

4. _____

5. _____

EXERCISE: **A Healing Monologue**

Matsakis suggests you stand in front of a mirror and repeat the following monologue to yourself three or four times a day until you can recite it almost automatically (1999, 222).

During _____, the following situation happened: _____.
Whenever I remember what happened, I usually think _____
(put in the thinking error here) and feel guilty. When I feel guilty about _____,
I need to remind myself that I am thinking incorrectly. Instead of thinking _____,
I need to view the situation as _____ (put in the more
positive, realistic thought). I also need to remember that I displayed the following strengths
during the event _____
and can give myself credit for those strengths. It would be a mistake for me to concentrate
only on these good things, though, because I am guilty (in reality) for _____.
However, it would also be wrong for me to concentrate on only the negative aspects of what
happened.

MAKING AMENDS

You also may deal with your survivor guilt by making amends. One way to make amends is to create a ritual for healing. Healing rituals are covered in chapter 11. Matsakis notes that making amends can lessen feelings of guilt and that "there is always something you can do to make amends, even if it is not perfect or powerful enough to change the past" (1999, 226). You might do something to work with the living (volunteer at a hospital), or for a cause that in some way deals with the trauma you experienced (for example, Mothers Against Drunk Drivers). Perhaps you can make amends financially (donating funds to help construct a trauma center for teens).

JOURNAL EXERCISE: **How I Would Make Amends**

If you were to make amends, describe in your journal or notebook how you would do it.

EXERCISE: **What I Learned from the Survivor Guilt Exercises**

What was it like to do the exercises having to do with survivor guilt? What did you learn about yourself by doing them? What did you learn about your guilt?

_____

_____

_____

Shame

Another emotional response to traumatic events that is common to many survivors, though not a symptom of the PTSD diagnosis itself, is shame. What is shame? Shame goes beyond guilt and is more difficult to overcome. Guilt means you feel bad for what you (supposedly) did or did not do during a traumatic event. Shame means that you feel bad for what or who you actually are. It is a deep feeling that originates from feeling flawed when you believe that only perfection is acceptable. Shame sometimes results from being used in an unacceptable or degrading manner (e.g., shame over feeling physical arousal while you were being molested).

Shame is a form of self-torment that includes feelings of inadequacy, inferiority, embarrassment, and disappointment and can lead to the formation of a shame-based identity—a situation in which your entire self-concept is based on your shame. Shame does not seem to get discharged through crying or expressing anger (Rothschild 2000). Feelings of shame may lead to aggression against yourself for violating your own inner standard of acceptable behavior. If you feel shame, you feel as if you are exposed to the world as bad. When you have been violated through a traumatic event, particularly if you were a victim of childhood abuse, you may feel shame about what happened to you. Your perpetrator may have told you messages during the abuse or afterward that now make you feel ashamed (e.g., you liked what happened to you, you chose it, etc.). You may have accepted those messages as true and as part of you rather than as messages that are false and have come from outside you. These introjects are lies that you no longer need to accept as your truths. Your own truth lies in you—you can make your own choices now about who you are and what you believe.

You may feel shame if and when you are put in a situation in which you have no power to choose. Then you feel wrong, bad, or worthless, or like you don't measure up, because the bad thing happened to you. Shame is a painful emotion because it involves very negative, critical judgments of yourself that lead to feelings of humiliation, inadequacy, and low self-esteem. Feelings of shame also can lead you to seek isolation and separateness. The roots of shame lie in your abuse, violation, assault, or betrayal and in your damaged, undermined, or destroyed sense of self.

EXERCISE: **My Shameful Beliefs**

Before you look at your personal shameful beliefs, first see if any of the following statements describe you. Put a check by each one that does. These statements may have originated in the messages told to you. If any of these messages came from abusers, note their source or sources after each belief.

☐ I cannot take risks. _____

☐ I am not allowed to be seen or heard. _____

☐ I am invisible. _____

☐ To avoid disapproval, I do things I don't want to do. _____

☐ I am not allowed to ask for what I need. _____

☐ I am inferior to others. _____

☐ I must treat myself negatively because I am bad. _____

☐ My beliefs about myself are all negative. _____

☐ I must be perfect. _____

☐ I am a disappointment to _____. _____

☐ My interests, choices, and wants are not of value to others. _____

☐ If something goes wrong in my world, it is my fault. _____

☐ I constantly look for ways to prove I am to blame for _____. _____

If you hold any other shameful beliefs, list them here:

_____

_____

Of the beliefs listed above, which are the three most powerful and shameful in your life? You do not have to come up with three: one or two such beliefs can control your life. If you have more than three, continue the list on another piece of paper.

1. _____

2. _____

3. _____

Now look at each of these beliefs and at their sources. What situation or situations led to their becoming a part of you? Who said them first? What facts lie behind them? Complete the exercise below for each of the beliefs you listed above. If you have more than three, you can complete the exercise on separate pieces of paper.

Belief 1: _____

The situation: _____

The speaker: _____

The facts of the situation: _____

The belief I can substitute for this shaming belief: _____

Belief 2: _____

The situation: _____

The speaker: _____

The facts of the situation: _____

The belief I can substitute for this shaming belief: _____

Belief 3: _____

The situation: _____

The speaker: _____

The facts of the situation: _____

The belief I can substitute for this shaming belief: _____

The primary ways to combat shame are to recognize it, identify it, name it, name or describe the events that created it, and then substitute a new belief or beliefs. According to Power, "Healing from shame is the primary journey of the wounded heart… Restoration is a process…begin with the recognition you are separate [from the shameful event], then deal with feelings of vulnerability, woundedness, and pain" (1992b, 60).

Use the following exercise to work out some new, healing beliefs and behaviors.

EXERCISE: Healing from Shame

Complete the following statements to help you heal from shame.

I can choose to assert myself when I am with people who still try to shame me by

1. _____

2. _____

3. _____

I can create positive affirmations to combat shaming. Three I am able to use (and am willing to at least try to believe) are

1. _____

2. _____

3. _____

If someone tries to shame me or if shameful feelings start to return, I can nurture myself by

1. _____

2. _____

3. _____

Answering the following questions may help you deal with your shame:

- Does your shame actually belong to you, or does it belong to someone else?

- What message does your shame hold?

- What questions does your shame seek to answer?

One question to ask is whether or not your shame has been placed on you by someone else, projected onto you by another to make that person look better (Kohanov 2013). If you are the recipient of projected shame, it is important that you stand up for yourself and refuse to be the scapegoat.

Helplessness

Another emotion associated with experiencing traumatic events is helplessness. If you truly were helpless and powerless during your traumatic exposure, you may want to complete the exercise below.

EXERCISE: **My Feelings of Helplessness**

Which of these thoughts do you have? Check those that apply to you:

- ☐ People ignore my needs.

- ☐ No one understands me.

- ☐ When they look at me, people don't really see me.

- ☐ People expect too much from me.

- ☐ People take advantage of me and use me.

- ☐ People want to control me.

- ☐ People are always yelling at me for things I didn't do.

- ☐ People don't do what I want them to do.

- ☐ People manipulate me.

- ☐ People bully me and are mean to me.

- ☐ People say cruel things to me.

- ☐ People have no respect for me.

- ☐ People don't treat me fairly.

- ☐ People don't hear what I say.

- ☐ People don't care about me.

- ☐ People don't help me when I need help.

☐ People reject me.

☐ People don't value me.

☐ People take me for granted.

☐ People think I am stupid.

☐ People see me as unattractive.

How many of these statements did you check? _____

What do the ones you checked say about you?

_____

_____

When the statement you checked says "people," go back and write down beside the belief the names of those people; for example, who takes you for granted or bullies you?

What did you learn about the people who hurt, abuse, or disregard you?

_____

_____

Are there few or many such people? _____

Do other people see this abuse and disregard for you? _____

The final major emotions we will present are those of sadness and grief and their accompanying losses.

Sadness

According to Kohanov (2013), sadness often occurs when a loss is imminent. What losses have you had because of your traumatic experiences? Sadness is often accompanied by what Kohanov tells us McLaren (2001) calls "the healing water of tears." If you are feeling sad, what questions do you need to ask of your sadness? Kohanov (2013) suggests asking

- What must you release?

- What do you need to rejuvenate?

Sadness can also motivate you to make changes and let go of what no longer serves you. On the other hand, grief is much deeper than sadness. The message behind grief is that you *must* let go of something that is so painful and has grown out of a death or loss. The question to ask of grief is "What else needs to be mourned?"

Grief and Loss

Trauma frequently includes loss. You may have lost your sense of safety and security, the meaning and purpose of life, your physical health, your ability to relate with others, your identity, your self-esteem, or someone or something you love. Loss leads to grief. Grief involves stages of disbelief or shock, anger or irritability, anxiety, depression, impaired concentration, and sleep disturbance—symptoms similar to those of post-traumatic stress disorder itself (Figley, Bride, and Mazza 1997). If the trauma you experienced involved death, the first reaction you may have had to that death was shock or denial, both of which function to protect you from distress and pain. The first goal for dealing with grief is to accept the reality that the one you love is dead. The shock or denial reaction is legitimate; it generally gives way to a feeling of disorganization and a need to adjust to a world without the loved one. In other words, you begin to move on.

JOURNAL EXERCISE: **The Grieving Process**

In order to begin working through your grief, you may want to write down everything you miss about the person who died. Use your journal, and start by completing the following sentences:

Since _____ died, I never can _____.

We never can _____.

You also may try to answer the following questions:

- Why me?

- Why did this have to happen?

- How can I go on?

- What can I do?

- What do I need?

- Who am I now?

- What does this all mean?

187

You also may draw the place of death with as many details as you remember, tell the story about the death in detail aloud or in writing, or write a letter to the dead person (Ayalon 1992).

The final phase of grieving involves acceptance, the establishment of an ongoing relationship with your loss and with your loved one, and the recognition that you will never be the same. It also involves transcendence beyond the death using personal spirituality and faith, as well as channeling your energy into and reaching out toward something positive, such as a new person, career, project, or mission. Finding transcendence often means changing your attitudes toward life, death, yourself, suffering, and spirit.

Sometimes it is possible to create positive statements about your grief. Some examples of these statements might be:

- *All emotions are natural, healthy, and necessary.*

- *Grief is one of my emotions and can be empowering.*

- *Grief can release my energy.*

- *It is necessary for me to feel grief, accept it, and express it to achieve resolution of what happened to me.*

- *Grief is a way to show how much I cared for* _____.

- *Grief is a step toward making changes and handling crises.*

What other positive statements about grief can you make?

_____

_____

As you work through your grief, the following suggestions (adapted from Grand 2000) may be helpful:

- Realize that no one can grieve for you and that you have the strength to do it for yourself.

- Remember that the purpose of grieving is to help you accept the reality of your loss.

- Keep in mind that trying to numb the pain of your loss will make the grieving process longer.

- Try to keep a normal routine while you grieve.

- Get help when you need it.

- Try to avoid making any extreme life changes or important decisions after your loss(es). Wait a few months at least.

- Remind yourself that grief is painful but that you will survive.

Using Feelings Appropriately

Learning how to use feelings to guide appropriate behavior is important. If your goal is to develop a self that has some personal power, it is important that you are able to experience both pleasant and unpleasant emotions without overreacting or underreacting and, if things really get rough, that you are able to self-soothe. The goal is for you to be able to look at possible ways to express your emotions and then make choices.

EXERCISE: **How Do I Regulate My Emotions?**

Ask yourself the following questions:

If I get very, very sad, how do I express that sadness? Do I become extremely depressed, or do I cry and grieve and then go on?

_____

If I get very, very happy, am I able to keep that happiness contained, or do I seem to get out of control?

_____

Sometimes the emotions that you feel are ones you associate with past traumas. For example, any time you feel the slightest bit of fear, it may take you back to an abusive situation in which you felt terror. Learning to know when the fear truly is due to something in your present and not something from your past helps you lessen the power of the past over you. If you were abused in childhood, it is possible that you may find it very difficult to contain your emotions, regulate your aggressive acting out toward yourself and others, and feel empathy for others.

One technique for controlling an emotion (adapted from Schiraldi 1999) has the following steps:

1. Allow yourself to feel enough of a certain emotion (joy, sadness) to get in touch with it, without either going out of control or detaching yourself from it.

2. Use the experience of feeling the emotion as a way to learn more about yourself. What other emotions are present? Do these other emotions grow from the original emotion? You can look at each of them separately.

3. Identify the source of the original emotion. Go as far back as is necessary, often to a trauma.

4. Say or do what you need to in order to get a sense of closure on the situation that led to the emotion.

5. Look for a way to find an outcome to the emotion—perhaps writing a good-bye letter to someone who has left or died, organizing a ritual (see "Healing Rituals" in chapter 11), or doing something for someone else.

6. Move on, away from the emotion; don't allow yourself to be stuck in it. Return to the activities of daily life.

EXERCISE: **Practicing Controlling an Emotion**

Can you think of a situation in which you have had an overwhelming negative emotion? Describe it here and name the initial emotion that arises from it.

_____

_____

Now apply the six steps just described to that emotion.

Was this exercise helpful? What did it teach you about that emotion? Can you think of another situation in which it might help you bring certain emotions under control?

_____

_____

If you are unable to write about your emotion, you might consider drawing the emotion or making a collage that expresses it.

Expressing Emotion

What are some other ways you might learn about, deal with, and express emotion in appropriate ways? Chapter 8 will give you some additional ways to deal with anger. Other techniques to help you with your emotions include:

- learning to identify cues and triggers that lead to emotions, then writing down the differences in what you feel with possibly different emotions (anger, fear, etc.)

- rehearsing ways to deal with emotions ahead of time when you are not sure how to handle a situation (e.g., saying out loud, "I need some time to think over what it is I need to do.")

- role-playing situations that involve emotion with others, including your therapist if you are in counseling

- discussing emotions with others

- practicing expressing emotions with those you trust and then asking for feedback

- using relaxation techniques to combat arousal when emotions become too intense

- monitoring your beliefs about situations: looking at what happens to those beliefs to lead to emotional reactions, and then attempting to challenge and change the beliefs so they do not lead to what Meichenbaum (1994) lists as the most damaging kinds of self-talk:

  - catastrophic interpretations of events (e.g., "This is so awful; I just can't stand it anymore.")

  - demanding and coercive language involving "shoulds," "ought tos," "have tos," "need tos," and so on

  - overgeneralizations using "never" and "always"

  - negatively labeling yourself as "stupid," "impossible," and so forth

  - categorical thinking, such as calling yourself labels like "asshole," "shithead, "SOB," and others

  - black-and-white thinking—seeing situations as either all good or all bad, with no gray in between

In chapter 12 we discuss problem-solving and coping techniques. You may turn to that chapter for additional ideas. It also is important that you look at exactly how you feel about feeling your feelings.

EXERCISE: **Feeling My Feelings**

This exercise (adapted from Miller et al. 1989) can help you gain a better understanding of how you feel about your emotions.

List any feelings that you enjoy having:

_____

_____

List any feelings that you may not enjoy having but that you at least are willing to accept having:

_____

_____

List any feelings that you find unacceptable to feel:

_____

_____

When you have feelings that you find unacceptable, what do you do with them?

_____

_____

List any feelings you may be embarrassed to feel:

_____

_____

If you have those feelings, what do you do with them?

_____

_____

List any feelings you may be ashamed to feel:

_____

_____

What do you do with those feelings if you have them?

_____

_____

Being Afraid to Have Feelings

Being afraid to feel and show feelings may really be related to your beliefs about your unmet basic needs for safety, trust, personal power, esteem, and intimacy (Rosenbloom and Williams 2010). You may be more afraid of being rejected, abandoned, punished, or criticized than of the specific emotion itself. What really would happen if you allowed yourself to show an emotion you feel?

For one day, try to express your emotions honestly (without hurting yourself or others). Record what happened in the space provided below.

Emotion I Expressed   **What Happened When I Expressed It**

_____   _____

_____   _____

_____   _____

_____   _____

_____   _____

Expressing emotions means taking a risk. Taking that risk can be productive; it can lead to emotional development and self-improvement. This type of risk-taking is in contrast to risk-taking that is not productive and that may occur just for thrills or an adrenaline high. Nonproductive risks often involve hazardous actions that can jeopardize health, career, relationships, and other major areas of life—or life itself (Ilardo 1992). Expressing emotions honestly can bring about gratification, either immediately or over time, as you become more honest with yourself and others and as you let go of emotional baggage that has collected over time. Expressing an emotion means taking a chance; however, the end result of release from being a hostage to your emotions is worth that risk.

Finding Joy and Happiness

Life hopefully does not bring you only negative emotions. As a trauma survivor, you may find it difficult to see joy or happiness in life. You may also find it very difficult to get outside of your feelings to be able to reflect on them and even think about them. One of the newer symptoms under category D is the persistent inability to feel or express positive emotions. What do you desire most in life? Do you have a bucket list of your life's goals?

How often do you try to accept your emotions for what they are and what they tell you? Positive emotions can lead to positive actions; positive attitudes have the means to heal your body (Capacchione 2001). Your basic worldview can impact your world's path.

What Is Your Worldview?

Your *worldview* includes your life's road map and your beliefs, expectations, thoughts, and life scripts. Allow yourself the opportunity to have positive beliefs about yourself. Positive beliefs inspire positive emotions. Do you hold any beliefs about yourself that are positive? Do you treat yourself with kindness and compassion?

Self-compassion, according to Kearney and others (2014), is associated with healthy psychological functioning and includes a lessening of self-criticism, satisfaction with life, and social connectedness. Loving-kindness is an emotional state of goodwill. It involves having positive intentions toward yourself. Do you ever tell yourself the following phrases, and if you do, how frequently?

- I may be safe in my world.

- I may be happy.

- I may have other positive emotions.

- I may be healthy.

- I may be open to new situations, experiences, and ideas.

- I may mindfully attend to my personal experiences.

- I may allow myself to receive positive social support.

- I may have a positive purpose for my life.

- I may be calm.

- I may have friends.

- I may develop my potential.

- I may lessen the amount of time spent on worrying.

Repeating these phrases consistently and frequently can lead to feelings of self-kindness. These phrases and other similar ones, because they are personal to you, are easily accessible. Thoughts and feelings do not have to have long-term effects and impacts; when negative thoughts are substituted with positive ones like the preceding phrases, negative emotions are more short-lived. The result of saying these phrases to yourself over and over leads to what is known as "built personal resources" (Kearney et al. 2014). Capacchione (2001) writes "as we believe, so we feel" (217). If you blame yourself for your trauma, you may want to review the section on self-compassion in chapter 6.

Dealing with Worry

One of the most time-wasting emotional states is worrying. In a sermon at the Warrenton, VA, United Methodist Church, Pastor John Chadsey (2014) said, "If you want to keep from stressing out, refuse to worry about anything…the number one source of stress is worry." He noted that "worry" is an Old English word that means to choke or to strangle. He listed several negative attributes of worry:

- Worry is unreasonable.

- Worry is unnatural.

- Worry is unhealthy; it cannot change the past or control the future, but it does mess you up today.

- Worry is unnecessary.

EXERCISE: **Do You Worry?**

Do you worry? If so, in the space below, write down up to three major worries and then look at the four attributes of worry just listed. How do your worries fit into those attributes?

_____

_____

_____

_____

What can you do with your worries? Here are some ideas:

- Allow yourself to let them go, because you really have no control over what you're worried about, or look at whether or not there are areas pertaining to the worry where you have some control.

- Talk to someone you trust about those worries and then let them go.

- Be thankful for what you have and are; speak and show gratitude daily. As Pastor Chadsey stated, "Have an attitude of gratitude." We recognize that gratitude is one of the healthiest emotions. Look at your blessings rather than what has happened to you that might be construed as negative. Instead, concentrate on your blessings. What are some of your blessings? List five things, people, etc. for which you are grateful.

    My blessings include: _____

- Think about the good things in your life.

- Be content with what you have, with your life's circumstances, and with who you are.

- Be mindful and enjoy what you have right now.

- Turn your worries over to your Higher Power or to your God.

- Look beyond yourself to gain a sense of contentment.

EXERCISE: **Looking at More Positive Emotions**

What are three positive emotions that you seek the most? Love? Happiness? Joy? Contentment without worry? List and define them below:

1. _____

2. _____

3. _____

Being able to express love to another human being or living thing is one of life's greatest joys.

Briere and Scott (2015) wrote about the need for trauma survivors to develop self-respect, positive regard, and compassion. It is important that you, the trauma survivor, recognize your own bravery, even if you need to avoid certain memories as a protective form of avoidance. If you are in therapy, hopefully your therapist will acknowledge that bravery and encourage your positive regard.

Another positive emotion is hope. It is an important task for your therapist (if you have one) to help you instill hope in your life, your future, and your present rather than exist in a state of continuous despair. Helping you to develop a positive view of yourself, while not promising a given outcome, can lead to potential symptom reduction. Briere and Scott add that "hope is a powerful antidote to helplessness" (2015, 102).

Helping yourself on your own or by working with a therapist to help you identify negative emotions, and to seek and find the messages they send to you, is part of affect regulation. How many different emotions can you name and recognize in yourself and others? Part of this process is to learn to identify the thoughts that trigger them. Refer to chapter 4 for a discussion of triggers.

EXERCISE: **Examining the Links Between Emotions and Triggers**

Things in your environment can trigger negative or positive emotions, depending on what happened in the past.

1. Choose a memory that is triggered by something in your present environment.

   Examples: K is a Vietnam veteran who served in Vietnam primarily during monsoon season. He was constantly wet, and he developed jungle rot on his feet. He remembers the smell of the wet jungle, the dampness of the air, the pain of his feet, and the stickiness of the mud that he tried to slog through. When it rains constantly for days on end, or when it stops raining and he smells the dampness in the air, it triggers him back to Vietnam. R is another veteran who liked the food in Vietnam. He went to an area near his neighborhood that has Vietnamese restaurants and smelled pho (the Vietnamese soup). He felt a sense of contentment.

Briefly describe your memory that was environmentally triggered:

_____

_____

2. Write down the thought that is associated with the memory, even if it is a negative belief about the self:

_____

3. Identify your current associated emotion: _____

4. Challenge that negative belief or reinforce the positive one:

_____

_____

Substituting Happiness for Sadness

When are you the happiest? How long does your happiness last? Is it fleeting? What is happiness to you?

Happiness is not a single simple thing. It sometimes seems very difficult to feel happiness after experiencing a traumatic event or events, and happiness may even seem to be elusive. Experiencing unhappiness may be your norm; an overall sense of "doom and gloom" may pervade your life. United Methodist Pastor Jiyeon Kim, in her sermon "Happiness Can Be Learned Through Christ: The Habits of Happiness," spoke to what it takes to be happy (Chadsey and Kim 2014):

To be happy, it is important to turn the focus away from yourself. What does this mean to you?

To be happy, it is important to become someone that people trust. Do you have people who trust you?

To be happy, it is important to live with integrity, with your actions and your words being congruent. Are you congruent? If not, what do you need to change?

To be happy, it is important to keep promises. What does this mean to you?

To be happy, it is important to work well with others. When do you work well with other people?

To be happy, it is important to earn the gratitude of others.

To be happy, it is important to show yourself and others what really matters and choose well how to spend time and money.

To be happy, it is important to give to others. What do you give of yourself?

To be happy, it is important to be considerate of others. When are you a considerate person?

To be happy, it is important to live for something worth dying for. This difficult aspect means finding meaning. What does this aspect say to you?

Schiraldi says that happiness is "what people around the world want most" (2011, 47). Happiness means feeling positive emotions fairly regularly and having an overall satisfaction with life and self. Happiness is necessary if you really want to enjoy your life fully. Schiraldi (2011) also notes that about half of your ability to be happy is in your genes.

EXERCISE: **My Happiness Checklist**

The following checklist is adapted from a number of lists of what happiness includes. Check which apply to you. The more you check, the happier you (theoretically) are.

- ☐ I find good in any situation.

- ☐ I consciously create my own happiness.

- ☐ I have ambitions and like to take control to attain them.

- ☐ I know what I want out of life and choose to live life to the fullest.

- ☐ I know that complaining wastes my energy.

- ☐ I am not controlled or limited by my fears.

- ☐ I take responsibility for my mistakes.

☐ I take calculated risks.

☐ I am a life-long learner either formally (taking classes) or informally (reading, watching, listening).

☐ I am solution focused.

☐ I would rather have long-term happiness than short-term pleasure.

☐ I can manage my emotions.

☐ I embrace change.

☐ I am generous and kind.

☐ I concentrate my energy on what I can control.

☐ My career is not my identity; it is my job.

☐ I know how to relax.

☐ I have happy friends.

☐ I know how to speak for myself.

☐ I appreciate what I have and recognize my blessings.

☐ I am patient with others and those around me.

☐ I forgive myself.

☐ I love myself for who I am.

☐ I embrace change.

☐ I celebrate the accomplishments of others.

☐ I do not dwell on my experiences of being a victim.

☐ I live in the present.

☐ I know that everything happens for a reason.

(DeNicola 2014)

What have you learned about feeling and expressing positive emotions? What have you learned that is important to you?

Loss of Interest in Doing Things

A markedly lowered interest in activities that you used to enjoy doing before the trauma is another symptom that you may experience. One common theme in the lives of many trauma survivors is restricted participation in the "doing" of life. Sitting on a couch and watching television or countless movies, sometimes not even actually knowing what is playing, may become the sum total of your daily experience.

Life is not easy for most of us. Sometimes it is helpful to stop and look at what being alive means to you. Knowing this may help you define your life's purpose.

- How do you "do" life?

- Do you feel that life is passing you by?

- Do you see your world shrinking around you?

- Is your hypervigilance so great that you fear leaving your personal cocoon?

- What types of activities do you enjoy?

- When do you do them?

- Do you do them alone or with others?

What do your answers mean to you?

_____

_____

It is very difficult in many situations to participate in new or even familiar activities if you have any negative emotions. Even if you have the urge to do new things, you may find it difficult to get started. It is important to review any beliefs you have about safety, trust, and power and control of self, others, and the world. Please turn to chapter 6 and review how you believe your safety, trust, and control are challenged in new situations. When you are ready, choose a safe situation to try first. Then move to more challenging ones.

Feelings of Detachment or Estrangement from Others

Many trauma survivors report that they no longer feel comfortable with other people, particularly if those other people are not trauma survivors themselves. They may feel unable to relate to others if they perceive situations to be unsafe, if they have a history of being harmed by people whom they were encouraged to trust, or if they feel threatened. Do you have these or similar feelings? With whom are you comfortable? With whom are you safe? To whom are you attached?

If you feel estranged from others, and you don't feel safe in relationships or have basic issues with trusting others, you may need to return to the exercises in chapter 6 to work on negative beliefs about yourself and others. This section focuses on techniques to help you improve your relationships with others.

How would you describe a healthy relationship? According to Boon, Steele, and Van der Hart (2011), there are certain characteristics that make a relationship healthy. Some of them include

- mutual respect, empathy, and equality

- clear boundaries

- a balance of autonomy, dependence, and interdependence

- a continuous sense of the other person, even when not with you

- use of negotiation to resolve difficulties

- basic trust

Do you have any relationships that have these or other similar characteristics?

An authentic relationship, according to Kohanov (2013), has certain attributes. Participants in the relationship

- use emotion as information

- sit on uncomfortable emotions (of self and others), without panicking

- sense and flow with the emotions of others, without panicking

- view misbehavior as a form of communication

- have boundaries that are sensitive, flexible, and responsive

- understand how shared emotions in a relationship work and may include catching emotions from others, empathy, projection, transference, and conditioned emotional patterns

- resist the temptations to fix others in the relationship

- support others in the relationship and "hold the sacred space of possibility"

Other elements of a good relationship according to Jim Rohn (2014) include eight essential factors:

1. love as a commitment to treat the other with honor

2. a serving heart, focusing on serving others

3. honest communication

4. friendliness with the other

5. patience

6. loyalty as a commitment

7. common purpose

8. fun, including some element of enjoyment

Setting Good Boundaries

By setting appropriate boundaries, you have a better chance of maintaining good relationships with others. If you have a good relationship, you and the other person respect each other and accept each other as you are. You are able to communicate with the other person—including communication about what has changed, what could change, what needs to change, what you each want to change—without demanding or disrespecting.

If a relationship is to last in any form (between friends, partners, coworkers), it is important that each party accepts change and adjusts to change in the other person, if that change is healthy for you both. If the other person changes in such a way that the change puts you at risk (emotionally, physically, spiritually), then you have the right to end the relationship or change its boundaries. Remember, you have the right to get out of a relationship if you are not happy in it or with it. You do not have the right to try to change the other person to fit your idea of what is a good relationship, and the other person does not have the right to try to change you.

Your relationships in the past may have been shaped by those who hurt or abused you through their actions and the beliefs they put into your head. Their repetitive traumatic abuse of you may have brainwashed you and led to feelings of terror and helplessness. You may have learned from them that the only way to survive was to be helpless, or you may have been so terrified of their rejection and abandonment that you were submissive and bonded with them so tightly that it has been hard to break away. You no longer have to be enslaved by those beliefs or by these earlier threats, actions, and control. You have the right to be your own person and to set your own personal boundaries. If you need to remind yourself of your rights in any relationship, you and the person in that relationship may choose to fill out, sign, and agree to follow the following contract.

EXERCISE: **Our Relationship Contract**

This contract is made between _____

and _____ and becomes valid

on the date we sign it. It will remain valid for _____ (period of time).

1. We care about this relationship and want it to succeed.

2. We admit that we are each responsible for half of the success or failure of this relationship.

3. We can improve our relationship by doing the following four things, upon which we agree:

   a. _____

   b. _____

   c. _____

   d. _____

4. We are willing to make compromises on the following four things:

   a. _____

   b. _____

   c. _____

   d. _____

5. We will not abuse one another in this relationship in any way.

6. We will not bring up problems that we had with our relationship in the past.

7. We will take time to participate in this relationship on a regular basis by:

   a. _____

b. _____

c. _____

d. _____

8. We will set time to communicate about our relationship if either one of us needs to talk, as long as that talking follows good rules of communication.

Signed: _____ Date: _____

Signed: _____ Date: _____

Communication Techniques

Relationships can be enhanced through effective communication. This involves talking directly with another person when something needs to be said. When you communicate effectively, you use clear messages that say what you mean; make statements when a statement is needed (rather than asking a question); clearly state your wants and feelings; do not intend to hurt the other person; and listen actively as well as talk.

ACTIVE LISTENING

When you listen actively, you listen with openness, as you try to see the other person's point of view, with empathy, as you try to understand the other person's emotional state or feelings, and with awareness, as you try to be aware of how what the person says fits with your known facts. As you listen, keep eye contact, maintain safe physical boundaries, and ask questions if you need to do so. Active listening also involves paraphrasing. When you *paraphrase* what another person says to you, you restate what you understand the other person's comment to mean. It does not just echo what the other person said but asks a question through which you test your understanding. For example, you may say some variation of the following: "If I hear you correctly, you're saying that you really don't want to go to the party tomorrow night, because your ex-wife may be there. Am I right?"

Paraphrasing may include an example, a general idea of what you have heard, or a specific idea you believe you heard from the other person. You want to show that you are interested in what the other person is saying. Paraphrasing what you heard can help others hear how they are being heard and can then help them correct any misunderstandings or inaccuracies. The objective is to get clarity. This process also can help you cool down a situation and help you get more information before you react.

ASKING QUESTIONS

If you want to communicate with someone, you may want to ask probing questions to get better information about how the other person thinks or feels. *Probing questions* ask others to think and become more aware about what they have just said, and to clarify it. Asking a probing question does not mean that the other person was "wrong." In asking for clarification, you may ask the other person to explain something in particular, or you may say, "What do you mean by what you said?" You may ask someone to refocus their answer or to increase their awareness of the meaning of their words ("What are your reasons for saying that?") You also may ask the same question of other people in order to compare the answers.

DESCRIBING FEELINGS

Another basic communication skill is to describe your feelings by making an *I-statement*, such as "I feel happy when I am with you." The aim of making such a statement is to start a conversation that will improve your relationship. If someone is to take you and your feelings into account as worthy of consideration, they need to know how you feel. Describing feelings is a report on your inner state, and gives information that can help build communication and a relationship.

DESCRIBING BEHAVIOR

Behavior description is another basic skill for improving communication. If you use this skill, you report the specific, observable actions that the other person has done without valuing them as right or wrong, bad or good: "I've noticed over the last couple of days that every time I've offered a comment, all I've heard is disagreements and opposition." The aim of behavior description also is to open up discussion about how each person affects the other and about the relationship. It is important that you describe the behavior clearly, using evidence and actions that are open to the observation of others. When you use this skill, it is important to avoid trying to infer beyond what you observe.

USING HUMOR

Using humor can help communication by relaxing tension, reducing bad feelings, increasing a feeling of fellowship, or reinforcing a point. Humor also can help you express feelings more openly and spontaneously. You may use exaggeration, irony, wordplay, or other types of humor. People who have been traumatized may use *black humor*, humor that makes jokes about what happened to themselves or others, which is frequently misunderstood by those who have not been traumatized (or who do not work in the trauma field). Humor should not be a way to attack the other person. It should be used with playfulness and should not evoke ridicule or sarcasm designed to hurt the other. Humor can make a situation more joyful and can improve a relationship. Laughter is good for the immune system; it reduces stress hormones and, over a prolonged period of time, burns calories. It seems there are many reasons to laugh.

USING I-MESSAGES

An *I-message* is a specific, nonjudgmental message that focuses on the speaker, not the person listening. When you use an I-message, you describe how the other person's behavior is affecting you, without blaming the other person. With an I-message, you state the behavior that affects you, how it affects you, and why, in three parts:

1. *When you* _____ (state the behavior),

2. *I feel* _____ (state the feeling),

3. *because* _____ (state the consequences).

For example, instead of saying, "Why are you always so rude to me?", You could say, "When you say _____ (restate what the other person said) in front of my coworkers, I feel angry and humiliated, and it makes me not want to be around you."

EXERCISE: Practicing Communication Techniques

Which of the communication techniques on the preceding pages are you willing to try in the next week? With whom?

_____

_____

What is the purpose of trying those techniques?

_____

_____

After a week of trying one or two of them, in the following space, write the results of your attempts at good communication. Did your relationship with the person improve?

_____

_____

_____

Communication Styles

Miller et al. (1989) note that there are four styles of communication. After reading the description of each, think of when you use that style and with whom.

SMALL TALK

Small talk tends to be used in social situations in order to build rapport and keep in touch. It is generally relaxed, cordial, and playful and includes greetings, stories, and talk about conventional topics or daily routines. It also may include talking about special events that have occurred or will be occurring. *Shop talk* is a form of small talk that occurs on the job. It can be either casual or used to gather or give information and monitor work-related activities and schedules. It may include a team meeting that asks who, what, where, when, and how questions in order to report on and describe what is going on. If you use shop talk, you are showing others how competent, informed, and productive you are.

When do you use small talk and with whom? Shop talk?

_____

_____

_____

CONTROL TALK

Control talk is used to lead, direct, persuade, evaluate, instruct, reinforce, show authority, get compliance or agreement, sell, or caution. The intent of control talk is to show that you are in charge while also being both helpful and persuasive. It uses statements, questions, directions, and assumptions. Control talk can become *fight talk* when you want to force change on or defend yourself against another. It then includes statements that are demanding, attacking, blaming, threatening, or intimidating. The aim of fight talk is to justify yourself, hide your own fear or vulnerability, put the other person down, or use abuse to control. Fight talk often involves accusatory statements and questions like "Why did you do that?" Another form of control talk is *spite talk*. Spite talk is used to make someone else feel guilty, to get even, to protect yourself, to cover over your hurt, or to stop change from occurring. It can include gossiping, complaining, sulking, keeping silent, or showing defiance.

How do you use control talk and with whom and when? Fight talk? Spite talk?

_____

_____

_____

SEARCH TALK

The third type of communication style is *search talk*. If you use search talk, you are trying to get insight, clarify what has happened, look for options or causes, evaluate alternatives, or ask questions. You want to explore, brainstorm, and expand upon what you already know. Your mood in using this style is calm, supportive, and inquisitive, and you are open to possibilities.

When do you use search talk and with whom?

_____

_____

_____

STRAIGHT TALK

The final communication style is *straight talk*. Straight talk is open, direct, honest, assertive, responsive, and respectful. If you use straight talk, you aim to disclose information, connect with others without trying to control them, collaborate with others, and look toward the future. Straight talk includes observing, using active listening and the other communication techniques described above, and has a "now" orientation.

When do you use straight talk and with whom?

_____

_____

_____

Final Thoughts on Communication

Remember, communication is inevitable. You cannot *not* communicate. If you do not respond verbally to someone or something, you are still communicating. Communicating is a continuous process that occurs even during sleep (particularly if you sleep with a person or an animal). Communication is irreversible. Once you have communicated a message, it cannot be taken back or erased. It can be challenged, modified, or reexpressed, but the original message is out there.

Communication has many levels: the words said, the setting, the style and technique of the communication, the level of trust that exists between the giver and receiver of the message, and the perceptions of each all play roles. The sender and receiver of a communication never share the same perception completely, and there is therefore always room for communication error. Communication is most effective when what is sent in words (verbally) and what is sent in action (nonverbally, through body language) are the same or reinforce one another. Communication also is most effective when the listener gives feedback to and interacts with the speaker. One major purpose for communicating is to build more communication—and, hopefully, better communication. Finally, communication is a very personal process that is impacted by who you are; it is impossible for you to totally separate what you say, or put out, from who you are as a person.

Before you look at what you have learned about yourself by completing the exercises in this chapter, consider the Ten Commandments of Good Listening (adapted from Virginia State CISM Team Members 1998):

1. Be quiet and stop talking.

2. Put the person who is speaking at ease through your attention and body language, eye contact, and respect.

3. Show that person you want to listen to him or her.

4. Remove possible distractions (noise, television) if you are having anything more than a superficial conversation.

5. Show empathy through body language and vocalizations (sounds you make such as "oh," "wow," "hmm").

6. Have patience with the person talking and let him or her take time to get out what it is he or she wants to say.

7. Keep your anger under control.

8. Try not to argue or to criticize.

9. Use the communication techniques listed above, including asking probing questions, para-phrasing, and describing emotion and behavior.

10. Stop talking.

EXERCISE: What I Learned from This Chapter

What did you learn from this chapter and chapter 6 about how you deal with traumatic events?

_____

_____

_____

_____

8

Lessening Arousal: What to Do If You Can't Sleep, Can't Relax, or Are Angry and Irritable

Trauma overstimulates your autonomic nervous system. This overstimulation means your arousal levels are chronically high, which can have serious impacts on your body. These can include having difficulty falling or staying asleep; feeling irritable or having outbursts of anger; having concentration and memory problems; being hypervigilant; being startled easily; and feeling that you have no reserve of energy to help you heal. If you find it is too difficult for you to protect yourself, your body may begin to shut down through illness or even through dissociation. Some survivors of trauma seem to express the trauma through immune system–related illnesses such as chronic fatigue, fibromyalgia, irritable bowel syndrome, headaches, and severe tension. Identifying triggers, as you learned to do in chapter 4, can help you control your body—these triggers can lead to hypervigilance and jumpiness as well as to fear and terror.

The body of a trauma survivor—your body—needs soothing and care. This chapter helps you look at and deal with some of the physiological symptoms of the increased arousal involved in PTSD. This chapter will also cover reckless behavior as a newly added arousal symptom (*DSM-5* 2013). Doing the exercises provided can help you calm down or reconnect with and get a measure of control over some of your body's reactions. The end goal of these exercises is to help you normalize how your body reacts so that you can return to some level of calm and order, or *homeostasis*.

If you have symptoms of any type of physical disease or if your physical symptoms have persisted for longer than a few days or weeks, seek medical care from a physician who understands the impact of trauma.

Techniques to Improve Sleep

The first arousal symptom you may want to look at deals with sleep disturbances. In the next few pages, you will find ways to help you if you have trouble falling asleep or if you wake up and then cannot get back to sleep. Many survivors of trauma have trouble falling asleep or staying asleep. In fact, Matsakis says that "sleeping problems are perhaps the most persistent of PTSD symptoms" (1994a, 167). To be sure, getting to sleep and staying asleep can be a challenge even if you don't suffer from PTSD.

It is possible for anyone to sleep better by improving their sleeping environment: by removing triggers from that environment, creating an atmosphere conducive to sleep, and using good sleep practices. As a trauma survivor, it is important that you prepare yourself for sleep. One way is to avoid seeing, hearing, and thinking about traumatic things before going to bed. If you watch television or videos late at night, choose things that are light and free from the triggers of your traumas. For example, if you've survived a natural disaster, don't choose something with sirens or fire or devastation. Think about positive things in your life as you go to bed. Put on soothing music or an audio recording of waves, sounds, a gentle rain, or other soothing sounds. You also may want to try a different sleep schedule. If you are a night person, wait until midnight to go to bed and then get up at seven or eight if possible, if you need that much sleep. Try to avoid using over-the-counter or nonprescribed drugs or substances to numb yourself into sleeping. However, you may turn to a cup of warm milk or some turkey (both of which contain L-tryptophan, a soothing amino acid) to help you relax. Or you may take melatonin, if your doctor agrees that it does not interfere with any medications you may take.

If you were traumatized during sleep or in a bedroom, it is very important for you to identify any parts of that bedroom or of sleep that might trigger you. Develop a trigger list for sleep or for the room (see the journal exercise "My Trigger List" in chapter 4). For example, if your room now happens to be the same color that the room you were traumatized in was, you can paint it a different color. If your furniture is arranged in a similar fashion, you can change that arrangement. Begin to change things that are possible to change.

If your partner is not a safe sleeper, you may want to talk with him or her about alternatives, including using twin beds or agreeing on ways to wake up your partner when there are triggers.

Kelly liked to sleep on a mat in the corner of her bedroom. She couldn't understand why, in the middle of the night, she would leave her queen-size bed and end up on the floor on this mat. As she began to work on her past traumas, she realized that she had been molested on a queen-size bed as a child. She began to work on ways to make her bed and bedroom safe: she got rid of the queen-size bed and bought a twin bed, which she put against a wall. She then slept with her back to that wall to protect herself.

Researchers have worked out many ways that might improve your chances of a good sleep. The following list is adapted from Matsakis (1994a) and from the Metropolitan Washington Council of Governments Health Care Coalition (2001). If there are things that have worked for you in the past and have made your sleeping easier, try them again. If there are things that have not worked, don't try them, even if others suggest them.

- Physically exercise sometime during the day but not right before bed.

- Listen to relaxing music.

- Listen to a relaxation audio recording.

- Practice relaxation techniques before going to bed.

- Pray.

- Medicate with prescribed medications or the hormone/antioxidant melatonin that can be used as a sleep aid.

- Talk to others if they can soothe you or calm you before you go to bed; don't argue.

- Write or make an audio recording about your day, but not about your traumatic experiences.

- Eat something light and avoid caffeine.

- Try not to drink anything in the two hours before going to bed, so you don't have to get up to go to the bathroom.

- Do a boring task.

- Read a very boring book.

- Get up at a set time (try to make it the same time every day), no matter what time you fall asleep.

- Sleep in the same place; don't bed-hop or place-hop (the bed, not the living room couch, is for sleeping).

- Set the thermostat at a comfortable, cool temperature. Monitor that temperature (Riggenbach 2013).

- Use a night-light if necessary.

- Take a walk in the late afternoon or early evening to tire yourself out and raise your body temperature. Falling body temperatures (after you stop your walk) sometimes make you sleepy.

- If you find you have trouble falling asleep because you worry a lot, schedule a "worry time" during the day and use up that time at least two hours before you plan to go to bed.

- Keep a record of the number of hours you sleep each day and how you feel after you have slept so that you can look for sleep patterns.

- Check with your doctor to see if any medications you are taking get in the way of sleep.

- Use a white-noise machine or wear earplugs (if it is safe not to hear) to drown out noises that might get in the way of sleeping (e.g., the music from a noisy neighbor or street traffic noises). Try to minimize other noises.

- Take a warm bath about four hours before bedtime; as your body cools down after your bath, you may find it easier to fall asleep.

- Follow a set bedtime routine, such as the following:

    1. Choose a regular bedtime that works for your needs, and then go to bed at this time for at least one week.

    2. About two hours before that bedtime, use the ability you have to contain, numb, or avoid traumatic reminders to put away any issues about trauma recovery.

    3. Do something relaxing.

    4. Begin to get ready for bed at least an hour before your actual bedtime by doing your personal care routines (get your clothes out for the morning, brush your teeth).

    5. Check out your room and make sure it is safe and comfortable: check your closets, windows, and doors; put away anything that might trigger nightmares, flashbacks, or intrusive thoughts (pictures, drawings, belongings).

    6. Gather anything you want to have in bed with you (special cover, stuffed animal, pets).

    7. Continue to contain any thoughts and feelings that might trouble you.

    8. Use a relaxation technique to help you get to sleep.

    9. Lie down and give yourself permission to sleep.

    10. If you use music or another type of audio recording, turn it on.

    11. Close your eyes and go for it.

Which of the above have you tried? Did any of them help you go to sleep?

EXERCISE: My Bedtime Plan

Use the space below to design your own bedtime plan. Be specific as to what you will do.

1. _____

2. _____

3. _____

4. _____

5. _____

6. _____

Try this plan for ten nights. After ten nights, come back to this page of your workbook and write down what happened to your sleep patterns. Did you sleep better?

Another Sleep Routine

Baker and Salston (1993) suggest that you try the following sleep routine, which integrates several of the suggestions already made.

Before you try this strategy for the first time, come up with ten things you hate to do around your home. These things might be cleaning and defrosting a freezer, cleaning the toilet, dusting a room, balancing a checkbook, or similar things.

Two hours before going to bed, start preparing yourself. Tell yourself, "I am now going to get ready to go to bed and go to sleep." Take a warm bath or shower and get into your sleeping clothes. If you do not wear clothes to bed, get into a bathrobe until you are ready to turn out the light. Stop all liquid intake, with the exception of warm milk or a few sips of water. Now do a relaxing activity. Read a long historical novel, knit, or listen to soft music. Don't watch TV or a video and don't watch the news.

Once you go to bed and turn out the light to go to sleep, you have thirty minutes maximum to get to sleep. You may choose to do a relaxation exercise during those thirty minutes if you find you do not fall asleep right away. If you are not asleep in thirty minutes, you have to get up and do the first thing on your list.

If you fall asleep and then wake up at some point during the night and can't seem to fall back asleep, you have fifteen minutes to get back to sleep. If you aren't asleep in fifteen minutes, you must do the first thing on the list and then go to bed. If you already did the first thing on the list earlier that night and then fell asleep, you are to do the second thing on the list, then go back to bed. Again, you have fifteen minutes to go to sleep. Continue doing the things on your list until you go to sleep and stay asleep.

Each night you can't sleep, begin again at the top of the list. Even if you have cleaned your refrigerator every night for five nights, on the sixth night you are to clean it again as if it were filthy. If this technique does not help you sleep soundly within four weeks, see your doctor and get some medication to help you sleep.

EXERCISE: My Ten Things to Do When I Can't Sleep

Now make your list. Remember, these are the ten things that you hate to do the most. They must be things to do inside your home that will not wake up others who are sleeping. Also, you must be able to complete them within about thirty minutes. If a chore will take longer than twenty to thirty minutes, break it down into parts. The one you hate the most should be number one; you'll always start with this one when you can't sleep.

1. _____
2. _____
3. _____
4. _____
5. _____
6. _____
7. _____
8. _____
9. _____
10. _____

Good Sleep Hygiene

Saindon (2001) has suggested numerous self-help tips that include some of the previously listed sleep hints. She notes that sleep problems are a common symptom for those recovering from traumatic events and that many usual methods for falling asleep may no longer work after the occurrence of a trauma. Instead, nightmares, sleep terrors, or thoughts of reenactment, rescue, or renewal may interfere with the sleep cycle. To practice good sleep hygiene, she recommends:

- No reading or watching TV in bed. Reading and watching TV are waking activities. Use your bed only for sleeping. (If you can't sleep after being in bed for thirty minutes, use the routine suggested above.)

- Go to bed when you are sleepy or tired, not when it is your habit to go to bed. Don't nap during the day.

- Wind down during the second half of the evening before bedtime. Don't get involved in anxiety-provoking activities or thoughts ninety minutes before bed, and don't exercise within three hours of bedtime.

- Do at least five repetitions of deep breathing exercises before you go to bed.

- Try to relax your muscles, beginning with your toes and ending with the top of your head.

- Keep your room cool, not warm.

- Counting sheep is stimulating; don't do it when you are lying in bed.

- Don't use alcohol, drink coffee, or smoke cigarettes two to three hours before bedtime.

- Add a positive, desired ending to any repetitive nightmares or bad dreams you realize you are having. Think of the dream before you go to sleep and add the new ending, in case it comes up again.

- Write about your hopes and dreams every night before you go bed to free up your mind.

- Listen to calming music or a self-hypnosis audio recording.

Hopefully one or more of these suggestions will be helpful to you.

Anger: A Signal Emotion

Anger is a *signal emotion* that is also one of the arousal symptoms. It warns you of a threat to your well-being or of actual danger. Your anger is real. As mentioned in chapter 7, anger can range in expression from annoyance and irritation to fury and rage, and when associated with trauma, angry outbursts can be out of proportion to what provokes them.

In reality, anger can be helpful to you if or when

- Your anger is natural and a part of you.

- Your anger is a signal about what is happening around you.

- Your anger helps you know yourself better.

- Your anger tells you to protect yourself.

- Your anger tells you to make necessary change(s).

- The reasons for your anger can be shared with those who matter to you.

EXERCISE: **How Anger Has Helped Me**

Think of any ways anger has helped you. What are they, and when did the situations in which anger helped occur?

My anger has helped me deal with what happened to me by

1. _____

2. _____

3. _____

What do your answers tell you about how you may want or need to change the way your anger helps you?

Resolving Anger

Working out trauma-related anger is not easy. As Schiraldi (2000) notes, to resolve anger, you must do the following:

1. Reexperience and express enough anger to get in touch with your feelings.

2. Develop an understanding of yourself and what happened in order to figure out why you really are angry.

3. Do what you need to do to give a sense of closure and finality to the situation.

4. Try to bring the trauma to completion by looking for justice, confronting someone or something, or getting an apology. Sometimes these things are not possible. Your perpetrator may be dead or unwilling to apologize. The legal system may not give you justice.

5. Take responsibility for the anger you have and choose how to express it.

6. Put that anger into words or pictures that describe the feelings behind it. If you write about your anger, describe what triggered its occurrence, what body sensations happened, and who was involved. This is a safer way to get out the anger without hurting yourself or others.

7. Generally, anger is the way you express fear or hurt. It is important to identify what lies beyond your anger. *Who* do you believe hurt you? Is there an appropriate target for your anger? If so, who or what is that target?

8. Look at the unhealed hurt lying behind your anger—this hurt, according to Schiraldi (2000), is generally from your past. Be sure to self-soothe before you look at the hurt.

9. Put your anger outside of yourself. Don't turn it against yourself or use it to think badly about yourself. Let those who hurt you know why you are angry, without criticizing or attacking them. Listen to what they have to say about what happened.

10. Learn how to protect yourself in other ways, so it feels safe for you to let go of anger.

It's important to remember that you choose to get angry and to react as you do. When you get very angry and lose control, you can become powerless. Therefore, it helps to learn what you can do to express your anger appropriately rather than lose control.

EXERCISE: **Alternative Expressions of Anger**

The alternatives I can use when I am angry include:

1. _____

2. _____

3. _____

4. _____

5. _____

If you had trouble thinking about alternatives in this exercise, suggestions in the following pages may help you. You might express your anger about what happened to you in words, pictures, or actions. You may use space in your journal to write about your anger or draw a picture of your anger. You also may take one or more pictures from a magazine that symbolize your anger, decide how and why the pictures are representative, and glue those pictures in your journal or notebook. You also may say the following statements, or something similar, to yourself:

When I am very angry, I can do things to take care of myself, just as I have done in other situations. When I am very angry and want to defend myself with excuses, I need to remember that I can just listen; ask questions; check to see if I understand what is being said to me by repeating back what I have heard and then asking if I have heard correctly; and look for some point of agreement. (Schiraldi 2000, 132)

Other things you can do when you have to deal with anger might be to go to a gym and work out, take a long walk, or change anger into something that is functional and helpful. You also need to follow the level of activation of your body; if physical exercise raises it even higher, it may make it harder to control anger. If you were to change your anger, you might look at its physical signs (e.g., a tight jaw or clenched fists), its cognitive signs (e.g., having suspicious thoughts, jumping to conclusions, or seeing things as black or white), and its behavioral signs (e.g., taking a fighting stance, puffing yourself up, or giving people dirty looks).

EXERCISE: **My Anger Signs**

Which of these signs do you have and how could you change them?

_____

_____

Other things I could change about my anger include

1. _____

2. _____

3. _____

4. _____

5. _____

What do your answers say about you and the way you deal with anger?

_____

_____

Coping with Irritability

Irritability is related to anger and is a common arousal symptom. To change your feeling of irritability, you can take the steps in the previous exercise in order to recognize its physical, cognitive, and behavioral signs. Other techniques, such as relaxing, getting exercise, and mindfulness, can be used to cope with irritability as well as with anger.

Relaxing to Control Anger and Irritability

One way to deal with anger and irritability is to do relaxing breathing. Breathe in slowly through your nose, hold that breath for five seconds, and then breathe out very slowly through your mouth. If you repeat this five times, you will help to calm yourself and defuse your anger.

Sometimes, it is good to turn to this relaxation exercise before anger takes over. It can help to have a relaxing place or scene already in mind prior to when you need it. This scene is generally not your safe place, because you do not want to introduce irritability, anger, and rage into it (McKay and Rogers 2000, 31), as shown in the following exercise.

EXERCISE: **My Relaxing Scene**

Where and when does your scene occur? (Choose the time and place.)

_____

_____

What do you see in that scene?

_____

_____

What do you hear?

_____

_____

What do you feel on your skin? What can you touch or are you touching?

_____

_____

What do you smell? What do you taste?

_____

_____

What feelings are you having (e.g., peacefulness, joy, calmness)?

_____

_____

What else would you add to your relaxing scene?

_____

_____

Now, think of a positive trigger word or phrase that you can use to jet-propel yourself to your scene, when you need it. My word or phrase is

_____

_____

Anger and Self-Care

As you know, taking control of anger is difficult, because anger can be a very disabling emotion. To get anger under control, it is important for you to change your irrational thinking and the negative messages you say to yourself. For example, do you say that you deserve to be treated badly because you are such a bad person and have done so many horrible things? Do you believe you should be punished by others or that you deserve their angry outbursts? Becoming aware of these thoughts and messages is a first step toward changing them. You must also realize that another person does not cause the angry feelings you have unless your anger is righteous anger against someone who has committed an atrocity or who has done something that is unforgivable. How you react is your decision.

EXERCISE: **My Anger-Producing Messages**

What anger-producing self-messages do you have?

1. _____

2. _____

3. _____

Now identify your personal sequence for expressing your anger-producing self-messages. Here is a possible sequence; you may not need to fill in all the blanks, but consider each carefully:

1. I say to myself _____.

2. Then I think _____.

3. Then I put the blame on _____.

4. Then I make this judgment on whatever or whomever I have put blame:

    _____.

5. Then I act out my anger by _____.

6. To release my anger, I usually _____.

What does this exercise tell you about the messages that you say to yourself?

_____

_____

You have the ability to change each message to a positive one. Take any of the negative messages you say to yourself that you have listed previously and see how you might change it:

_____

_____

EXERCISE: **A Situation That Caused Me to Feel Angry**

Now, keeping in mind all of the information about anger you have read and the exercises you have done, you may apply all of this to a specific situation.

The situation that really upset me and caused me to feel anger:

_____

_____

Write a few sentences that describe you in the situation.

_____

_____

_____

_____

_____

_____

Now try to think of that situation in a different way. McKay and Rogers (2000) suggest that you ask yourself the following questions (if you need more space, write in your journal):

What were my needs in this situation? _____

How was I trying to get them met? _____

What were my fears? _____

What was my level of stress? _____

What traumatic events were influencing me? _____

_____

What nontraumatic events were influencing me? _____

_____

What did I not know at the time that would have helped the situation? _____

_____

What skills did I use to react? _____

What skills did I lack? _____

What emotional limitations impacted me at that time? _____

_____

What physical limitations influenced me? _____

_____

What values and beliefs influenced how I behaved? _____

_____

What rewards or sources of pleasure did I hope to get? _____

_____

What resources did I have to help me? _____

_____

What other resources did I need? _____

_____

What would these questions lead you to say or write about the situation overall? _____

_____

_____

_____

_____

Now think about some alternative ways to deal with the situation that could help you resolve the anger without resorting to an outburst. Which of the following might work for you? Place a check mark next to the appropriate alternatives.

☐ Leave the situation so you can cool down and not act impulsively or aggressively.

☐ Overcontrol the situation and your anger.

☐ Take time to be alone because it is hard to be angry if you are alone and don't have a target for your anger.

☐ Exercise your anger away. If you can't do something physical, do some isometric exercises. For example, put your hands against a wall and push very hard until you are exhausted.

☐ Yell and scream by yourself until you are worn out.

☐ Hit a pillow, pound or tear a phone book, or throw bottles into a recycling bin.

☐ Ground yourself in the reality of your present environment. Become aware of whether or not you really are safe or if you truly are in danger.

☐ Take your child up on your lap and hold her/him tenderly; hug your significant other or yourself (in a butterfly hug) for over twenty seconds; stroke your dog or cat to get oxytocin flowing to relax your body.

☐ Use your image of your safe place and/or safety person.

Using Mindfulness to Lessen Anger and Irritability

According to Mizuki (2013), and in agreement with the definition of mindfulness in chapter 2, mindfulness is the "skill of attending fully to an experience (thought, emotion, action, sensation) in the moment (as it is happening) in an open and accepting manner" (229). Being mindful means remaining a curious observer rather than emotionally engaging with something. Being mindful of emotions can help lessen their power and impact because you aren't judging the emotion or your behaviors; instead, you are silently observing them. Regular relaxation and mindfulness exercises help you to learn to calm your body down when it reacts to mild signs of anger or irritability; when the body is calm, anger is weaker and easier to control.

Mizuki (2013) suggests that, when rage and anger surface, you can step back in your mind from the emotions, allowing them to be present without reacting to them or engaging with them. This practice can allow you to improve your regulation of emotions so that you get less angry or have better control over the anger you do have. In addition, practicing mindfulness on a regular basis can help build up gray matter in the brain in areas associated with memory, emotional regulation, introspection, self-appraisal, and thinking (Moore and Malinowski 2009; Hölzel et al. 2011). In order to practice this type of mindfulness, take five minutes right now and just *listen* to the sounds around you. Set a timer if you think you may not listen mindfully for long enough. When you finish the five minutes, write in your journal about your observations. Do this in a variety of places with a variety of emotions and then look at what you have written.

Reducing Anger by Setting Boundaries

Being able to set an appropriate boundary is another way to lessen anger. (The issue of setting boundaries as a way to help build relationships was already discussed in chapter 7.) By not permitting others to violate emotional, physical, spiritual, or other boundaries, by preserving personal space while respecting the personal space of others, anger will lessen. Setting boundaries is a form of self-care. It involves setting limits without being manipulative. Boundaries need to be specific, reasonable, logical, and enforceable (Kohanov 2013). Boundaries also need to be clear, consistent, and congruent.

Think of a situation when your boundaries were being violated and you were getting angry. Now, what type of boundary might you set or did you set? Has that boundary been enforced? Are you consistent in your enforcement?

Healthy boundaries, according to Riggenbach (2013), can lead to healthy individuals who

- interact with others effectively

- frequently get what they want

- know the limitations of their actions

- know what actions they will tolerate from others

- respect the personal spaces of others

- are responsible to others but not responsible for them

- allow you to say "yes" or "no" at appropriate times

Do you have healthy boundaries? Boundaries can be physical or emotional, or both.

PHYSICAL BOUNDARIES

A *boundary* is any type of division or separation that you set between what is permissible or possible and what is not. You have many different types of boundaries around you and within you. One type of boundary involves physical space. It is important for you to recognize the amount of physical space that you need around you in order to feel comfortable when you are with others.

EXERCISE: **My Physical Boundaries**

Answer each of your following questions, using your journal or notebook if you need more space.

How close is too close? _____

If someone comes too close, how do you feel? _____

_____

Are there situations in your life at the present time in which people come physically too close to you? What are they?

_____

_____

What do you do when a person approaches you and you do not want to be approached? Are you able to be assertive and maintain your physical space?

_____

_____

What is your definition of unwanted physical contact?

_____

_____

How do you react if someone violates your boundary of physical contact? For example, how do you react if someone:

- brushes up against you _____

- stands too close to you _____

- touches you on your body in a nonsexual way when you do not want to be touched

  _____

- tries to touch you in a sexual manner and you do not want to be touched

  _____

- stares at you _____

- hits you _____

- talks too close to your face _____

If you have very tight physical boundaries, you may feel very uncomfortable if someone touches you, even in a social situation (e.g., if someone puts a hand on your shoulder). You may avoid physical closeness, keep a very stiff body posture, and try to keep a "stone face." If you have very loose physical boundaries, you may touch others without asking permission, may let others touch you even when you do not want to be touched, may invade the private conversations and spaces of others, may personalize (take what others do as being a personal attack on you), and may overreact to others. If you have a healthy physical boundary, you know the limits of your own personal space and make your boundary clear to others.

EXERCISE: **What Is Your Personal Space?**

What amount of space between you and another person is necessary for you to feel comfortable or safe?

_____

Do you always need or want the same amount of space between you and others?

_____

How can you keep that space? Does keeping it make you tired?

_____

_____

How do you let others know if they get too close to you—in words or in actions? If you don't let others know, what stops you?

_____

_____

If someone gets too close to you physically, what happens to you inside? What feelings do you have? What messages do you say to yourself?

_____

_____

EXERCISE: **Recognizing My Personal Space Needs**

Mundahl et al. (1995) suggest that you do the following exercise with another person whom you think you might trust.

1. Ask the person to stand about twenty feet away from you and stay still. Now slowly walk toward that person with your arms held out in front of you. Keep walking toward the other person until you begin to have any feelings of discomfort and lack of safety. Then stop. This is your personal space. How large is that space? When we work with children in elementary school and teach them about "good touch" and "bad touch," we teach them that the personal space they are entitled to have is the distance between them and another person if both people have their arms outstretched. Is your personal space more or less than this distance? How did doing this exercise make you feel? What did it teach you about yourself?

    _____

    _____

2. Now, repeat the exercise with your friend or support person. Let that person walk toward you. How does his or her personal space compare with yours? How did you feel in this role?

    _____

    _____

A healthy physical boundary means respecting your own personal space and that of others. You ask permission before touching others or invading their personal space. You also are respectful of their boundaries and needs. If someone begins to invade your personal space, you have various choices of ways to react. You may back up or put an object (e.g., a chair or table) between you and the other person. You may say, "I feel uncomfortable because you are so close to me physically." If you were physically or sexually abused as a child, your boundaries were invaded in many ways and you may find it difficult to set boundaries now. Practice the preceding suggestions and be assertive in saying what you want from others and how you want them to respect your physical space. One way to determine where your boundary lies is to pull your elbows in to your sides and extend your forearms forward. The tips of your fingers probably indicate the minimum distance at which your boundary lies.

You have the right to be safe and to feel safe. You do not have to allow others to get closer to you than your personal space zone (usually between eighteen inches and four feet) permits. If you want others to have closer contact, you have the right to say when and with whom and for how long.

EMOTIONAL BOUNDARIES

A second type of boundary is an *emotional boundary*. Having an emotional boundary means that you are able to set limits without worrying whether or not you might hurt or disappoint another person. Asking for what you want or deserve is another way to set an emotional boundary. When you have good emotional boundaries, you can do this without worrying about whether or not you will be abandoned, disliked, hurt, or attacked. If you have good emotional boundaries, you can refuse to be sexual, without fearing that the person who wants a sexual relationship with you will be so hurt or angry that he or she will abandon, reject, or punish you. You have the right to say no emotionally as well as physically.

Part of setting boundaries is to create a personal "bill of rights." This bill of rights can allow you to set boundaries and take risks. In one of the next exercises, you will have the opportunity to choose from the rights listed below or add your own to create your bill of rights:

- I have the right to choose my own sexual partners.

- I have the right to say no to a request for sex.

- I have the right to keep others out of my personal space.

- I have the right to stop any sexual activity in which I am involved if and when I have a flashback.

- I have needs and can take steps to meet them or try to meet them.

- I have the right to express my feelings as I feel them.

- I have the right to make mistakes.

- I have the right to change my mind (and what I believe).

- I have the right to change who I am.

- I have the right to ask for help.

- I have the right to set a boundary.

- I have the right to be alone if I want to be.

- I have the right to let go of the past.

- I have the right to seek support from myself.

- I have the right to seek support from others.

- I have the right to set goals and then prioritize them.

- I have the right to give myself a compliment.

- I have the right to forgive myself when I am not perfect.

- I have the right to stop making unrealistic demands on myself.

- I have the right to stop blaming myself for things for which I was not responsible.

- I have the right to believe that I can succeed.

- I have the right to judge myself appropriately.

- I have the right to care for myself before giving to others.

If you say no in a firm manner when it is right to say no, you will be able to survive the reactions of those around you. It may feel very strange to think that you are able to say no to someone or something. You may find that saying no brings up many different emotions.

EXERCISE: **How I Feel When I Say No**

When you say no, which (if any) of these emotions have you felt in the past? Circle those that apply to you.

scared

nervous

angry

empowered

disliked

anxious

ashamed

powerless

rejected

pressured

strong

guilty

relieved

abandoned

manipulated to change my mind

There are positive and negative ways to say no. Listed below are examples of each. Which have you ever used and when? Put a check in front of each that you have used and then, in your journal or notebook, write a sentence or two about when you have used it.

When I say no (or try to say no):

☐ I become passive.

☐ I shut down.

☐ I get angry and turn that anger toward another person.

☐ I explode in rage.

☐ I escape through substances.

☐ I withdraw.

☐ I make clear statements.

☐ I make good decisions.

☐ I state what is good for me.

☐ I negotiate if that is necessary.

☐ I communicate what I want.

☐ I listen to the wants of others.

☐ I take a time-out if necessary.

☐ I keep my needs and safety in mind at all times.

☐ I know I have the right to say no.

EXERCISE: **My Personal Bill of Rights**

Which of the previously listed rights would you include in your personal bill of rights?

_____

_____

_____

_____

What other rights you would like to add?

_____

_____

_____

_____

What has completing the last few exercises taught you about setting boundaries?

_____

_____

_____

_____

If you have emotional boundaries that are too tight, you may be emotionally numb. You may seem to be insensitive, unaccepting of others, and not interested in others. You may avoid reacting or showing your feelings to others and have problems asking for or giving help. If you have emotional boundaries that are too loose, you may be unable to contain your feelings and you may overreact to yourself or others. You may tell others too much about yourself, may depend too much on others to meet your needs, and may trust too quickly or get into intimate, sexual relationships too fast. You also may agree to do things when you really want to say no. If you have boundaries that are too loose emotionally, you also may give too much to others, take too much from others, and not respect your own or others' personal rights.

How do you separate your own feelings from the feelings of others? If you are in a good mood and someone else around you is having a bad day, does your mood immediately change or are you able to maintain your happiness or contentment? If you feel good about yourself and something happens in one part of your life to challenge that feeling (e.g., your boss treats you rudely), do you feel bad about every part of you? Do you allow your boss's unfair comments to ruin how you feel about every part of yourself and your world?

Your emotional boundaries are impacted by your beliefs. If your beliefs tell you that anything that upsets your emotional boundaries is correct and that you do not deserve to maintain a healthy boundary, then it is important for you to challenge those beliefs. Your beliefs are the filters through which you see the world and help determine whether you react defensively, appropriately, or without a boundary.

EXERCISE: **My Boundary Script**

When others invade your emotional boundaries and impact you, you might say something like this to them:

When you _____ (talk rudely to me in front

of others), I feel _____ (embarrassed, humiliated,

unfairly treated, judged). I need _____

(for you to treat me with the respect you treat others in the office). If you (continue to)

_____ (be so rude to me),

I will _____ (go to your supervisor, file

a complaint, etc.).

If you use this exercise, try to make sure that your end options of behavior are realistic and will not bring you undue harm or criticism.

If you have healthy emotional boundaries, you are able to share how you feel with others in direct, appropriate words and body language. You are able to be assertive and make appropriate choices between possible actions. You also are able to admit your mistakes and then correct them, if at all possible, without seeing yourself as a totally horrible, awful person. You also are able to accept others' opinions and views, even though you may not agree. You can look at the pros and cons of others' views, and decide how to act in response. If you have appropriate emotional boundaries, you are a caring, feeling person who is empathic and sensitive, without being either overly distant or overly involved. You do not assume that you know how others think or feel or what they need. You respect their rights as well as your own. You ask for help when you need it but don't depend on others alone to meet your needs or to give you constant support and reassurance. You can keep your own values and morals.

EXERCISE: My Emotional Boundaries

Look at the following checklist and mark which of these statements are true about you. I believe my emotional boundaries are rigid, loose, or healthy because:

☐ I have good boundaries in the following areas: _____

☐ I tell others only what makes me comfortable to disclose.

☐ I do not have an intimate, sexual relationship immediately or shortly after beginning a relationship.

☐ I take my time to learn to know someone before I decide to trust that person.

☐ I do not change my behavior and values to please others.

☐ I am sexual only when I want to be.

☐ If someone tries to invade my personal space, I will tell that person that I am uncomfortable or back away.

☐ I do not accept touch from others when I do not want it.

☐ I make choices about my own life and the direction in which it is going.

☐ I do not expect others to anticipate my needs.

☐ I do not expect others to fulfill my needs.

☐ I do not fall apart to get others to take care of me.

☐ I am not self-abusive; if I did self-abuse, I have stopped doing so.

☐ I consciously try not to repeat patterns of abuse that happened to me in the past.

☐ I expect realistic assistance from others.

☐ I have realistic expectations of myself.

How many of these did you check? Ideally, you checked all of them. If your boundaries are good, you checked at least twelve or thirteen of these statements. If you left any blank, write those sentences below and look at the belief that lies behind why you did not check them. Then consider what you might do to challenge each belief.

The statements I did not check include:

1. _____

2. _____

3. _____

The beliefs that stopped me from checking each statement:

1. _____

2. _____

3. _____

What I am willing to do to challenge those beliefs:

1. _____

2. _____

3. _____

What did completing these exercises about physical and emotional boundaries teach you about yourself?

_____

_____

Remember that you have the right to set limits when it comes to your physical and emotional space and ask others to respect those limits.

Distractibility and Trouble Paying Attention

If traumatic images, thoughts, dreams, flashbacks, and other intrusions are constantly in your head, or if you are using energy to keep them out of your head, you may find that you have difficulty concentrating or paying attention. If you seem to have excess energy and are always on the go, you may get labeled as having attention deficit/hyperactivity disorder, when you really are just trying to avoid dealing with, thinking about, or reexperiencing your traumas. If these statements seem to be true about you, you can use some of the following techniques to increase your ability to concentrate:

- Do relaxation visualization exercises.

- Make lists of what you need to do.

- Make lists of what you need to remember.

- Read several paragraphs in a book and then summarize what you have read in writing.

- Practice thought stopping if you have intrusive thoughts that get in the way of thinking.

Hypervigilance, Heightened Awareness of Danger, and Startling Easily

During the traumatic events that happened to you, were you very aware of what was going on around you? In the present time, are you very observant or overly aware? Are you always on edge? Being overly aware or hypervigilant may be one of the symptoms of PTSD you are experiencing. Meichenbaum has listed metaphors that might help you identify these feelings (1994, 112). Do you ever feel as if or believe any of the following?

- You are a time bomb about to explode.

- You are over the edge.

- You are a volcano about to erupt.

- You are about to have a meltdown.

- You have a short fuse.

- You are in attack mode.

- You are at your breaking point.

- You are on alert.

- You are ready to snap.

- You are ready for a fight.

- You are walking on eggshells.

240

- You are ready to flee.

- You are coming apart at the seams.

Do any of these describe you or do you have other terms that describe you? If you find that these or other images of you indicate that you are extremely watchful and hypervigilant, you may use the following techniques to calm down:

- Do whatever you need to do in the house to feel safe: check the locks on the doors, make sure windows are shut, etc.

- Use a paradoxical intervention when you are checking safety—checking doors and windows five times is not enough; make yourself check them ten times. (In other words, instead of doing less checking, do more.)

- Ground yourself in the reality of your present environment—become aware of whether or not it really is safe or if you truly are in danger.

Reckless, Risk-Taking, or Self-Destructive Behaviors

Reckless, risk-taking, or self-destructive behaviors are a new qualifying arousal symptom for a positive PTSD diagnosis. These behaviors can range from doing "too much of something" (e.g. overeating, overmedicating) without harmful intent to doing something deliberately that would harm yourself (self-mutilating, attempting suicide) to not doing something (not taking life-preserving medications, such as insulin, or not following a necessary diet), among others. The following questions are included here to get you to begin to think if any of these arousal symptoms of reckless or self-destructive behaviors are ones you use:

- Do you need stimulants or stimulation in order to feel alive?

- Do you take risks in order to create a sense of excitement in your life? (Briere and Scott 2015)

- Do you self-injure as a way to feel alive? If so, how?

Self-Harm

Self-harm does not mean only hurting your body or doing things to your body that bring you pain. It is deliberate injury that ranges from minor to severe. It also includes the effects of taking minor or serious risks that potentially culminate in serious physical harm (e.g. unprotected sex that leads to an

STD, speeding that leads to an arrest or a car crash, going out alone to unsafe locations and ending up being attacked, abused, or raped). There are many ways that you can harm yourself and sabotage yourself as a trauma survivor. As suggested in the writings of Zampelli (2000), you may choose to complete the following exercise to see exactly what self-defeating behaviors you use and which ones you use most often. Then you can go back again and ask yourself what these behaviors say about you (Rosenbloom and Williams 2010).

EXERCISE: My Self-Defeating Behaviors

Check all that apply to you:

- ☐ I waste time.

- ☐ I avoid working toward a goal I have set by doing meaningless things.

- ☐ I get physically ill when I have something pressing to do.

- ☐ I change the subject when I am uncomfortable.

- ☐ I use a "geographical cure" when I am uncomfortable rather than face a situation (that is, I physically go someplace else).

- ☐ I refuse to look people in the eye when I talk to them.

- ☐ I avoid emotional intimacy.

- ☐ I communicate indirectly.

- ☐ I do something distracting during a conversation (bite my nails, play with jewelry).

- ☐ I overeat.

- ☐ I use substances to excess.

- ☐ I use alcohol to excess.

- ☐ I am a shopaholic.

- ☐ I lie to cover up, impress others, and get out of a problem.

- ☐ I smoke.

- ☐ I am disorganized.

- ☐ I am generally late to appointments.

- ☐ I put myself in risky situations.

- ☐ I miss important meetings and appointments.

- ☐ I do not make important phone calls.

- ☐ I don't write things down.

- ☐ I have excessive debt.

- ☐ I forget important things on a regular basis.

- ☐ I overspend without getting into debt.

- ☐ I remain in a harmful situation even though it is self-destructive.

- ☐ I go along with what others want, even when it is bad for me.

- ☐ I don't try to change myself.

- ☐ I ask for help from the wrong people.

- ☐ I take on more than I can handle.

- ☐ I believe I am special, unique, entitled.

- ☐ I believe things have to be perfect around me.

- ☐ I am impatient and "want it now."

Now rank your top six self-defeating behaviors and describe the situations where you do them:

1. _____

I use this behavior when I _____

2. _____

I use this behavior when I _____

3. _____

I use this behavior when I _____

4. _____

I use this behavior when I _____

5. _____

I use this behavior when I _____

6. _____

I use this behavior when I _____

Now, taking those six self-defeating behaviors, use the following strategy for each. (You may do this with the first one here; do the others in your journal or notebook.)

Write the behavior: _____

Ask yourself the following questions:

1. What does that behavior say about me?

   _____

2. Now what does *that* say about me?

   _____

3. And what does *that* say about me?

   _____

The answer to the third question gives you your core belief—the deep belief that underlies the behavior.

Self-Injury as a Type of Self-Harm

Self-injury is a special type of self-harm. It is direct, controlled, and repetitive, it does not have the intent of suicide, it is not related to being impaired mentally or cognitively (e.g., being retarded or autistic), and it is socially unacceptable (Suyemoto and Kountz 2000). Self-injury generally happens when you feel a deep loss that leads to feelings of tenseness, anxiety, anger, or fear, and you express those feelings by harming your body in a very controlled manner. The most common form of self-injury is cutting. Cutting, and self-injury in general, has the following functions (adapted from Suyemoto and Kountz 2000, and Alderman 1997):

- a way to manage painful emotions that you can't express in words by doing something that is concrete and active

- a way to stop feeling feelings and therefore control them

- a way to prove you are alive

- a way to reenact trauma and abuse

- an addictive action that can become compulsive

- a boundary violation of your body

- an expression of self-blame

- a way to self-soothe

- a way to communicate an emotion

- an expression of self-hate

- a way to resist taking care of yourself in a positive way

- a way to maintain a stable sense of self if you are threatened with the loss of your identity

- a way to escape the pain of a perceived rejection

- a way to have physical evidence of emotional injury

- a way to distance yourself and set boundaries between yourself and others who will reject you for self-injuring

- a way to stop, induce, or prevent dissociation

- a way to release endorphins so you do not feel pain

- a way to self-punish for doing certain behaviors or having certain thoughts or feelings that were punished in childhood by others

As Alderman writes, "Most self-inflicted violence is the result of high levels of emotional distress with few available means to cope" (2000, 7). You may use or experience self-injury as a way to get control over your body, challenging those around you to care enough to notice and do something. Do you see hurting yourself as a way to express your rage toward powerful others through hurting yourself? Self-injury of any kind can be a substitute for anger toward another as well as a desire (unconscious or conscious) to inflict pain on that person. Sometimes, the desire to hurt yourself is a way to fight depression and anxiety or a way to numb yourself out through a type of self-medication. Sometimes self-injury is a way to show how much you hate yourself. Eating disorders involving self-starvation and purging yourself to the point of physical pain also can be a form of self-injury. You also may self-injure as a way to reconnect your body and mind. Some people say that they are able to believe and recognize that they are real and alive if they see blood. Self-injuring, to them, may calm their intrusive trauma-based thoughts by giving them the endorphin release that brings calming and lessens their arousal.

If you self-injure, complete the following exercise. Above all, it is important for you to go to a qualified therapist to get help. No self-abuse is okay; it is a way of revictimizing yourself. There are other ways for you to communicate your pain and anguish without taking it out on your own body. When you have very strong emotions of any kind, you do not have to act on them. Setting up a plan of alternative reactions to strong feelings is one way to bring self-injury under control.

EXERCISE: My Reasons for Self-Injuring

List ways you self-injure here:

_____

_____

_____

Now ask yourself the following questions about each of these behaviors (do this for the first behavior here in the workbook, and do the others in your journal).

How does the behavior help me survive?

_____

How does the behavior give meaning to my trauma?

_____

How does the behavior give me a sense of mastery and control and power?

_____

How does the behavior release endorphins and make me feel better?

_____

How does the behavior give me revenge?

_____

How does the behavior reinforce my feelings of guilt, shame, and self-blame?

_____

How does the behavior punish me?

_____

How does the behavior reenact what I learned earlier in life?

_____

How does the behavior bring me affection, care, and emotional closeness?

_____

Check all the items that you feel apply to you in the list below.

I injure myself because:

☐ I want to show that I own my own body.

☐ I want to express my rage at myself.

☐ I hate myself.

☐ I want to distract myself from other pain.

☐ I want to numb out my feelings.

☐ I have a message to give that I can't say directly.

☐ I am asking for help.

☐ I want to be rescued.

☐ I believe my body is a battleground.

☐ I want to cleanse myself.

☐ I want to somehow atone for my sins.

☐ I want to express my shame.

☐ I am trying to express my pain.

- [ ] I am taking over where my abuser left off.

- [ ] I am retaliating against myself for telling secrets.

- [ ] I am doing what my abuser brainwashed me to do, if I told.

- [ ] I am trying to connect my mind with my body.

- [ ] I am trying to make sure I am real, through bleeding.

- [ ] I am trying to bring my emotions under control.

- [ ] I am trying to prove that I am alive.

- [ ] I am trying to get a "high."

- [ ] I am trying to manage my flashbacks or memories.

- [ ] I am trying to release intolerable emotional tension.

- [ ] I am trying to buy myself time by focusing attention on physical rather than emotional pain.

- [ ] I need a release valve. I need to get into a "neutral zone."

Now take each of the reasons for self-injuring that you checked and think of five other things you might do to express that emotion or action. For example, if you checked "I want to cleanse myself" as a reason for self-injuring, what are five other things you could do to cleanse yourself that do not involve self-injury? They might be to take a bubble bath, take a sauna, go to a day spa, use herbs to purify your body, or do some other form of cleansing ritual. You may think of others that might apply to you. There is space below to write your reactions to one of your reasons. You may describe the others in your journal or notebook.

My reason for self-injuring and what I do to self-injure: _____

Five things I could do instead:

1. _____

2. _____

3. _____

4. _____

5. _____

What did completing this exercise teach you about yourself?

_____

_____

_____

Beliefs Leading to Self-Injury

You also may have a belief system that allows you to injure yourself. These beliefs frequently are distorted and may even have come from your abusers (as introjects you have taken into your brain and now experience as your own beliefs). They are generally black-and-white or all-or-nothing beliefs.

EXERCISE: My Beliefs About Self-Injury

Check which of the following statements you believe, if any:

- [ ] Self-injury doesn't hurt anyone but me and it really doesn't hurt me.

- [ ] It's my body; I can do what I want with it.

- [ ] It's no big deal and shouldn't upset anyone.

- [ ] If I don't hurt myself this way, my pain will be worse.

- [ ] The scars are there for a reason; they remind me of (telling, needing to be punished, my shame, etc.).

- [ ] No one knows about it, anyhow.

- [ ] I need to be punished for what I did.

- [ ] It just shows how bad a person I am.

- [ ] It keeps people away.

None of the statements in the preceding list is accurate or true. Each is a distorted belief. Self-injury is never a healthy way to express pain or hurt. If you checked any of these statements, it's important that you work with a therapist to help change these beliefs. Other things you might do with that therapist include developing an impulse control log (write what you did instead when you felt the urge to harm yourself) and thinking of ways to express your feelings that are not harmful to you. In the impulse control log, you may want to identify any triggers that led you to self-injure. Here are some other techniques to control self-injury:

- Try to focus your attention on something other than the need to self-injure—e.g., focus your attention on doing a crossword or jigsaw puzzle or some other intellectually stimulating challenge. This minimizes emotional pain.

- Make a list of alternatives to self-harm.

- Write or draw the abusive intent rather than act on it.

- Substitute physical activity to get the same adrenaline high, if that is the motivation.

- Make a collage of acceptable methods of self-expression.

- List the introjects (messages from others that you listen to in your head) that lead to self-harm.

- Develop a safety contract with your therapist or some other significant person and agree not to self-injure for a specified period of time; include rewards for following the contract and consequences if you break it.

- Develop a collage of each emotion that you find difficult to handle or express, including ways to release that emotion without self-harm.

- During a period of time that you don't feel self-destructive, prepare a list of reasons why you don't want to self-injure. Then, when you feel the urge to hurt yourself, go back and review this list and try to add another one or two reasons to it.

- Prepare a list or photo gallery of positive accomplishments in your life. When you feel the urge to self-harm, look at that list or album and then tell yourself, *I've accomplished all this good in my life and don't deserve to suffer more; I'm a good person.*

- Learn to identify the early warning signs that a feeling is becoming intolerable and then self-soothe or do something else. This technique involves identifying patterns of self-injury as a first step to changing those patterns. How often do you self-injure (daily, weekly, sometimes, rarely)? Then look at what you were doing, thinking, or feeling both right before the self-injury happened and right after it happened (Trautman and Connors 1994).

- Look at the backlash that happens after you harm yourself—from others and from yourself. Do you feel crazy, hurt physically, feel shame, try to hide from others? Use memories of that backlash as reminders of why you do not want to hurt yourself.

- Create a safe toolbox that includes a nonharm agreement, an impulse control log, a list of your self-harm alternatives, writing materials, and art materials, so you can get out your feelings and thoughts in other ways, and a life plan (Alderman 1997).

- If you must see blood on yourself, get a tube of fake blood and use it to visualize the effects of self-injury without actually carrying out the act.

- Use affirmations to change your beliefs about why it's okay to harm yourself.

An excellent resource for those who self-injure is http://healingselfinjury.org. See the resources section of that website for an archive of past issues of their newsletter, *The Cutting Edge.*

EXERCISE: **My Affirmations Around Self-Injury**

In the space below, write three affirmations that you want to say to yourself or write to yourself that you eventually hope to believe. Remember to put them in present tense and use the word "I."

1. _____

2. _____

3. _____

Now write each affirmation five times to begin to get familiar with it:

1. _____

_____

_____

_____

_____

2. _____

_____

_____

_____

_____

3. _____

_____

_____

_____

_____

Unmodulated Sexual Involvement

Schiraldi writes that some studies "have indicated that males and females with PTSD are more likely to experience sexual problems than those without PTSD...[including] sexual disinterest, aversion, dissatisfaction, performance difficulties (including painful intercourse and impaired arousal)" (2000, 318). If you were a victim of any type of sexual abuse or sexual assault, you may feel shame if you have sexual feelings, and sex can become a trigger that is associated with humiliation, danger, and the need to keep a secret.

You may have flashbacks during sexual relationships. If so, it is important that you ground yourself in the present as soon as you become aware of the flashback, perhaps by focusing on your safe place and on relaxation. It is important to stop any sexual response or activity you might be having until the flashback is done. It also is important to let your sexual partner know immediately what you are experiencing, asking him or her to comfort you and reassure you that you are in the present (Dolan 1991).

Some trauma survivors believe that they must self-injure if they have sexual feelings or arousal. Learning to substitute pleasure-oriented touch and imagery for self-injurious images and actions can be a long, hard process. Trauma may have impacted your ability to express yourself sexually to the point that you either ignore your sexual needs and wants or act out your sexual needs and wants aggressively, impulsively, or nonintimately. The next paragraph contains questions about your sexual feelings and behaviors. You can read and think about them, or write about them in your journal or notebook.

What behaviors are involved in any sexual behavior you have? Are there specific triggers that lead to your having or wanting to have a sexual encounter or relationship? When you want to be sexual, what thoughts motivate your behavior? Do you expect a negative outcome from any sexual experiences you have?

When you are sexual, how much control do you feel you have over what happens? If you feel out of control in a sexual encounter, what feelings do you have? Do you get confused, do you feel pain and shame, or do you feel anger toward yourself or your sexual partner?

Then what do you do? Do you continue to have sex even though you don't enjoy it? Do you get angry toward your sexual partner? Do you try to manipulate the situation? Do you stop the sexual act itself? Do you physically leave?

If any of these things happen, then how do you feel? Do you feel vulnerable and powerless? Do you believe that your partner will no longer care for you or love you? Then what do you do? Do you seek to protect yourself through distancing from your sexual partner? Do you use substances, numb out, sleep, or isolate yourself? Do you self-injure?

BOUNDARIES AND HEALTHY SEXUALITY

Appropriate boundaries are an important part of healthy sexuality. Healthy sexuality can be fun, playful, and authentic; it usually exists within the boundaries of a loving, respectful, giving relationship. It is part of relationship building and maintaining because it involves shared vulnerability and control. If you want to work on normalizing your sexual feelings, you might consider following the strategies suggested by Schiraldi (2000). These include:

- Think of your genital area as a normal part of your body; use its proper name and acknowledge its unique functions.

- Neutralize any feelings of disgust you have toward sex. Start by considering whether you think all sex is disgusting, or just certain aspects of it.

- Look at any feelings of shame that you have about sex and then develop positive affirmations to shift your focus toward the positive aspects of yourself and your sexual being.

- Develop your own description of what healthy sexuality is.

- Keep the following "sexual paradoxes" in mind to help you develop a satisfying sexuality (Engel 1995):

  The harder you try to make good sex happen, the less it happens, so relax and take your time.

  You can cure your sexual dysfunctions by not trying to cure them.

  The way to have sex when you want to is to learn to know when you do not want to have it and then say no.

  The way to please your partner sexually is to learn what feels good to you.

- Before trying to have sex, learn to touch yourself and your partner sensually.

- Learn the differences between sex, love, affection, and attention.

- Be prepared for the inevitable flashbacks that will occur during sex (the techniques you have learned in chapter 4 should help).

- Develop your own personal healing sexual imagery or stories to use if you need some fantasy during sex; these stories are typically built around what would lead to your safety.

An Aside About Suicide

Many trauma survivors feel suicidal and have suicidal thoughts and plans. Some act out those thoughts when they are particularly stressed and triggered; some act them out on a regular basis. It is important to develop ways to cope with and control your suicidal impulses. In order to do so, if you have had these impulses, it is important that you ask yourself about the meaning and role of those impulses. Do the impulses and fantasies related to planning suicide lead to an adrenaline rush or a sense of calm and peace? If you have these impulses, what else might you use to bring you relief?

Learning to find ways to relieve any intolerable feelings you have through less destructive means is the first step to bringing suicidal impulses under control. Writing in the online newsletter *Survivorship*, Mari Collings (2010) has created the following list of reasons not to kill yourself:

- Because you deserve to live.

- Because your life has value, whether or not you can see it.

- Because it was not your fault.

- Because you didn't choose to be battered and used.

- Because life itself is precious.

- Because they were and are wrong.

- Because you are connected to each and every other survivor and so your daily battle automatically gives others hope and strength.

- Because you will feel better, eventually.

- Because each time you confront despair, you get stronger.

- Because if you die today you will never again feel love for another human being...or see sunlight pouring through the leaves of a tree.

- Because you have already won. No one can take that away.

- Because the will to live is not a cruel punishment, even if it feels like that at times; it is a priceless gift.

- Because we need survivors to offer testament against this horror and despair.

- Because no one knows better than you the meaning of suffering, and agony deepens the heart.

- Because you deserve the peace that will come after this battle is won, and it will be won, but only minute by minute.

- Because you are furious that you have to suffer the pain of another's evil and filth.

- Because you, too, will one day feel fury.

- Because it is critical that you survive.

How do you relate to this list?

_____

_____

What else might you do to help yourself survive?

_____

_____

_____

According to Kohanov (2013), suicidal urges may develop from a chemically related imbalance and/or chronic pain. If you feel these suicidal urges, it is important that you seek medical, psychological, and spiritual support. Some people commit suicide to end their physical pain. However, more likely than not, suicidal urges arise in a desire not to end existence but to resolve conflicts between your authentic, real self and who you have become as a false, materialistic self. The false self is

- inflexible, rigid

- out of touch with purpose and meaning

- more concerned with appearances than introspection

- projects the negative self onto others

- repeats wounding patterns

- has negative beliefs programmed into the self

What are the questions to ask of your suicidal urges? Possibilities include:

- What do I want to end?

- What is it in me I want to kill?

- What messages lie behind any suicidal urges I might have?

If you have felt such urges, have you sought help?

The extreme level of distress lying behind suicidal urges may lead to the development of serious stress-related illnesses that, over time, may actually lead to physical death. Kohanov (2013) writes that your refusal to take care of yourself "is arguably a passive form of suicide." If you ever feel strong suicidal urges, let them speak to you about lost dreams, threats to your being, and/or forgotten goals.

EXERCISE: **What I Learned from This Chapter**

What has this chapter taught you about yourself and your arousal-based reactions to trauma?

_____

_____

_____

_____

9

Stress, Trauma, and the Body

(by Andrew Heyman and Mary Beth Williams)

We all experience stress in our daily lives. In 1936, Hans Selye helped create a new understanding of stress, which he described as a nonspecific response of the body to the body's demand for change. When stressed, your body releases hormones in the form of an adrenaline rush, which can lead to positive health consequences in terms of surviving a threatening situation. However, if the adrenal glands keep releasing stress hormones, eventually you may experience stress-related fatigue or even adrenal failure, and the consequences can become disastrous, if not potentially deadly. Risk factors that can influence how you respond to a traumatic event and whether your stress response is positive or negative are included in the list of pre-event factors in chapter 1. Some are emotional, others are social (e.g., support), and still others are physical (female gender, younger age, and earlier episodes of depression and anxiety, among others). People who are more resilient are able to withstand the impacts of stressors better, particularly the emotional impacts. This extends to stressful work environments, including being at war (Headquarters, Department of the Army 2012).

This chapter combines parts of the original chapter in the second edition with material written by Dr. Andrew Heyman. It is well accepted that stress can lead to chronic health problems and that one's potential ability to cope with the chronic physical aftereffects of trauma and stress may evolve over time. This chapter also summarizes healthy coping skills that will help you deal with doctors and hospitals. The major part of the chapter deals with integrative medicine and ways to deal with stress to improve general health.

The Impacts of Stress on the Body

Did you know that between 75 and 85 percent of all doctor's visits are related to stress in some way? Stress impacts every aspect of you: your body, your emotions, your relationships, and your view of yourself. Good stress, sometimes called *eustress*, can motivate people to take some kind of action. However, stress more often wears people down, impairs the immune system, and leads to many different kinds of illnesses. Stress, in all of its forms, including its most severe forms, has been the subject of attention of doctors and individuals for over 4,000 years. Back then, there was no distinction made between mind and body, and it was thought that the vital energy of the individual could be directly accessed, contacted, and manipulated through a variety of methods and techniques to ward off illness and extend life.

Today, an enormous amount of research has been conducted to help you understand the physiological and psychological parts of the stress response. As the scientific community has begun to appreciate the complexity and interplay between these two areas, it has also provided both a better understanding of how integrative therapies may lessen the stress response and new ways of thinking about how to treat stress.

The Physiology of Stress

The term *stress* has been used to describe anything that causes a disruption of normal functioning, also called *homeostasis*. However, the lack of a clear definition of this term oversimplifies the nature of the underlying positive and negative physiological effects of lasting disruption on you as a person (Edwards, Heyman, and Swidan 2011). Consequently, the alternative terms *allostasis* and *allostatic load* were proposed to describe the protective maintenance of homeostasis and the resulting deterioration of an organism due to overwhelming stress (McEwen 1998). Genetic influences, developmental and life experiences, and individual lifestyles and personalities indirectly influence and directly contribute to this internal balance.

The brain is the central regulatory organ in the stress response not only because it houses essential structures needed to regulate the stress hormone cortisol, but also because it determines whether and to what extent a stimulus is potentially harmful to you. Upon exposure to a perceived stressor, stimulation of the pituitary gland by the hypothalamic corticotropin-releasing hormone (CRH) results in secretion of adrenocorticotropic hormone (ACTH), which in turn promotes adrenal gland production of cortisol. This is the complex biological process that occurs when you are under stress (Edwards, Heyman, and Swidan 2011). In easier to understand terms, a perceived stressor causes the brain to tell the stress system to make cortisol, our main stress hormone.

Cortisol is the key regulatory hormone responsible for maintaining internal balance. Cortisol helps direct energy to where the body needs it most to deal with a stressor and can even change behavior to improve our response to stress. It also indirectly affects the release and action of other hormones as they attempt to reestablish homeostasis, which means cortisol affects just about every other hormone in the body (Edwards, Heyman, and Swidan 2011). Under normal circumstances, cortisol levels typically peak before awakening and decrease over the course of the day. When chronically elevated, cortisol has potent metabolic effects as a catabolic hormone, which means that it can break down all body tissues except the liver. Some systemic effects of elevated cortisol include increased gastric acid secretion, decreased collagen production, reduced diuresis, reduced bone formation, and memory center damage. Cortisol also impairs thyroid hormone production and function and causes numerous problems with immune system regulation and function (Edwards, Heyman, and Swidan 2011).

Other Basic Facts About Stress

When a stressful event occurs that is traumatic, your body and brain respond immediately, often with terror, fear, and other negative emotions. Your body releases cortisol from your adrenal glands. If traumas keep happening or you keep getting triggered, your adrenal glands may become so stressed that you might develop very low cortisol levels:

- Low cortisol can make you more susceptible to diseases, colds, allergies, flu, senility, decreased collagen, and reduced bone formation.

- Endorphins are natural pain relievers in your body that can give you a "high" after doing heavy physical exercise. Their presence can lead you to detach and dissociate from a situation and, in combination with cortisol, can keep you from consciously remembering traumatic events. However, they don't stop the emotional brain and the limbic system from remembering parts of events (Woll 2009).

- If your immune system "turns on you" and you develop an autoimmune condition, in which your immune system is attacking your own body, you may get caught up in a downward spiral of poor health and disease, as well as chemical sensitivity, worsening allergies, and hormonal imbalances.

- Autoimmune diseases impact about five million Americans, or 20 percent of the population, mainly women. They are usually chronic and are one of the ten leading causes of death in US women under age sixty-five (American Autoimmune Related Diseases Association 2012).

Stress and the Head, Gut, and Heart Brains

Many people now realize that we actually have some form of brain cells in three different parts of the body: the head brain, the enteric nervous system brain (gut), and the heart. The brain that is in your head is your body's control room. Its left side includes the hippocampus, which holds facts and language-based memories of traumatic events. Exposure to stress may cause molecular changes in the head brain that weaken the prefrontal cortex's ability to regulate behavior, thought, and emotion. The right side of the brain includes the limbic system and holds half of the amygdala—the half that seems to be most primary in emotional reactions to traumatic events (e.g., terror and fear). It also holds nonverbal, emotional, and picture memories.

259

Stress also impacts what is known as the *enteric nervous system*, a network of cells and neurons in the gut. This system's nerves influence a large part of your emotions, particularly "gut feelings." The enteric nervous system operates on its own as a second brain and has over thirty different neurotransmitters, including 95 percent of your body's serotonin (Gershon 1998). When the enteric nervous system is impacted by traumatic stress, it can lead to the development of diseases such as irritable bowel syndrome, Crohn's disease, gut obesity due to excess cortisol production, and ulcerative colitis. Having butterflies in your stomach or getting diarrhea before a stressful event are examples of gut reactions.

Stress also impacts your heart. Your heart has independent cells that influence how you process information. In fact, 60 percent of the cells in your heart are made up of neurons (Cooper 2001). Your heart sometimes acts as if it had a mind of its own and sends messages to the brain in your head. There is a strong connection between the brain and heart, mind, and spirit. Stress can interrupt the communication between the two, and stress reduction techniques have been shown to improve coherence and reestablish healthy communication.

EXERCISE: **Assessing Stress-Related Fatigue**

Look at the list below and check off any of these conditions if they describe you:

- [ ] feeling excessive fatigue and exhaustion
- [ ] showing low stamina
- [ ] feeling run down
- [ ] feeling more energy in the evening
- [ ] feeling tired after a good sleep
- [ ] being slow to recover from stress
- [ ] having concentration problems
- [ ] having a high susceptibility to colds, flu
- [ ] having sensitivity to cold
- [ ] experiencing unexplained weight gain
- [ ] experiencing suppressed immunity
- [ ] having heart problems, such as spikes in high blood pressure
- [ ] having weakened bones
- [ ] having gastrointestinal problems

These are all symptoms of possible stress-related fatigue. This occurs after you, the trauma survivor, have dealt with overwhelming stress. However, there is hope for you. You have the ability to reverse this problem and rebuild your immune system. For an excellent program of rebuilding, you can read *Overcoming Adrenal Fatigue: How to Restore Hormonal Balance and Feel Renewed, Energized, and Stress Free* (Simpson 2011).

EXERCISE: **Do You Have an Autoimmune Condition?**

Many times in visits to physicians, neither doctor nor patient links illness symptoms with traumatic stress. They neither see the connections between those events and the mind, heart, gut, and body in general nor consider that responding to traumatic events may have lowered cortisol levels into the danger zone. This exercise will help you determine whether traumatic stress may have impaired your immune function and led to any autoimmune conditions. The following list is from American Autoimmune Related Diseases Association (2012). Check off any of the conditions you've experienced, either now or in the past.

☐ atypical chest pain, hypertension, cardiac rhythm changes, EKG abnormalities

☐ body stiffness

☐ cardiomyopathy

☐ chronic fatigue syndrome or Epstein-Barr virus

☐ chronic Lyme disease

☐ chronic nonrestorative sleep

☐ chronic pelvic pain without a physical cause (especially if you are a victim of sexual abuse)

☐ chronic unexplained pain

☐ Crohn's disease

☐ delayed wound healing

☐ endometriosis

☐ esophageal pain mimicking heart attack, including spasms and constrictions

☐ extreme or chronic chemical sensitivity and environmental sensitivity

☐ fibromyalgia

☐ Graves's disease

☐ Guillain-Barré syndrome

☐ Hashimoto's thyroiditis

☐ herpes simplex virus outbreaks

☐ increase of hepatitis B symptoms

☐ irritable bladder syndrome

☐ irritable bowel syndrome

☐ multiple sclerosis

☐ psoriasis

☐ rheumatic fever

☐ sarcoidosis

☐ scleroderma

☐ systemic lupus erythematosus

☐ thyroid problems

☐ type 2 diabetes

☐ ulcerative colitis

☐ unexplained dizziness

☐ unexplained irregularity of vital signs (heart rhythm, blood pressure)

☐ unexplained tinnitus (ringing in the ears)

How many of these conditions did you check off?

If you checked off several of these conditions, be sure to talk to your doctor about what you've learned in this workbook and what connections might exist between your traumatic experiences and any physical illnesses. Also be sure to ask to have your cortisol levels checked.

Trauma and Chronic Illness

If you have developed chronic illnesses or autoimmune conditions due to your traumatic experiences, your relationship to these health issues is likely to evolve through four phases: developing chronic health problems, experiencing some degree of stabilization, reaching resolution or remission, and integrating any ongoing symptoms or limitations (Fennell 2001). Let's take a quick look at these four phases.

Phase 1: Developing Chronic Health Problems

You may have experienced one or more illnesses arising from the impact of traumatic stress on your immune system and that have become chronic. If so, you may have lost or had to quit your job, found yourself disabled, applied for and possibly received disability, and have a limited capacity to function as you once did. You may have deep feelings of grief over the loss of your past self, and your family may be angry that you have changed and that your changes have also changed their lives.

Phase 2: Experiencing Some Degree of Stabilization

If you have developed one or more chronic autoimmune illnesses, you may have had to restructure your goals and activities to some degree. You may not be able to do certain things you once could do. You may not be able to drive or leave the house for an extended period of time. You may not be able to stay awake for more than a few hours at a time or participate in fun things you once did with your family.

Hopefully, you have been able to set some boundaries for yourself within a framework of self-compassion. Have you identified your energy boundaries and what you can or cannot do? Have you sought support, including spiritual support? If you've reached this phase and are beginning to experience stabilization in your chronic illness, it's a good time to review, revise, and rewrite your personal narrative using the writing exercises in chapter 3. It will also be helpful to examine the impact of your traumatic experiences on your life and consider what you can do to incorporate those impacts without totally relinquishing control.

Phase 3: Reaching Resolution

Over time, if your PTSD-related illnesses remain chronic, you may reach some plateau or leveling of your symptoms. Your illness may have even gone into remission. However, if your symptoms continue to afflict you, you may wonder if your life will ever get better and wonder if the person you once were will ever exist again. If you've gained some strength and energy, you may want to take more control of your medical care and decision making. This would be a good time to look at the use of metaphor as part of healing. You may want to use the metaphor of the bog (see chapter 10) as a visual way to illustrate the impact of autoimmune illness on your life. In creating your bog picture, you may realize that never again will you be the person you were before your illness, or you may find that you are closer to an exit from the bog than you realized. After working with the bog metaphor, you may want to rewrite your life narrative to include the bog of your illness.

Phase 4: Integrating Any Ongoing Symptoms or Limitations

In the integration phase, you have a clearer picture of your chronic physical conditions. There still may be questions about the course of treatment or healing, but you are involved in decisions about your medical condition. In this phase, you can continue to rewrite your life narrative and work on reconstructing your life to make it as meaningful as possible, given your physical condition. Keep a gratitude log and record any daily "acts of bravery" that you undertake (Fennell 2001, 164). Study your health conditions, say no to unnecessary treatments and procedures, and search for ways to find meaning in life through whatever actions you are capable of taking.

How the Body Stores Trauma

The nervous system communicates somatic memories of trauma between the brain and all other parts of the body. When the memories of trauma are stored as sensations, similar sensations can trigger these memories, causing what is known as *state-dependent recall* of the trauma. Your body can remember a trauma that your conscious mind is not remembering. So you're experiencing an implicit (body) memory or trauma without the explicit (thought) memory needed to make sense of it. Various body parts may hurt or have symptoms that are in some way connected to the trauma without your knowledge of how those parts of the body were involved in the trauma. Emotions that are connected to trauma also may be carried in the body. Rothschild writes that "emotions, though interpreted and named by the mind, are integrally an experience of the body" and that "each emotion also feels different on the inside of the body" for each individual (2000, 56). She points out that many expressions in our language link emotions and the body (2000, 57):

- "You are a pain in the neck." (Anger gets expressed in muscular tension.)

- "I am all choked up." (Sadness is often felt as a lump in the throat and tearing eyes.)

- "You make me sick." (Nausea often accompanies disgust.)

- "I have butterflies in my stomach." (Fear often is felt in a racing heart, upset stomach, or in trembling hands.)

If some of your symptoms of trauma have turned back onto your body, it is important that you allow those symptoms to speak: that you identify their origin and their relationship to what happened to you. It also is important for you to learn to develop a baseline state of calm by working on the exercises in chapter 2. Additionally, it is important that you have one good medical doctor who understands trauma and the impacts of trauma, rather than a number of different doctors who treat you for the trees without seeing the forest. Trauma can cause you to amplify and generalize your physiological symptoms. The best course of action is to make sure that you have no serious medical condition and then to look to the trauma basis of your symptoms, working on the memories from which they come. You can use the techniques in chapter 4 to do this work.

Chronic Pain

What is pain? Generally, when you have a pain in your body, you immediately think that something is wrong medically, and you want to fix it. However, as a survivor of ongoing, complex trauma, there may be no physical cause for the pain you feel, or the amount of pain you feel is not necessarily in direct proportion to the physical injury you have. Pain is a psychological problem as well as a medical or physical problem. Curro (1987) found that pain had four dimensions: motivational (your desire to avoid or escape from pain), cognitive (your experience with and memory of pain), affective (the feelings you associate with pain, including fear, anxiety, and stress), and discriminative (your nervous system's response to what causes the pain and its onset, duration, intensity, quality, and location). What do you do if you have chronic pain and a doctor tells you that it's all in your head? How do you get relief when the tendency of the medical community is not to prescribe enough pain medication to control the pain stimulus? One way to work with pain is to use what are known as cognitive behavioral techniques, or cognitive behavioral therapy. The adherents of cognitive behaviorism say that your thoughts influence your feelings and behavior, and your feelings and behavior influence your thoughts. If patterns of thinking and behaving are destructive or maladaptive, they can be challenged and changed. Cognitive behavioral therapy teaches people with pain to question and challenge those thoughts, feelings, behaviors, and reactions and to also use relaxation, imagery, and distraction (Grant 1997).

Researchers who have learned about trauma have helped us see that mind and body are one. Emotional learning occurs with a part of the brain called the amygdala; another part, called the hippocampus, is responsible for thoughts associated with those emotions (LeDoux 1997). These two parts of the brain are also involved in processing information after a trauma. The hippocampus is able to "remember" the facts of the situation and the context of the trauma. Van der Kolk (1996) has found that beliefs and cognition give meaning to the affect (emotion) that a trauma brings. Thoughts activate the amygdala and trigger emotions.

So what does this all mean to you? The emotions or emotional memories of a trauma get incompletely processed and then are constantly getting reactivated through triggers. Chronic pain is part of this conditioned emotional learning and "is a kind of recurring 'trauma,' since the traumatic event consists of recurring pain attacks or constant physical discomfort" (Grant 1997, 36). Trauma and its associated pain get associated with emotions and the cognitive appraisal (that is, the judgment or perception) of pain. Over time, the true pain that occurred with the trauma becomes a psychological response as well.

If pain doesn't get better over time, and if it gets more and more associated with emotions such as anxiety or fear, you may eventually have less awareness of your body and bodily sensations. You may even begin to dissociate from your chronic pain. Over time, dissociation maintains your traumatic stress reaction. Eventually, you may be told to "learn to live with your pain" or "try to manage it" because no one can find a cure or way to stop it through pills or medical treatments.

So again, what does that mean for you, the trauma survivor with pain? If you have endured serious trauma, your emotional responses are the major source of information for your thoughts and the meanings you attach to things. Your thoughts *appraise* (look at, value, question) your emotional responses. If you are to change your emotional responses, it is important to look at your emotions and to work on challenging and changing the meanings associated with those emotions. If you are to understand the sources of your pain, you need to go back and process your traumatic experiences (as in chapter 4) and reconnect with as much information about your traumas as is possible.

Relaxation strategies (chapter 2) may help you reduce the intensity of your pain because they reduce emotional tension (Gatchel and Turk 1996). Exposure to and desensitization of parts of your traumatic experiences or your triggers also can help lessen suffering and tension (Grant 1997). As Grant has written, "chronic pain can be a somatization of unresolved trauma, and treatment of the trauma can lead to significant reduction in physical symptoms" (1997, 63).

EXERCISE: **My Pain**

Do you have any pain that cannot be diagnosed medically? If so, please describe it here:

_____

_____

_____

_____

Have you ever looked at the sources for that pain outside your actual physical body? What was the result?

_____

_____

_____

_____

Eye Movement Desensitization and Reprocessing

One way to work on pain is through eye movement desensitization and reprocessing (EMDR), a technique developed by Francine Shapiro (1995). She observed that certain eye movements are able to reduce the intensity of disturbing thoughts that have not otherwise been dislodged or released. When information in the brain is associated with trauma or chronic pain and gets frozen in time along with its associated emotions and memories, EMDR seems to change the way the information is processed. EMDR can change pain sensations and the way a person experiences and perceives pain. It is a technique that must be done in the context of a therapeutic relationship. The five tasks of pain management using EMDR are

1. Check that your pain is being adequately managed.

2. Check your medical diagnosis to see if it is correct and if you accept it.

3. Identify and prioritize targets for EMDR.

4. Do relaxation exercises and change pain sensations through desensitization.

5. Develop resources for psychological pain management through EMDR.

If you are interested in working on your pain using EMDR, contact the Eye Movement Desensitization and Reprocessing Institute.

Coping with Trauma-Related Chronic Illness

If you have developed a chronic illness as a result of exposure to traumatic events and that illness has impacted you physically, some or all of the following suggestions may be helpful:

- Set more appropriate physical and emotional limits.

- Take as much responsibility for your health-related decisions as you can.

- Treat yourself compassionately (see chapter 6 for more on self-compassion).

- Get an evaluation by and help from your local rehabilitation services agency.

- Identify any necessary accommodations that will help you function in society under the guidelines of the Americans with Disabilities Act.

- Define your "new normal" and act accordingly.

- Define what activities might create more meaning in your life.

267

- Connect with others; for example, join a support group.

- Look for things for which you can feel gratitude and seek opportunities to show that gratitude.

- Maintain hope.

Dealing with Medical Professionals

Consider choosing a primary care doctor who is familiar with trauma, wants to know about your trauma history, and treats you as a whole person, recognizing the mind-body connection and the link between traumatic events (through PTSD as a mediator) and poor health, including autoimmune illnesses (Friedman, Schnurr, and McDonagh-Coyle 1994).

Read books on autoimmune diseases, such as *Living Well with Autoimmune Disease*, by Mary J. Shomon (2002), so you will be well-informed when talking with medical professionals. This will give you more confidence in being assertive and advocating for yourself.

Choose medical professionals who look beyond pharmaceutical drugs alone for effective treatment methods. Learn what supplements or alternatives are available for your condition(s). You may want to ask your physician about taking supplements such as inositol, which can be calming. Although sometimes referred to as a B-complex vitamin, inositol is actually a carbohydrate that functions as a calmative agent. In high doses, it's been shown to improve clinical depression symptoms without changing liver or kidney function or affecting the blood (Levine 1997). Seasonings also can be used as alternative therapies (Amen 2010): saffron taken twice daily lessens mild to moderate depression as well as Prozac does. Chewing cinnamon gum helps regulate blood sugar levels, offsetting imbalances caused by elevated cortisol levels. Taking magnesium, a vital mineral and enzyme catalyst, can help relax tense muscles and serve as a sleep aid.

Ask your doctor to consider giving you a checkup that looks at autoimmune disease symptoms, and request that your cortisol levels be checked. If your cortisol level is low and you have allergies, chronic pain, sleep difficulties, fatigue, or muscle pains and aches, these symptoms may indicate that you have an autoimmune condition. If so, ask your doctor to investigate ways to lessen the symptoms.

If your doctor prescribes medication, be sure to ask questions before agreeing to take it: How long has the drug has been on the market? What are its benefits? What are the potential side effects? Are there other drugs that are as effective? To reduce the chances of adverse side effects, you may wish to only take drugs that have been on the market for seven years or more (Barry 2011). Also, ask your doctor and pharmacist about any potential interactions between medications, and consider researching all of these questions yourself. Above all, try to avoid a "drug cascade syndrome," in which drugs are prescribed to combat the side effects of other prescribed medications.

If your doctor orders diagnostic tests, again, be sure to ask questions: Are the tests really necessary? Do they have the potential to be traumatizing in and of themselves? Avoid overexposure to radiation through unnecessary MRIs or CAT scans (e.g., to determine a sinus infection). As an article in *Newsweek* noted, "For many otherwise healthy people, tests often lead to more tests, which can lead to interventions based on a possible problem that may have gone away on its own" (Begley 2011, 32).

Dealing with Your Body

The following suggestions may help you take more control over your own physical health and healing:

- Recognize when you are overstressed and when adrenaline is speeding up your body. If possible, recognize when you are worrying too much over little things, are getting the shakes, or are having serious problems sleeping. Other symptoms of adrenaline overload include racing heart, pounding head, sweaty palms, dry mouth, tense muscles, and tense jaw. When you notice these symptoms, use relaxation techniques such as deep breathing or find other ways to slow down and be less reactive. Eating a healthful diet will also help support your body in dealing with stress.

- Burn off adrenaline through large-muscle activities, such as running, walking vigorously, doing calisthenics (jumping jacks, push-ups, and so on), doing housework that burns energy, or doing isometric exercises. Walking at least 7,000 steps daily is great both for overall health and for reducing stress (Lasse Nurmi, personal communication).

- Eat complex carbohydrates, such as carrots and potatoes, to boost your thinking abilities. Go easy on sodas, salt, alcohol, and processed sugars. Drink lots of water, and, as much as possible, try to eat unprocessed foods (those that aren't refined and don't have artificial ingredients and other added chemicals).

- Take time to rest and restore your body's balance. This can help alleviate pain, lower blood pressure, and lower heart rate.

- Get enough restful sleep. Fatigue is your enemy (McGraw 2008). Your brain's emotional centers become 60 percent more reactive when you are sleep deprived (Epstein 2010). Getting less than six hours of sleep a night can lead to making serious errors and can put you at risk for becoming overweight and developing diabetes (Epstein 2010).

- Go to a private location and scream, smash something that doesn't have value (e.g., a box of unmatched dishes bought at a yard sale), or use a punching bag. The key is to do this in a private location and clean up any mess afterward.

- Avoid nicotine if at all possible. It may seem to be calming, but it can change certain areas of the brain that are disrupted by PTSD and depression, potentially compounding your problems (Neergaard 2009).

- Avoid the use of unnecessary antibiotics. When exposed to antibiotics, pathogens can develop resistance to the drugs. Then if you experience a truly threatening infection in the future, the antibiotics won't be as effective when they are needed.

- Practice deep breathing regularly. Take in a deep breath through your nose. Hold that breath and slowly count to five in your head. Breathe out through your mouth as slowly as you can, feeling your shoulders drop and your body relax as you exhale.

Using Integrative Therapies

Integrative therapies, also known as complementary and alternative medicine (CAM), are a commonly used medical resource in the United States, mostly as a complement to standard care (Astin 1998). Estimates show nearly four out of ten Americans use some form of integrative medicine (Barnes, Bloom, and Nahin 2008), totaling nearly $34 billion in out-of-pocket dollars in 2007. The total number of annual visits to IM providers has been estimated at 425 million, exceeding the total number of visits to all primary care physicians combined (Eisenberg et al. 1993).

The spread of integrative medicine has led to the institutionalization and adoption of integrative services within health care systems as well. The American Hospital Association 2010 survey reported that up to 42 percent of hospitals are offering CAM services (American Hospital Association 2011). These hospitals include all of the top eighteen hospitals on the *US News* "America's Best Hospitals" list, with each offering some form of IM (Comarow 2008).

In academic medicine, the Consortium of Academic Health Centers for Integrative Medicine (CAHCIM) boasts 57 academic medical centers and affiliate institutions including Harvard University, Yale University, Duke University, the Mayo Clinic, and Stanford University. Within the US health care system, a study published in Health Services Research found that 76 percent of health care workers and 83 percent of doctors and nurses personally used CAM, compared with 63 percent of the general population (Johnson et al. 2012). Still, the formal entrance and offering of CAM into healthcare delivery systems is often challenging.

The National Center for Complementary and Alternative Medicine (NCCAM), established by Congress in 1998, has been a leader in advancing research in integrative therapies. NCCAM (now known as the National Center for Complementary and Integrative Health) defines CAM as "a group of diverse medical and health care systems, practices, and products that are not generally considered part of conventional medicine" (2008). NCCAM classifies therapies into five categories or domains:

1. Alternative medical systems, or complete systems of therapy and practice

2. Mind-body interventions, or techniques designed to facilitate the mind's effect on bodily functions and symptoms

3. Biologically-based systems, including herbalism

4. Manipulative and body-based methods, such as chiropractic and massage therapy

5. Energy therapies

This includes natural products and supplements, diet-based therapies, mind-body practices such as meditation and yoga, and traditional medicine practices such as Ayurvedic medicine from India, traditional Chinese medicine, homeopathy, and naturopathy.

How does this all impact you, the trauma survivor? Integrative therapies can be helpful in reducing stress and stress-related health problems. Weakness in the stress response, leading to insufficient cortisol production, can make you more susceptible to diseases such as the common cold, allergies, influenza, and senility (Edwards, Heyman, and Swidan 2011). Some scientists have proposed that infection, emotional trauma, and toxemia, when added to the mix, lead to even more serious results, such as hypocortisolism, which reflects a serious impairment in the body's ability to appropriately respond to stress (McEwen 1998).

Low cortisol levels also can allow inflammation to go unchecked, since cortisol generally regulates the inflammatory response (McEwen 1998). According to Stien and Kendall (2004), cortisol can "eat away at the neural networks in the brain," in particular the hippocampus, which has more cortisol receptors than any other area of the brain. Cortisol also causes functional changes in the prefrontal cortex, amygdala, and locus coeruleus, leading to impairment in decision-making, emotional stability, and proper processing of memories.

With lessening cortisol (hypocorticolism), the inflammatory response is activated and leads to susceptibility in the development of autoimmune diseases as well as chronic pain, increased mortality, and metastasis in breast cancer patients. In fact, "the more flattened the cortisol curve, the worse the prognosis and the earlier the mortality." Since cortisol is the body's natural brake, insufficient amounts leads to unregulated immune activity, higher levels of IL-6 and TNF, and heightened TH1 response, all of which have been associated with various autoimmune conditions. Cortisol normally suppresses the release of catecholamine; when cortisol lessens, therefore, the levels of catecholamine go up, particularly in patients with PTSD (Edwards, Heyman, and Swidan 2011).

Cortisol creates additional autoimmune potential through its relationship to the digestive tract. Elevated cortisol directly and indirectly affects gut permeability, making the gut more leaky or vulnerable to absorption of food lectins (allergenic proteins found in food) that trigger both an innate and an acquired immune reaction, leading to B cell and T cell sensitivity (Mayer 2000). Through the process of molecular mimicry, the immune system becomes more reactive to food, such as gluten, but can also confuse protein structures on various body tissues with the food proteins themselves, establishing an autoimmune process whereby your own immune system mistakenly attacks normal tissue, having lost its ability to distinguish between self and not self.

When you experience ongoing, unrelenting stress, or an overwhelming stressful event, it is possible to alter the stress response and damage key structures such as the brain and gut lining, often leading to perpetual inflammation. From a therapeutic perspective, it is important to pay attention to each of these vulnerable areas by offering integrative therapies that are neuroprotective, calm the excited autonomic response, improve nutrition, and heal the gut lining, while limiting the effects of excess inflammation.

Mind-Body Therapies

Mind-body therapy is one category of integrative medical techniques that directly influences stress, reduces sympathetic tone in the nervous system, and increases well-being. Mind-body therapies have a global effect on the stress response, are safe, and are easy to perform. There are a wide variety of contemplative practices, such as yoga and meditation, visualization, body scanning, and more that focus on breathing techniques, sitting, calming the mind, and expanding awareness. Thoughts, through meditation, should become like "clouds in the sky." Their presence is noted, but they are silent and leave no trace. Often, an overactive mind is likened to a "drunken monkey," rolling around in the head attempting to attach to anything and everything. When one becomes mindful, the drunken monkey learns to sit still and be quiet. This is not an easy task to accomplish and takes daily practice.

There are additional forms of mind-body therapy that sometimes are easier to learn and perform. A good example is tai chi, a moving meditation that was developed over 2,000 years ago in China. The practitioner performs slow movements that flow from one to the next, to develop and strengthen your internal vitality, or *chi*. Each movement is meant to reflect an animal or form in nature and is designed to improve the health of the practitioner and ward off illness. If the postures and movements are sped up, tai chi also becomes a form of martial arts. Even the Mayo Clinic recommends tai chi for stress reduction. When learned correctly and performed regularly, tai chi can be a positive part of an overall approach to improving your health. The Mayo Clinic cites these benefits of doing tai chi:

- Decreased stress and anxiety

- Increased aerobic capacity

- Increased energy and stamina

- Increased flexibility, balance, and agility

- Increased muscle strength and definition

Some evidence indicates that tai chi also may help to

- Enhance quality of sleep

- Enhance the immune system

- Lower cholesterol levels and blood pressure

- Improve joint pain

- Improve symptoms of congestive heart failure

- Improve overall well-being in older adults

- Reduce risk of falls in older adults

(Mayo Clinic 2015)

What all mind-body therapies have in common, though, is a focus on the breath, improving awareness of yourself, your thoughts, feelings, and bodily sensations, and an attempt to calm psychic turmoil through routine practice. Many of these techniques are well studied as to their effectiveness to reduce stress and improve stress resilience.

Lifestyle Improvements

Mind-body therapies can be very effective for reducing stress. They often work even better when we improve our diet, sleep deeply, and exercise on a regular basis. Interestingly, on a physiological level, it has been shown that these strategies also reduce inflammation, reset the stress response, and even can repair the brain when injured from stress (Edwards, Heyman, and Swidan 2011).

NUTRITION

Your body needs minerals, vitamins, amino acids, good fats, and other building blocks to survive. Stress will deplete the body of these key factors and make your system work harder to manage stress. Vegetables and fruits are full of fiber, minerals, and vitamins. Consider eating probiotic foods like sauerkraut and kimchi, and if you do not have issues with dairy, add yogurt and kefir. And not all fats are bad! Butter contains butyric acid, which is food for your gut lining. Avocados, coconut oil, and fish oil are building blocks for your brain and every membrane in your body (Bowthorpe 2014).

Maintaining a normal blood sugar is also important. When we are under stress, cortisol temporarily increases insulin resistance, which in turn makes more sugar in the blood immediately available to service the fight-or-flight response. But chronic stress will lead to chronically elevated blood sugar. This potent scenario causes weight gain, fatigue, and achiness. Recent studies have also shown that, like cortisol, excess insulin damages the brain. Additionally, with a carbohydrate-heavy diet, swings in blood sugar are very stressful. In an effort to stabilize these large swings, excess cortisol production results. Processed foods are the enemy of a normal stress response. To help stabilize blood sugar, eat whole foods, stay away from sugar (starches and alcohol), and boost your diet with lots of vegetables and some fruit and healthy protein (De la Monte and Wands 2008).

Cortisol, as stated before, also injures the gut lining. Since it is a catabolic hormone, it can degrade the tight junctions designed to keep foreign invaders and other immune triggers from being absorbed into the body. Stress loosens these junctions and can induce the immune system to respond to foods, thus triggering a cascade of inflammation. Between 70 and 80 percent of the immune system is

273

assigned to monitor your gut. The immune system is the guard that makes decisions as to what should enter our body and what should not. Specialized white blood cells work together to make immuno-globulins that tag invading viruses, parasites, bacteria, and undigested food so that other white cells can destroy them. If your immune system is stimulated by food particles, and the food particles look similar to cells in your body, your immune system attacks normal cells (Bowthorpe 2014).

The top five offending foods that trigger the immune system are gluten, dairy, eggs, peanuts, and soy; however, people can have sensitivities to many other foods as well. What to do? Try the 4R approach by Jeff Bland, PhD:

- Remove: Take out foods that your body can't digest well.

- Replace: Add in digestive enzymes and stomach acid to help you break down your food completely.

- Reinoculate: Make sure you have good bacteria (probiotics) in your gut.

- Repair: It takes a minimum of two to three weeks for your gut to heal. L-glutamine and omega 3 fish oil are some of the supplements that can help.

EXERCISE

Exercise is meant to be healthful. But at its core, it is designed to be a metered dose of stress to the body. After a workout, you need to rest and recover for a period of time to allow your system to adjust and respond to the exercise load. The important thing is to listen to your body. If you are completely exhausted after exercise and have to go to bed immediately afterward or find that you really can't function for the rest of the day, then your exercise regimen is too much. Remember, your body needs to rest and repair. In fact, *overtraining syndrome*, which is the technical term for exercising too heavily without allowing time for recuperation, is very similar to chronic stress symptoms. Even the physiology looks similar: cortisol abnormalities, chronic inflammation, gut dysfunction, and lack of motivation and poor mood.

This is not to say that we shouldn't exercise. Most of us do not obtain enough movement in our lives. Sometimes more gentle forms are better for the stressed-out individual. Ten thousand steps per day is a healthy walking program. You can start with tai chi or yoga and then progress to harder work-outs as you improve your fitness.

Exercise helps regulate stress hormones and sleep cycles and helps manage heart rate. At least thirty minutes of exercise daily, five days a week, is typically recommended, but your doctor may advise an alternative exercise program specific for you.

SLEEP

For a discussion of techniques for sleeping better, refer back to chapter 8.

VITAMINS AND MINERALS

This list of dietary supplements can be used to help decrease your risk for chronic stress and sleep problems and developing health conditions related to stress and sleep imbalances:

- **Vitamin C (ascorbic acid).** Antioxidant; helps support adrenal function and decrease high cortisol levels.

- **Benfotiamine (water soluble thiamin).** Studies report thiamin (as an injection) to be an effective nutrient in decreasing adrenal exhaustion.

- **Niacin (as niacinamide).** Reported to enhance sleep; shunts tryptophan to serotonin.

- **Vitamin B6 (pyridoxal-5-phosphate).** Cofactor in the synthesis of neurotransmitters GABA (gamma-aminobutyric acid), serotonin, and dopamine.

- **Folic acid.** Helps regenerate BH4, essential for neurotransmitter formation (serotonin, dopamine, norepinephrine, and epinephrine).

- **Vitamin B12.** B12 is reported deficient in those with sleep disorders; reported to exert a positive influence on circadian rhythm and melatonin secretion.

(Lavalle and Heyman 2013)

NUTRACEUTICALS

Phenyl-GABA. Helps support the calming brain chemical GABA formation; reported to improve relaxation and sleep.

5-HTP (5-hydroxytryptophan). This is the immediate precursor for serotonin, the brain chemical that helps regulate moods and emotions, satiety, and carbohydrate cravings and sleep. Administration of 5-HTP as a dietary supplement has been reported to improve levels of serotonin. Precursor for melatonin, which helps regulate the sleep/wake cycle, and functions as an antioxidant for immune support. Reported to be beneficial in insomnia and effective in panic disorder treatment.

Melatonin. Natural "sleep" hormone produced by the brain. Reported in clinical studies to help regulate sleep/wake cycle and improve ability to fall asleep. Also antioxidant, helps balance immunity. Studies report levels of melatonin can be significantly reduced in those with night-eating syndrome.

(Lavalle and Hawkins 2013a)

BOTANICALS/HERBS

Combination of Magnolia officinalis (bark) extract and Phellodendron amurense (bark) extract. Magnolia officinalis and Phellodendron amurense are herbs that have been used in traditional Chinese medicine for over 1,500 years. The combination is generally nonsedating, but use caution if driving an automobile or operating heavy machinery. Helps balance cortisol levels, control stress-related eating, and decrease weight gain.

Theanine. L-theanine is an amino acid component of green tea (Camellia sinensis); reported to improve brain chemicals (serotonin, dopamine) and enhance alpha wave activity, thereby improving sleep and reducing anxiety. Also reported to decrease stress/anxiety in a small clinical trial of twelve individuals.

Combination herb extract of Magnolia officinalis and Ziziphus spinosa. Magnolia officinalis and Ziziphus spinosa are traditional Chinese herbs used for sleep and relaxation. The combination may help improve cortisol at night and produce a sense of relaxation. Also reported to reduce calcium flow into neurons, which reduces hyperexcitability of brain cells. It also helps to stimulate GABA activity, which helps calm the brain.

Holy basil (Ocimum sanctum) leaf. Reported in laboratory studies to decrease cortisol levels during chronic stress. Human study reported that in 25 patients with generalized anxiety disorder taking holy basil lowered stress and decreased symptoms of anxiety. A study of 24 patients reported that holy basil administration improved immunity during stress.

Rhodiola (Rhodiola rosea) plant. Traditional folk medicine in China, Serbia, and Ukraine. Adaptogenic, improves body's resistance against stress, including psychological, physical, and environmental stressors. Reported to decrease fatigue, improve mental performance, and decrease anxiety.

(Lavalle and Hawkins 2013b)

In summary, an integrative approach to stress includes an assessment of the psychological and physiological aspects of your personal stress response. Often, salivary cortisol is measured to understand the physical resiliency and integrity of the body's stress mechanisms better. If stress, in any form, is identified, a comprehensive plan is offered to the patient. This usually includes attention to adequate sleep, diet, and exercise. Stress management techniques are routinely recommended, which may include breathing techniques, meditation, or movement therapies such as tai chi and yoga. It is not uncommon for herbs and supplements to be suggested, to augment these lifestyle interventions and boost the individual's ability to cope with ongoing stress.

Body Sensations and Body Awareness

Building awareness of all kinds is the first step to controlling trauma-based reactions. Developing body awareness will help you establish a positive relationship with your body. Body awareness can help you discharge stored up emotions and reconnect to numbed parts of yourself and possibly help you lessen, and even eliminate, some trauma symptoms, restoring you to a more normal level of functioning. Body sensations may remind you of your prior traumas. If you are going to work with your own bodily sensations when they are triggered by trauma, it is important that you develop awareness of your body's sensations and what those sensations communicate to you.

Does your body tell you when it is hungry, tired, and sad or when it is satiated, rested, and happy? How does it do so? If you cannot feel your body sensations, try the following exercise.

EXERCISE: **My Body Sensations**

Draw an outline of a gingerbread person below on the right side of the page. On that drawing, use the following colors to identify where your body feels the following emotions:

Anger (red)

Sadness (blue)

Fear (black)

Calmness (pink)

Pain (orange)

Happiness or joy (yellow)

What does completing this exercise tell you about your body? What do you see in your drawing? Where do you carry your emotions? Any idea why?

_____

_____

_____

_____

EXERCISE: **Developing Body Awareness**

Rothschild suggests the following exercise to develop basic body awareness (2000, 102–103). The exercise is from her book *The Body Remembers*.

1. Do not move. Notice the position you are sitting in right now.

2. What sensations do you become aware of? Scan your whole body: notice your head, neck, chest, back, stomach, buttocks, legs, feet, arms, and hands.

3. Are you comfortable? Do not move yet.

4. How do you know if you are comfortable or not? Which sensations equal comfort or discomfort?

5. Do you have an impulse to change your position? Do not do it yet; just notice the impulse.

6. Where does that impulse come from? If you were to change your position, what part of your body would you move first? Do not do it yet. First follow that impulse back to the discomfort that is driving it: Is your neck tense? Is some part of your body becoming numb? Are your toes cold?

7. Now follow the impulse and change position. What changes have occurred in your body? Do you breathe easier? Is a pain or area of tension relieved? Are you more alert?

8. If you have no impulse to change your position, you might just be comfortable. See which bodily cues you get that signal that you are comfortable: Are your shoulders relaxed? Is your breathing deep? Is your body generally warm?

9. Next, change your position, whether or not you are comfortable (changing it again, if you already did it above). Change where or how you are sitting. Move somewhere else: try a new chair, stand up, or sit on the floor. Take a new position and hold it. Then evaluate again: Are you comfortable or not? Which bodily sensations tell you whether you're comfortable? Consider tension, relaxation, warmth, cold, aching, numbness, whether your breathing is deep or shallow, and so on. This time also notice whether or not you are more alert or awake in this position than you were in the last one.

10. Try a third position. Evaluate as above.

11. Jot a few notes about your experience, keeping in the language of bodily sensation: tension, temperature, breathing, etc.; for example, *When I was sitting in my chair, I felt tense in my shoulders and my feet were warm. When I moved to stand on the floor, my feet became cold and my shoulders relaxed…*

_____

_____

_____

_____

After doing this exercise, are you more aware of your body? If so, why are you more aware?

_____

_____

Trauma and Hyperarousal

Normal body reactions to traumatic events include fear-based reactions, such as shock, and *shutdown* (the total numbing that comes from extreme stress). If your body played a central part in the way you responded to a traumatic event when it occurred, then it is essential for your body to be included in the healing process (Van der Kolk 1999). Trauma is often experienced in the body as physiological arousal. You may become addicted to getting a similar state of arousal and do things to get that feeling. Some of the things you may do to get your body to respond can be very risky, if not potentially dangerous and life threatening. This is called being addicted to trauma or being an adrenaline junkie.

If you are not aware of which sensations are safe and which are dangerous, you may perceive them all negatively. Your body sensations are supposed to tell you when you are hungry, full, tired, alert, cold, warm, comfortable, uncomfortable, scared, or calmed. Rothschild concludes that "life would be very dangerous if…sensations and emotions could not be perceived" (2000, 106). Having an awareness of body sensations also can anchor you in the present. It is more difficult to stay lost in your past if you are aware of your body sensations in the present. Learning to recognize hyperarousal as a part of body awareness is a skill that is acquired through practice (Rothschild 2000).

EXERCISE: How My Body Speaks About My Trauma

If your body or a body part could speak about how it was treated during the trauma or traumas, what would it say?

_____

How was your body a battleground during the trauma? (It may not have been one; if that is the case, you don't have to answer this question.)

_____

Are you alienated from your body in any way? Do you see any or all of your body as toxic, ugly, or powerless?

_____

How is who you are on the outside different from who you are on the inside of your body?

_____

Right now, is your body

☐ relaxed, with deep, easy breathing, slow heart rate, and normal skin tone?

☐ slightly aroused, with quickening breathing or heart rate, skin color that is normal or paling or graying, and slightly moist skin?

☐ moderately aroused, with rapid heartbeat and respiration and paling skin?

☐ hyperaroused, with accelerated heart rate and respiration, pale or grayish skin, and cold sweats?

☐ hyperaroused to an endangering degree, with all of your body systems on alert?

Does the way your body reacts change when your past trauma is triggered? If so, how?

_____

_____

What other body reactions might you have in reaction to your past trauma? Do you have

☐ headaches?

☐ worry lines carved into your forehead?

☐ tics and involuntary movements?

☐ red splotches when you are stressed or talk about trauma?

☐ hives that come and go?

☐ sores that arise in places where you were hurt?

☐ physical reminders that appear out of the blue (for example, rope marks around your wrists or welts on your back that appear and disappear)?

☐ aching legs?

☐ genital or reproductive problems that can't be explained by doctors?

☐ stomach problems?

☐ too frequent trips to the bathroom?

What do any items you checked say about your traumas?

_____

_____

The Importance of Body Awareness

Again, building awareness—of all kinds—is the first step to controlling trauma-based reactions. Developing body awareness will help you establish a positive relationship with your body. Body awareness helps you feel your emotions and then self-soothe. Getting in touch with your body can help you retrieve memories, ground yourself in the present, problem-solve about physical reactions that cannot be otherwise explained, and limit your use of body-related dissociation. Use of massage as a healing strategy may help you learn that some forms of touch are not associated with abuse. If you are in therapy, you may suggest that your therapist do a session together with a psychotherapist specializing in sensorimotor psychotherapy or a physiotherapist.

EXERCISE: **What I Learned from This Chapter**

In this chapter, have you learned anything about the role of PTSD as a "middleman" between various combinations of traumatic events, body reactions, and autoimmune illnesses? If so, make some notes about what you learned in the space below:

_____

_____

_____

_____

10

For Veterans Returning from War: Tools for Personal Survival

(by Priscilla Bryant-Schoenly and Mary Beth Williams)

This chapter in the second edition summarized much of the content of the workshop Slogging the Bog of War in Order to Return to the World of Work (Williams 2012). The chapter now examines five tools to help you in your journey. These include challenging or correcting beliefs through the use of cognitive processing therapy (CPT); using narrative and storytelling (as types of exposure therapy); using metaphors; using sound and music; and working with service/support animals. These powerful techniques will help you help yourself either on your own or in group or individual therapy. This chapter was expanded with the help of Priscilla Bryant-Schoenly, social worker at the Community Based Outpatient Clinic in Stephens City, VA.

What We've Learned About PTSD from Veterans of OIF, OEF, and Desert Storm

Desert Storm (also known as the Gulf War) began on August 2, 1990 and ended February 28, 1991. Operation Enduring Freedom (OEF), a multinational military operation in Afghanistan, began on October 7, 2001. It officially ended toward the latter months of 2014, when the mission changed from one of military engagement to support of the Afghani forces. However, many American troops and contractors remain in country. Operation Iraqi Freedom (OIF) began on March 20, 2003 and officially ended with the pullout of combat troops.

If you've served in OEF, OIF, or Desert Storm, it's likely that you don't consider yourself to be a hero, even though you've survived one or more tours of duty. Your heroes are those who survived with multiple wounds and loss of limbs or brain functioning, who survived many, many tours of duty, or are lying at rest in Arlington National Cemetery or other cemeteries. You have come home changed and, as Lighthall (2012) notes, "do not assume that is a bad thing." You now may be more confident and have better problem-solving skills, a sense of gratitude for what you used to take for granted, and a greater sense of purpose and direction than you did before. On the other hand, combat stress, combat overload, and the many other stressors of war have undoubtedly had an impact on you. Asking for help in dealing with war's impacts, as well as using this workbook in some way, is a sign of your courage. Asking for help doesn't mean you're permanently damaged or that you'll experience a backlash and stigma, particularly if you remain in the military, reserve forces, or National Guard. As the US Army WRAIR booklet "10 Tough Facts About Combat: What Leaders Can Do to Mitigate Risk and Build Resilience" states, "Combat poses moral and ethical, and spiritual challenges… Every soldier needs to come home with a war story that he or she can live with" (US Army WRAIR Land Combat Study Team 2006).

A Look at the Facts

If you've been diagnosed with PTSD or suspect you might have PTSD, you are not alone. A 2008 estimate that 300,000 veterans experienced PTSD as a result of serving in Iraq and Afghanistan seriously underestimated the consequences of these two wars (Headquarters, Department of the Army 2012). A 2010 estimate was that at least 20 percent of the two million service members who deployed have or will develop PTSD—at least 472,000 service members across all branches as of September 2011. By mid-2011, over 187,100 veterans from Iraq and Afghanistan had already been diagnosed with PTSD by the Veterans Health Administration.

However, these estimates now appear to be low. A study by the Pew Research Center (Taylor 2011) found that 44 percent of post-9/11 veterans believe their readjustment to civilian life has been difficult, and 37 percent believe that they are suffering from PTSD, even if they haven't been officially diagnosed. Post-9/11 veterans who were in combat have even higher rates: 49 percent say they have PTSD, and 52 percent have had emotionally traumatic experiences in the military. It is a well-known fact that the VA is at least 100,000 claims behind in looking at service-connected disabilities for veterans of all wars; plus the VA is looking for ways to cut its costs, including taking back percentages of disability ratings of individuals believed to have "improved" and making eligibility criteria much more rigid. A National Health Study for a New Generation of US Veterans (US Department of Veterans Affairs 2015), suggested that 1:6 Iraq and Afghanistan veterans may have PTSD and that the number actually could be underreported. It is now estimated that about 30 percent of Vietnam combat veterans have PTSD, and more are seeking evaluation and compensation as they retire and find memories coming back more readily to fill the void previously occupied by work. In addition, the US Department of Defense is beginning to reconsider other-than-honorable (OTH) discharges for upgrades for undiagnosed PTSD. This may add many additional veterans to the already filled VA treatment slots. It is estimated that up to one-third of Vietnam veterans with OTH discharges may have PTSD. Secretary of Defense Hagel noted that the discharges to be considered are for low-level misconduct only.

What has led to these high numbers, in spite of efforts by the armed services to prepare warriors to be resilient, using programs such as Comprehensive Soldier Fitness? One factor is repeat deployments. Other factors are female gender, the presence of assaultive violence, short home time and rest time between deployments, the cumulative impact of combat exposure, a war of insurgents without clearly defined enemies, and continued feelings of being stigmatized for seeking help in spite of steps taken to reduce that stigma. Breslau (2012) found that there is a consistent relationship between intensity of combat exposure and the risk of PTSD. As a veteran, you are very aware that the more deployments you've had, the more likely it is that you've seen battle buddies die or get seriously wounded. You also might have been impacted by reduced rates of death and high, increased rates of nonfatal injuries—injuries that are severe and often involve loss of limbs. Redeployments also lead to increased physical stress and its autoimmune illnesses, sleep disturbances, fatigue, exhaustion, and mental health injuries (Cantrell 2009).

You Have Survived!

As a veteran of any one of the recent and not-so-recent wars, you have returned home as a person who has been changed in some way. During deployment, you used your military and personal skills to face challenges and work toward completing any mission that was part of your general orders. According to the Department of the Army's field manual *Survival (FM 3–05.70)*, your survival means you exhibited a variety of skills and strengths (Headquarters, Department of the Army 2002):

- sized up situations

- used all your senses to check out your surroundings to ensure safety

- remembered where you were and how to act in that environment based on your earlier training

- vanquished or at least controlled fear and panic so you could stay present and react accordingly

- improvised when needed

- valued staying alive

- acted like "the natives" (belonged)

- lived by your wits

You also survived because of your sense of duty and allegiance to your values as a member of the armed forces, swearing allegiance to your commander-in-chief, as well as allegiance to the values of your specific branch of military service. These values differ to some degree between branches but generally include duty and loyalty to your fellow warriors and your country. Now that you are home, you may be having difficulty finding civilians who uphold those values; however, those values are probably still important to you.

What military values do you still try to uphold, either as a member of the armed services or as a civilian?

_____

_____

How successful have you been in this?

_____

_____

What Was It Like for You to Go to War?

According to Hoge, "Coming back from combat deployment is like returning to the three-dimensional world after experiencing a fourth dimension" (2010, xiv). What might that statement mean to you? How do those two realities differ?

In order to be able to kill, you had to learn to make the enemy less than human. You learned to make the enemy a "carrier of evil" (Tick 2005, 82). Your education began at boot camp when you were stripped of your former identity and participated in countless killing exercises that were often very realistic. You had so many target practice exercises that shooting became a reflex. You overcame not wanting to be aggressive to others. Killing became a moral obligation. However, according to Grossman (1996), only 2 percent of soldiers become comfortable with killing, and they do about 50 percent of the killing. If you did kill, according to Marlantes (2011), you became a "lethal instrument of war," and death became "an abstraction, except for those at the receiving end" (19). Meagher (2007) writes that the pressure of the modern battlefield on warriors is very intense because of factors of time, space, target, and speed:

- **Time:** Operations are continuous, leaving no time to relax and unwind. Combat can occur around the clock.

- **Space:** There is no traditional front line, and the environment has many difficult features, such as no electricity or ways to shower.

- **Target:** The enemy can be anyone, and attacks may occur in guerilla style.

- **Speed:** War occurs anywhere and everywhere, causing combatants to become hypervigilant and leading to frequent or perhaps constant adrenaline rushes (which, as discussed in chapter 9, can lead to autoimmune diseases).

How Are You Adjusting As You Move from Battlefield to Home Front?

What is your life like now that you've returned home? The war is no longer present in your environment, but within, it may be continuing to plague you. How do you view yourself: as damaged goods or as a gallant warrior? What are your personal costs of war? Have you applied for any kind of assistance, such as VA benefits? Are you participating in activities that give you an adrenaline rush and remind you of combat, such as paintball, video games, or fast driving?

JOURNAL EXERCISE: How Battlefield Skills Impact Your Home Life

According to James Munroe (personal communication) of the New Haven VA, reentry into civilian life can be a challenge if any of the following eight battlefield skills interfere and if any of the five basic psychological needs (safety, trust, power, esteem, and intimacy) are lacking (Rosenbloom and Williams 2010). As you read through the list below, take some time to consider the questions asked and to write about them in your journal or notebook.

1. **Assessing danger** (the first psychological need, for safety): Are you finding life at home to be safe for you? Do everyday situations make you feel that you are in danger? Do you constantly check your environment to see how safe you are?

2. **Being guarded about trusting** (the second psychological need): Do you trust those around you, or do you see everyone around you as different and therefore the enemy? Do you trust battle buddies only?

3. **Having a mission orientation:** Your primary task during deployment was to finish the mission. Are you still looking for someone to give you orders?

4. **Making decisions** (the third psychological need, for power and control): How are decisions made in your home life or family? What type of input are you contributing to family decisions? Do you believe you have control over any parts of your life?

5. **Responding with tactics:** When you were at war, you acted with maximum firepower first and then thought about what you had done later. You had to make sure that all of

your gear was in its place, in working order. What is it like at home for you now? If there is a mess around you, can you stand it? Do you overreact in tense situations?

6. **Avoiding predictability and controlling intelligence:** Do you find you vary your route or routine so that others cannot harm you? Do you withhold information from others? Do you need chaos to survive?

7. **Controlling yourself emotionally** (an aspect of the fourth psychological need, esteem): When deployed, you were exposed to many events that may have led to fear, guilt, grief, sadness, anger, and other emotions. However, the desire to survive often meant you had to stuff away those feelings. Now that you're home, what emotions have you expressed? Do others fear your emotions? Does it feel dangerous to have positive emotions, such as happiness? Do you like who you have become or who you are?

8. **Talking about war** (the fifth psychological need, for intimacy): When you were with battle buddies, you could talk openly and freely about combat. Is there anyone in civilian life you can talk to? Have you found anyone, including family members, who can understand your experiences as you talk about them, if you choose to do so? Do you find that you are comfortable only with battle buddies who also have returned home? How close are you emotionally to your family members?

Five Techniques to Help You Help Yourself

As noted above, this chapter gives you five powerful techniques that can help you help yourself, either on your own or in therapy. This chapter also will refer you to other sections of this workbook that expand on what is presented here. All five of these suggested ways to deal with your traumatic experiences are useful for veterans but not specific to them; other trauma survivors can use them as well: challenging and correcting beliefs, narrative and storytelling, using metaphors, using sound and music to heal, and working with service, therapy, and emotional support with animals.

Many treatments for war-related trauma try to help you make sense of the facts of what happened to and around you and try to help you increase your personal power over your emotions. You may have been educated about the signs and symptoms of PTSD when you were demobilized or went to a new assignment after you returned from "across the pond." You may have been asked to look at your thinking and beliefs about war and what you did or what happened to you.

The primary method used by clinicians to help veterans is called cognitive behavioral therapy (CBT), the evidence-based treatment method endorsed by the US Veterans Administration. According to Rothschild (2011b), CBT "targets the thinking process: by helping you to change your negative thinking patterns, thereby modifying your emotions that are a result of your thoughts; it is a deceptively simple concept" (75). As Bryant-Schoenly notes, it helps you understand how your thoughts, feelings, and behaviors are interrelated and impact various aspects of your life. For you, the veteran, CBT exercises are designed to help you look at your thoughts and beliefs about war and how they impact your behaviors so that you can change, if needed.

Each of the techniques described in this section aims to address the five basic psychological needs previously discussed in chapter 6 (category D): feelings of safety, feelings of trust (of yourself and others), sense of personal power, esteem, and the ability to have intimate relationships. These needs are the basis of constructivist self-development theory as adapted from McCann and Pearlman (1990, 1992) and Rosenbloom and Williams (2010) and are core elements of cognitive processing therapy (CPT). CPT underlies the first technique, which examines beliefs related to war and war's impact on your psychological needs, and shows you how to challenge and correct or change those beliefs if they are unhelpful. According to Bryant-Schoenly, CPT is one of the most effective treatment interventions to relieve your PTSD symptoms. CPT teaches you how to manage distressing thoughts (also called stuck points) while you gain a better understanding of your PTSD symptoms.

In looking at your symptoms, thoughts, and psychological needs, you will learn how to challenge irrational thoughts, as well as negative beliefs. This *cognitive restructuring* is one aspect of cognitive behavioral therapy. CBT is generally based on what is known as the ABC model (Ellis 2001). When something happens, you try to identify that event (A) and the dysfunctional beliefs that are associated with that event (B), as well as the action-related consequences of holding those beliefs (C). The activating event (*being in a fire fight*) is directly responsible for the actions that occurred (*I fired my weapon and killed that bad guy*); however, the truth is that the thoughts that occur between A and C determine the actions taken (e.g., *I will definitely be killed if I don't fire*).

Tompkins (2014), in a short article published by New Harbinger Publications, stated that you "believe what you believe" and seldom question the accuracy or basis of your beliefs in reality. CBT aims to "place a question mark next to a belief rather than trying to change it." For some people, actually changing a belief is not even possible. Questioning the accuracy and value of a belief may be more realistic. These false beliefs are as likely as truthful beliefs to motivate behavior (Ciarrochi and Bailey 2008).

Challenging and Correcting Beliefs

Your wartime experiences have impacted your beliefs about yourself, others, and the world. The belief system you have created is unique to you and determines how you view the world. It is how you explain reality. Your beliefs about your personal identity, spiritual framework, and meaning for your life can keep you trapped or set you free. The more survival value a belief holds for you, the more you'll want to hang on to it. Just as with other beliefs, the beliefs you have about war are not necessarily completely true (Brookman 2001). They can be based on feelings rather than facts and may lead to making either appropriate or inappropriate decisions. Beliefs can lead you to have feelings about certain things, which in turn can lead to taking action.

Some of your beliefs go back to childhood and were influenced (or even created) by your parents, schooling, and other social influences; others are a result of serving in a war. In all cases, they may not always represent reality, even though you regard them to be true about yourself or the way the world works. Take some time to consider what beliefs you developed while deployed. You may wish to complete the following statements, based on your experiences while you were deployed:

- I believe that…

- I think that…

- I doubt that…

- I am certain that…

_____

_____

_____

_____

Do any of these beliefs cause you problems now?

According to Ehlers and Clark (2000), identifying beliefs associated with key parts of the trauma, using cognitive restructuring methods, can help. This means you may want to look at alternative ways to view an event or events, as well as the beliefs associated with those events. You may decide you want to focus on beliefs that were changed by war if they are disrupting your life now that you are home.

What might you do to defuse some of your negative thoughts?

- Keep a log of your unhelpful thoughts.

- Take a mindful approach that lets you observe yourself in the present moment in contrast to being stuck on negative beliefs about self, others, and the world. Use meditation, deep breathing, or other methods to help you in this approach.

- When a negative thought arises, if at all possible, step back and observe your thoughts or feelings (Ciarrochi and Bailey 2008).

Have you created any new belief statements that are positive and future oriented? Do any of those beliefs contain intentions about your path forward? If so, describe them here:

_____

_____

_____

Do these new beliefs seem to work for you? What about old beliefs that you're still hanging on to? Are they working for you? If they are not, think of one or two beliefs you want to challenge or change and write them here:

_____

_____

_____

For more information on changing beliefs, see chapter 6.

You also may want to try some of the following suggestions to get rid of beliefs that are causing you problems:

- Set an intention to exchange an old belief for a new one, and then state the new belief over and over and over again to get it in your head.

- Challenge an old belief by looking for new evidence or facts to disprove it.

- Write your inaccurate belief and then burn it, rip it up, flush it down the toilet, or create some other type of ritual to free yourself of it.

- Try to identify the emotions that lie behind beliefs that you would like to challenge.

- Substitute a positive, present-day affirmation for a negative belief about yourself.

- List pros and cons about keeping an old belief.

- Use your energy to challenge a belief through action and activity. Do something to contradict your belief.

- Collect evidence for different ways to interpret a belief by brainstorming with people you trust.

Choose one or more ways to challenge or modify a chosen belief and then follow through with an action or actions. Later, come back to this page and describe what you did. How successful were your efforts?

_____

_____

_____

_____

_____

_____

_____

_____

_____

_____

_____

_____

_____

Substituting changed beliefs that fit your world now that you have returned home can help you begin to fit in, feel comfortable and safe, and have a sense of personal power. If your negative beliefs generally lead to conflict, they can potentially cause you to be at higher risk for heart disease, higher blood pressure, and increased sleep problems, unless you deal with them in some manner (DeAngelis 2013).

Narrative and Storytelling

Another way to heal is by "getting it out" and telling your story safely. According to Tick (2005), doing so helps you get in touch with your life and your soul, which is an essential step in healing. When your story is combined with the stories of others, together they create an even larger story of war. This method is a form of exposure therapy. Other forms of exposure therapy include practicing exposure with real-life situations (in vivo exposure), talking repeatedly about your trauma memories (imaginal exposure), and virtual exposure. Exposure therapy is designed to trigger memories of your traumatic events.

Exposure therapy is a means to help you face your traumatic experiences in small chunks without retraumatizing you. By writing a narrative of your traumatic experiences, you may find that your traumas take on new meanings and become more symbolic. According to Schauer, Neuner, and Elbert (2011), a typical trauma narrative includes these elements:

- experiences from the beginning of the threat to the first traumatic and terrifying event

- description of the terrifying event or events in detail

- how you escaped, survived, ended the experience

- life thereafter

- future goals, plans, and hopes

There are many ways for you to tell those stories of war: through poetry, writing, acting them out, drawing, making collages, painting, or sharing with fellow warriors in private or public gatherings. You can share your stories with family, friends, therapists, the media, church groups, school groups, and so on.

Capps (2013) writes that a narrative is testimony. It helps you to organize your thoughts into a meaningful narrative. Writing after returning home comes from a different space and time than journaling during your deployment (or at the time of the traumatic event). As such, it allows you to develop a different perspective on what happened. It can include both "cold" and "hot" memories. *Cold memories* may include information about general events (a campaign, battle, or life on a base). *Hot memories* are more emotional and specific. They contain detailed sensory information, perceptions, and personal responses and impacts (Robjant and Fazel 2010). Michael White (2013) presents the following summarized points about narrative therapy:

- The primary focus of narrative is the expression of personal life experiences.

- All of an individual's experiences are interpreted by that individual.

- Interpretations give experiences meaning.

- Giving meaning to an experience evolves over time, and the meaning may become clearer.

- Through narrative (or other types of) expression, you will process, shape, and reshape your experiences as well as your life path.

- The structure of your narrative provides an intelligible frame that allows you to link together the events of life in sequence as you tell and retell them, perhaps reframing your own personal history.

- Narrative writing may allow you to link your stories with the stories of others.

If you choose to write a narrative, consider including some or all of the following elements:

- describing yourself as a hero or heroine or as a main character in your narrative

- finding and including a symbol to describe an event or person that injured you psychologically or physically

- including objects or symbols that stand for resiliency and healing

- including symbols that stand for your ideas about safety and security

- including symbols that indicate your sense of mastery of your war-related problems

- including symbols of your military or nonmilitary culture that can help or empower you (clothing, badges, and so on)

- describing the arrival of a messenger to bring a solution to you

You also can use metaphors (described in detail in the next section) and other figures of speech as you create the story of what happened to you. You also might consider telling your story in a straightforward fashion using first-person or I-statements. You can put words to your emotions to help yourself and others understand what you still may not fully get or comprehend. Writing your feelings down makes the words a permanent expression of what is or was within you and may even help you build a container for what happened to you as you describe the indescribable.

Writing your story of war also helps make your remembered experiences more real. It transforms suffering into story. It gives information. It illustrates your motivations and values. If you choose to do so, write part or all of your story in your journal, perhaps using the writing exercises described in chapter 3. As you write, you may find that your traumatic experiences become more real and are now more outside of you and therefore more manageable.

According to Ehlers and Clark (2000), memories about what happened in the past (autobiographical memory) create an organized way to look at your life. However, war disrupts normal memory processes in such a way that war-related memories aren't situated in the correct time, place, and context, as other past memories are. They remain in the here and now and can be triggered by many things. You may "feel locked into the past…unable to resume a former life or start a new life—you feel you are 'frozen in time,' permanently changed for the worse by the trauma" (324).

Capps (2013) offers some alternative suggestions for writing about your war experiences:

- Write about the war event that you believe changed your life.

- Write a letter to the person who was most influential during your deployment.

- Write about any previously unremembered parts of events in detail.

- If you previously wrote about events in the first person (I-statements), try writing from the third person (referring to yourself as he or she).

Writing or telling the story of what happened to you while you were at war helps bring those memories into your mind in a way that allows you some control over what you reveal. Your narrative of your war experiences serves as a form of history and bears witness to what you experienced. Through witnessing, you may find a new mission and a new perspective on your memories.

In the following space, you may choose to note some ideas or topics you would include in your personal story or narrative and then write a longer or more complete story or narrative elsewhere in a journal, blog, or other format.

Using Metaphors

The third way to heal is through the use of metaphor as a way to restructure your thinking. We particularly recommend the bog metaphor, created by the primary author to help veterans and other trauma survivors.

Metaphor is a word or phrase that ordinarily stands for one thing and is then used to stand for another. An example is a blooming red rose representing love growing. Metaphors are often easily remembered. Metaphors, according to Hayes, Barnes-Holmes, and Roche (2001), are like pictures that will help you look at what happened to you in a different way. The bog metaphor helps you create a picture of a physical space that involves a physical struggle. A metaphor can externalize the problem of war, putting it outside yourself. As a way to solve a problem, a metaphor often orients itself toward the future. A metaphor may help you look at your personal strengths as you struggle against or fight a situation. It can help you make sense of your feelings and your personal experiences by offering new ways to put them into words or pictures in your head or brain.

Metaphors let you use mental images or pictures to reexpress something, including your war experiences, in alternative terms, such as a bog or a desert of sand dunes covered in blood. They can help clarify what you've experienced or provide new information. In addition, they can give form to beliefs (Wormeli 2009). Wise and Nash (2013) believe that metaphors are mediators, serving as middlemen between body memories of trauma and a verbal narrative of what happened, and that they are creative ways to use your imagination to counterbalance your "deeply frightening inner world of traumatic experience" (163). In other words, putting a specific pain into a metaphor may help connect that pain to an event that caused or resulted in it.

Loue (2008) notes that memories (and metaphors) can be organized in the following ways:

- **Content:** What happened?

- **Time:** When did things occur?

- **Person:** Who was involved?

- **Place:** Where did the event occur?

- **Activity:** What were you doing?

- **Mood:** How did you feel at the time?

Bruhn (1990) also considers attitude: What thoughts and beliefs did you have at the time of the event?

THE BOG OF WAR

In his book *The Pilgrim's Progress*, John Bunyan penned the following description of a deep bog: "This miry Slough is such a place as cannot be mended; it is...whither the scum and filth...doth continually run and therefore it is called the Slough [swamp] of Despond... there ariseth...many fears, and doubts, and discouraging apprehensions, which all of them get together, and settle in this place; and this is the reason of the badness of this ground" (1965, 46).

We believe that the bog is an extremely helpful metaphor for understanding where you are stuck in your trauma experiences due to war (for vets) or other traumatic events. In the exercise that follows, you will physically create a representation of your own bog in a poster, painting, collage, drawing, or mixed-media representation that describes in visual form how your self or soul is stuck. A bog might be a field of vegetation, such as a cranberry bog, or it might be a mess of glop, slime, and stench. It may look solid but actually be quicksand. If you step on it, you'll sink down into a sticky, jellylike ooze. Some bogs are shallow and more easily conquered. Others have deep holes or other dangers (e.g., hidden stumps, reptiles). Bogs can be made of dead plant material compressed over thousands of years, known as peat bogs. Peat can be used as a form of fuel to provide energy and heat. Bogs also can preserve bodies and other objects that become entombed in them. Yet peat bogs also support life, hold carbon, and help prevent climate change.

Another type of bog is a tar bog, which can be deadly, trapping animals and other creatures so they can't get out, eventually starving to death or sinking down into the tar as they struggle to escape. The La Brea tar pits in Los Angeles, California, have grabbed hold of many creatures and trapped them until they died of starvation.

EXERCISE: **Escaping the Bog of War**

In your mind's eye, what do you see when you read the word "bog"? How do you define the word "bog"? As a returning veteran, do you believe you're stuck in a bog of war? Multiple deployments can create a very deep, all-encompassing bog. The bog of war can trap you in your memories, physical sensations, and emotional horrors. Creating a visual representation of your bog can help depict what it was like for you to be at war.

To begin this exercise, consider the phrase "stuck in my bog" and list the first ten words that come to mind:

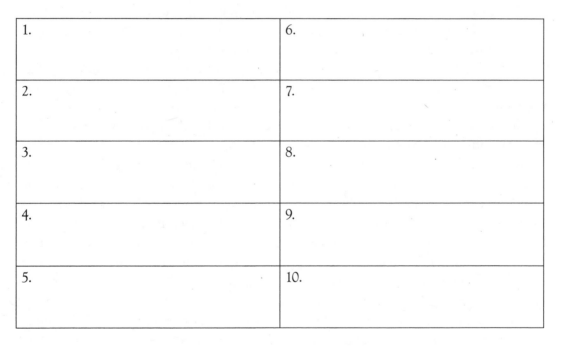

1.	6.
2.	7.
3.	8.
4.	9.
5.	10.

Military culture also can help create the bog and keep you stuck as you adhere to its values, culture, and missions. When you were at war, you put what you learned in basic training into practice. Your principle job when you were at war was probably to kill or facilitate killing. Have you needed to forgive yourself for anything (everything) you did while you were at war? What stressors keep you in your bog?

Your bog is yours alone. You do not need to share it unless you want to. With that in mind, we purposely have not given you extended directions on how to create a visual representation of it. Simply take a separate piece of paper or other materials and draw or otherwise create a visual representation of your personal bog. You could also write some type of short narrative to explain your bog, if you wish. In that narrative, do you see yourself as a bog survivor? Don't limit your imagination or creativity. It's fine to use any art medium, including collage, photography, sculpture, drama, poetry—whatever speaks to you.

As you depict or describe your bog, feel free to use any of the following questions for inspiration: What does your bog look like? What is it made of? Does it have a beginning and an end? What is its shape? Where is it located? How big is it? What does it contain on the surface? What's underneath the surface? How does it smell? Does it have anything to taste?

What are your chosen or given tasks as you are stuck in the bog? Is your task to get out, defend others, or wait for an opportune time to move? Is there anyone around who can help you get your tasks done? Are you alone in the bog, or are battle buddies, family members, friends, enemies, or others with you? Do you have weapons in your bog? What about the dead—friends or enemies? Are there "ghosts" who help or condemn you for your actions? Who or what might be trying to prevent you from leaving the bog?

Now that you've thought about what might be in your bog that keeps you stuck in your war experiences, take a minute to think about what you'd like to have on the other side of your bog or what you can see at its border. Do you feel as if you'll be stuck in your bog forever? Do you believe you're on a good path? Is there anything in the bog that might help you? Put all of these things into your representation of the bog. Take your time, and when you feel your representation of your bog is complete—at least for now—go ahead and put the finishing touches on it. You can always come back later and make additions or changes, or even create an entirely new representation.

What does your bog creation tell you? How have you visualized your bog? Can you think of any coping strategies you can use to overcome the obstacles the bog is putting in your path? How can you finish your tasks? How do you want the story to end, or how would you like to see yourself and your environment after you free yourself from the bog? Have you described or portrayed yourself as a survivor—someone who will eventually escape the bog and thrive? Drawing your bog and including all of its aspects, both good and bad, can help you bring memories and experiences out of your head and body and onto paper or into the present, so their impacts can lessen or be healed.

If you create new representations of your bog as you work on healing from PTSD, notice how those images change over time. Does your bog begin to look totally different? Do you stay in the same bog but get closer to the edge? If you are in counseling, please consider sharing these images with your counselor. They provide a visual, physical way to monitor your healing.

Your depiction also can be entirely imaginary. A pond covered with water lilies might be a bog. One former Air Force pilot sees himself as a frog in a pond, hopping between lily pads. Each one he jumps to is the current, most adrenaline-stimulating crisis in his life. When he conquers that crisis, he can jump to the next, growing and learning as he nears the shore.

Using Sound and Music to Heal

According to Joshua Leeds (2010), a pioneer in psychoacoustics and using sound for healing, "Sound is vibratory energy." We are constantly "being vibrated, on a cellular level, by heard and unheard sound frequencies: electromagnetic fields of all kinds, microwaves, radar, jet planes, jackhammers, horns, sirens, and loud sounds of many kinds, including music" (17).

You may wonder how music can be helpful to you, a veteran suffering the impacts of traumatic stress. Leeds says that Daniel Levitin (2006), a cognitive neuroscientist, has found that "music activates the same part of the brain and causes the same neurochemical cocktail as a lot of other pleasurable activities… Serotonin and dopamine are both involved" (Leeds 2010, 91). He also cites Luciano Bernardo of the Department of Internal Medicine at the University of Pavia, in Italy, who believes that "music is a powerful tool in the management of cardiovascular disease" (127) because various tones and types of music can lower blood pressure and reduce heart rates. Certain songs can influence the mind and emotions, leading to feelings of joy, sadness, peace and calm, and more, thereby influencing the physical body. Sound and music have emotional impacts.

What ambient sounds startle or alarm you: a siren, the sounds of fireworks exploding, the sound of a jackhammer, fingernails on a chalkboard, screeching brakes, or the sound of metal hitting metal? What sounds calm you: a lullaby, a quiet love song,, the purr of a cat, or the ambient sound of the ocean's waves hitting the shore? Music can be a form of self-medication. Music and sound are all around you and have been since you were in the womb.

Are there particular songs, pieces of music, or types of music that help you relax or make you feel energized? List a few of them below:

_____

_____

_____

Many cultures, both ancient and modern, use sound to heal. Indian wise men chant mantras by the hour or use singing bowls or drums for healing (Norris 2011). These practices go back to ancient times. In fact, some ancient Hindus believed that the universe was quiet until the first movement of the universe made the sound "om." Now some therapists are beginning to use sound frequencies and rhythms in their practices to help clients balance their bodies. It's possible that diseases have their own cellular frequencies and that sound can play a role in healing. The body heals best in a state of total relaxation. Certain types of music help individuals relax. Capacchione (2001) notes that "Music affects us physically, emotionally, mentally, and spiritually… The feelings evoked by music, the experience of the rhythm, can be translated into lines, shapes, colors, and textures" (134).

Greg McGraw (2012a), in his blog *The Fortress of Potential*, wrote that creation began with sound— according to science—with the Big Bang and, according to Eastern scripture, through the vibration of the primordial "om." McGraw believes that God is sound—a sound heard much more deeply than simply through the ears. In the next day's posting (2012b), he discussed how, when two people hug, they feel it without words and how that feeling is energy; energy is vibration; and vibration is the foundation of sound. A hug lets you feel unuttered sound, an emotional vibration that is God. He sees God as a vibration or energy that we have come to recognize as sound.

Sound can heal in many ways: through encouraging words, songs or other music that promotes relaxation or positive mood; a singing bowl of a certain frequency; a chanted mantra (a phrase or combination of sounds); affirmations expressed verbally; and perhaps even via the vibrations inherent in a silent, physical act. To put the power of sound to work in your own emotional and physical healing, you might try some of the following approaches:

- Chanting can help synchronize brain waves and promote deep relaxation by increasing the production of endogenous opioids (the body's own self-soothing chemicals). Try chanting a simple song, a keening sound of grief, or just the syllable "om."

- Similarly, try simply singing, humming, or making other sounds, such as sighing, moaning, or slowly saying "aah" for five to ten minutes. Then notice how you feel. If you like, take this a step further by chanting a single note or word for an extended time—perhaps as much as thirty minutes—and then notice where you feel the note in your body.

- Try playing a musical instrument or drums, and then notice how this changes your mood or physical feelings.

- Listen to music that calms you, makes you feel uplifted, or otherwise improves your mood. There are no rules here; maybe rap music or heavy metal is what works for you. The key is to find music that is healing for you personally.

- Go to an isolated or private place and try screaming as a way to express and release emotional pain and terror through sound.

- Use singing bowls, striking the rim three times and then running the mallet around the rim to create a sound with waves, oscillations, and energy. You can chant or say a mantra at the same time or relax with deep breathing if you like.

- Use a mantra or groups of syllables to express your life story. The sounds don't have to make sense or even be real words. Chant your life story for a while, and then change those primal sounds.

In addition, vocal music also conveys human emotions. We scream when frightened or excited; we laugh when happy or even when embarrassed. Words in and of themselves, without music, can change you in many ways. Hearing "I love you" brings an entirely different response than does hearing the words "Earthquake, run!" when you are inside an old, undulating building. We vocalize pain by groaning or moaning, or by crying or yelling. Take a minute or two and exercise your voice either individually or as part of a family or group: yawn, sigh, laugh, make the sound of the vowels in English or any other language you know. Also you may choose one sound ("om") or a series of sounds to use in a mantra meditation. You may want to create a personal mantra as a chant several times a day for a few minutes at a time; try to make the meaning of the mantra relevant to you. If this task seems overwhelming, you can listen to a variety of mantras on CDs.

Music can be therapeutic, as it helps you to release your emotions. Capacchione (2001) also writes that "half an hour of listening to Mozart can have the same calming effect as a 10 milligram pill of Valium (p 137)." We recommend that you experiment with these approaches to find which are effective and healing for you. Music has an innate ability to encourage our expression of feeling. Songs, at appropriate times, help express the inner emotions we feel. Their themes are universal; their abilities to elicit emotional release are beyond measure. As therapy, music can help to bring buried emotion to the surface. It is quite possible to transform sadness, grief, and depression through music. We suggest that you might choose to experiment with drumming and/or join a drumming circle. Drumming can help you to express the "hot" emotions discussed previously. If you don't choose to purchase a drum, you can use everyday kitchen items to make your own. Hot sounds from a drum can express anger, passion, and sexuality. And even if you elect simply to listen to music, there's no doubt that doing so can be profoundly healing. Before reading on, take a few minutes to do the following exercise and think about how music has helped or healed you, or how it might do so.

EXERCISE: How Music and Sound Can Help Me Heal

Has music helped you heal? _____

In what ways? _____

_____

_____

_____

When you're feeling upset or triggered, what types of music do you seek out?

_____

_____

Working with Service, Therapy, and Emotional Support Animals

The final tool is "man's best friend"—the dog—as a service or emotional support animal. Not every veteran needs 1:1 or group therapy. Not every veteran needs counseling. And not every veteran needs a canine companion. A PTSD service dog can perform a specific task, such as pulling a wheelchair, helping you cross the street, or even alerting you to an impending seizure, and it can be extremely empowering to have this companion with you to walk by your side, share your space, watch over you, guide you, let you know when you're dissociating, or ground you when you are triggered or having a nightmare. Animal-assisted therapy utilizes a trained animal to go either with you or with someone else into various facilities, such as a hospital, nursing home, or rehabilitation center. An emotional support animal can be part of your personal healing/treatment plan, if you have a diagnosed handicapping condition.

According to the Americans with Disabilities Act (2010), a service dog is "any dog that is individually trained to do work or perform tasks for the benefit of an individual with a disability, including a physical, sensory, psychiatric, intellectual, or other mental disability." The dog must be trained to perform a particular behavior that is not its natural response (Mills and Yeager 2012). It is now recognized by the ADA that an emotional support or companion animal can alleviate or mitigate some aspects of a mental or psychiatric disability. Under federal law, the individual who has this type of animal must have a verified, diagnosed disability, and the animal must provide the disabled individual some type of benefit. Section 504 of the Rehabilitation Act of 1973 extends reasonable accommodations (housing, public places, transportation) for individual and animal.

If you have a therapy dog, that dog also may be a service dog if, in addition to being a companion, it has been taught to perform a service. If your dog does not perform trained tasks and gives you emotional support and comfort, then that dog is now entitled to be with you anywhere you go, without challenge, if you have the necessary documentation.

The bond between humans and animals can be extraordinarily powerful, and a growing body of research indicates that dogs can help veterans overcome PTSD (Colin 2012). The presence of a dog may help physically buffer the effects of stress on traumatized veterans, whether the dog is a service animal or "merely" a companion (Knisely, Barker, and Barker 2012). According to Beck and colleagues, wounded warriors who participated in life skills programs with therapy dogs "had improved mood states, decreased stress levels, increased resilience, lowered levels of fatigue, and improved daily function for reintegration and transition to the next stage of their life as compared to [those] who did not interact with dogs" (2012, 40).

The new Walter Reed National Military Medical Center is leading the way in implementing human-animal bond programs in its wounded warriors programs. Currently, the service dog program works with accredited civilian organizations to provide dogs to wounded warriors with physical disabilities; however, programs to provide dogs to veterans with PTSD are being developed. One nonprofit organization that provides dogs is NEADS Canines for Combat Veterans (Yeager and Irwin 2011).

In 2008, Yount created the first program to train dogs to be used in a safe, effective intervention to treat symptoms of PTSD and traumatic brain injury in veterans. In 2010, he created a program to train service dogs at the National Intrepid Center of Excellence in Bethesda, Maryland. That program is now offered through the nonprofit foundation Warrior Canine Connection. Warrior trainers with PTSD participate in the program by training dogs to assist individuals with impairments in mobility. Research (Yount, Olmert, and Lee 2012) has shown that the trainers with PTSD experience improvements in a variety of areas:

- patience, impulse control, and emotional regulation

- ability to display emotion (and decreased emotional numbness)

- sleep

- depression symptoms

- startle responses

- use of pain medications and antipsychotic medications

- sense of belonging and acceptance

- use of assertiveness skills

- parenting skills and family dynamics

- in-the-moment thinking

- stress levels and sense of calm

Do you perceive dogs as trustworthy and safe? Would you like to have a companion with whom you can bond in order to buffer stress? Would you benefit from positive social interactions that can increase the natural antistress agents in your body? If so, you may be a candidate for animal-assisted therapy or an emotional support animal.

It is essential to remember that an emotional support animal is not a pet but an animal that performs a therapeutic function for an individual with a verified disability.

EQUINE THERAPY

According to Baker (2004), humans who work with horses therapeutically need to stay in the moment. She writes that "a relationship with horses provides meaning and solace to those who have (spend time with) them" (28). Horses can provide both emotional and spiritual healing. They require the people who interact with them to stay in the moment. Baker writes about Native Americans' relationships with horses and notes that that relationship "provides meaning and solace to those who have them" (2004, 28).

In *Riding Between the Worlds*, Kohanov (2003) writes that horses are geniuses at sensing the feelings of others (helping trauma survivors through on-the-ground equine therapy) with "everything from anger management issues and PTSD to depression" (xvi). Through work with horses, a frightened or hesitant trauma survivor can learn to trust through developing a relationship with a horse. During specifically designed exercises, such as leading a horse without a rope or standing in the midst of three or four horses and allowing yourself to feel them as beings, your safety and emotional vulnerability are always mindfully observed and acknowledged. If you decide to participate in an equine experiential learning program in your geographic area, you will be challenged to expand your nonverbal awareness. If you have an opportunity to be near a horse, try to connect nonverbally without touching the animal. If you participate in an actual program, you will learn, through reflective activities, how to build that connection. Walk up to a horse, step back and take a horse's pose (feet apart about shoulder width, knees and arms slightly bent and extending outward), and then breathe into your belly and notice what you feel.

Moving Ahead

We hope that the tools we presented in this chapter will be helpful in your healing. We have just a few more suggestions on other ways you might improve your situation.

If you're applying for compensation for a service-connected disability, consider getting an evaluation by a qualified individual who is familiar with veterans' issues, assessment of PTSD, the VA system, and military culture and issues. It's best to do this after registering with the VA but before participating in a compensation and pension (C&P) examination. Although it is no longer necessary to have explicit stressor details, it is helpful to provide information about your tour of duty and specific stressors you experienced. We also recommend contacting a local service organization that has a good track record (as indicated by word-of-mouth among veterans) to help you file and track your claims.

If you want to return to the workforce and are not sure how to do so, attend one or more of the Get America Back to Work recruiting events held by various military and nonmilitary organizations. There, you can talk to recruiters who can help place you and help you get any needed education through return-to-work seminars, including the Slogging the Bog Workshop mentioned earlier in this chapter.

If you need vocational rehabilitation, here are a few suggestions that will ensure a more productive meeting with officials at your local department of rehabilitative services (Krause 2009):

1. Decide you want to win this one.

2. Tap into your purpose, strengths, talents, knowledge, and experience.

3. Choose three areas of career options that interest you, research them, and determine whether a career in these areas is feasible, based on your emotional, cognitive, and physical condition. Ask for a vocational evaluation if you aren't sure about possible career paths for yourself.

4. Know the rules of vocational rehab and how you will be considered for benefits. What is your service-connected disability? Do you need a therapist to evaluate you and send a report to the agency first, before you can apply for benefits? How do your disabilities impact your capacity to work, such as time of day when you can work, type of job, or need for accommodations? Accommodations can become part of a return-to-work plan, called a 504 Plan. Be sure you know how to complete this statement: "My service-connected injury prevents me from working in my previous qualified field because…"

5. Know past vocational rehabilitation decisions in your area of disability. How likely is your local organization to approve your particular area of disability for assistance? This assistance might incorporate training, participating in educational programs, or completing an undergraduate or advanced degree. Know how to present your case. List how each form of assistance could help you obtain gainful employment.

6. Make your personal plan.

7. Refine how you will present your plan before your meeting. Be ready to describe your present situation, your employment history, and your employment handicap (Krause 2009).

Welcome home!

11

Finding Meaning

Traumatic events have the ability to change anyone who experiences them. You have been changed in some or many ways by those experiences, perhaps even at a core level. Still, if you are to heal, it is important for you to find some sense of meaning from what has happened to you. If your basic psychological needs for safety, trust, power or control, esteem, and intimacy cannot be met adequately by yourself, the world, or others, then finding that meaning may be a difficult task.

Working Through a Traumatic Event

The person who works through a history of trauma and comes out the other side as a (somewhat) whole person is resilient and has certain character traits and abilities that can be learned or developed by using many of the exercises in this workbook (the appropriate chapter number is listed after each ability). Such people have the ability to:

- Tolerate or lessen the intensity of painful feelings

- Recognize self-blame and shame and then counter it

- Stay connected with people who are both present and absent

- Be alone without being lonely

- Self-soothe when upset

- Anticipate consequences of actions and events

- Set and maintain appropriate physical and emotional interpersonal boundaries

- Provide mutual self-support with supportive others

- Have willpower

- Take initiative

- Have empathy for others

- Have a sense of humor

Which of these qualities do you have? Which do you want to develop?

_____

_____

_____

_____

You also may want to try to develop what Covey (1999) lists as the "seven habits of highly effective people." Those habits are:

1. Be proactive—decide what you want to do and do it. This is personal vision.

2. Begin with an end in mind (your legacy) and then make every decision and take every action with that final legacy in mind. This is personal leadership.

3. Put first things first and concentrate on what is important, though not always urgent, to do. This is personal management.

4. Think win-win. Seek solutions to problems that benefit everyone involved. This is interpersonal leadership.

5. Seek first to understand and then to be understood. Listen to others with the goal of understanding them and their position. This is empathic communication.

6. Synergize through teamwork. This is creative cooperation.

7. Commit to improving yourself constantly. This is balanced self-renewal.

The key to implementing these seven habits is to make a choice each day to try to live by them. Choosing to do so with awareness means you have that end result in mind. As you choose, look at the results of each choice you make. If you like those results, then keep up your good work. If you do not like the results, then learn from your mistakes and try again (Power 1992a).

Continuing to Heal

Healing from trauma occurs when you are able to have at least some level of power or authority over your memories, when you can manage any emotions connected with those memories, and when you can manage intrusive and avoidant PTSD-related symptoms. Healing occurs also when you are able to control your own behavioral responses (e.g., choosing when and how to express anger). To be healed means you are able to take care of yourself emotionally, physically, interpersonally, and spiritually. It also means that you respect yourself and have relationships with yourself and others that are safe (Matsakis 1998).

We have given you many suggestions and provided many exercises that will help with this healing. We have shown you how to deal with your own messages about what happened to you as well as the messages others instilled within you (your introjects). We have given you strategies to deal with your deserved and undeserved guilt. We have helped you learn self-care and gain boundaries (Matsakis 1999). It is our expectation that your healing will continue long after you finish this workbook, even if you come back to it on occasion for a brush-up. Challenging and even possibly changing some of your beliefs about those five basic needs has given you strength to continue to grow. You also have given voice to what happened to you consciously, with the intent of healing and bringing any intrusive memories, thoughts, or nightmares under more control. You have learned to set boundaries and are better able now to keep your traumatic experiences contained, letting out what happened to you only to those who need to know. You have developed strategies to resolve your grief and deal with your losses. Also, you have learned to be satisfied with taking small steps toward healing and are learning to accept yourself as you really are (Schiraldi 2000).

Speeding Up Healing

Power lists a number of ways to speed up healing without retraumatizing yourself (1992a, 92, 104):

- Become more and more aware of each choice you make.

- Choose to work for a "common good" that gives you a sense of meaning.

- Utilize self-management techniques to control or minimize the impact of flashbacks.

- Implement ways to be more functional on a daily basis.

- Look for what makes you resistant to doing your work, and then do something to modify that resistance.

- Manage your pain in constructive ways (exercise a "normal" amount, not to the point of injury or exhaustion, for example).

- Remind yourself consistently that you survived "the worst"—your original traumas—and that you now exist in this present time.

- Learn the names of your feelings, find out what those feelings feel like, and practice them.

- Practice turning the volume up and down on various feelings.

- Seek out positive experiences and enjoy them and the positive emotions that accompany them.

EXERCISE: **The Ladder**

Another way to look for meaning in your healing is with the ladder exercise developed by Busuttil (2002). The aim of this exercise is to identify short- and long-term goals that can be presented to others. In your journal or here, draw a ladder with several rungs. On the top rung, write in your long-term goal for healing or finding meaning. On the bottom rung, write in the lowest point of your life. On the intervening rungs, fill in the steps you want or need to take in order to achieve your ultimate goal. You will want to include many life dimensions as you climb the ladder, such as your marriage or other long-term relationships, social activities, spiritual endeavors, occupational and financial goals or pursuits, and your values. If you seek feedback from important people in your life, you may change what you have put on your rungs.

Thoughts About Finding Meaning

How do you find meaning in life? Where do you find meaning—through your faith, your family, your acts of service? What are the blessings you have experienced in your life? In the space below, list ten things, people, or acts that you consider to be blessings and for which you are thankful:

1.	6.
2.	7.
3.	8.
4.	9.
5.	10.

One way is to pursue some type of activity or project that grows out of your traumatic experiences. Mothers who have lost children to drunk drivers often become active in Mothers Against Drunk Driving (MADD). Family members of those lost in major airline disasters have formed support groups and have advocated for changes in airline regulation. Through this process, you will again recognize your abilities and your limitations. You may become a mentor to others or start your own organization or project. You may write poetry or throw pottery or draw. You may decide to enter a helping profession (once you are healed enough that your baggage does not influence how you practice your professional skills). Through these or similar activities, you give something back to the world.

You also may find meaning by developing your own self further or by enjoying some of the beauty and pleasures of the world (Schiraldi 2000). You may become a photographer of nature. You may develop a new loving, intimate relationship or foster the relationship you presently have. You may develop friendships, or you may commit to personal growth that helps you to understand yourself and others.

It is quite possible that you will never know exactly why you were a victim; on the other hand, you may have some knowledge about what lay behind your abuse, torture, or trauma. Bad things do happen to good people (Kushner 1981). At times, growth comes from suffering.

How have you grown as you have done the work in this workbook? Have you changed?

_____

_____

_____

_____

It is possible to grow through trauma. If you have been responsible to any degree, through negligence or intent, for the event or events that happened to you or around you, and you own up to your responsibility, you have grown. When you realized and accepted that you were betrayed, violated, victimized, and abused and that what happened to you was due to the actions of others and was not of your own doing or causing, you have grown. If you no longer blame yourself for what was not your responsibility, you have grown. When events were due to chance and you can accept just that—that you were a victim of a random act of trauma—you have grown. As Tedeschi, Park, and Calhoun (1998) recognize, you grow when your trauma is no longer an incomprehensible present but becomes, instead, a comprehensible part of your past.

Spiritual Development

One way many people find meaning is through pursuing some form of spiritual development. Developing spirituality can be a lifelong pursuit as you learn to ask questions about how you view a Higher Being, Creator, or God. Perhaps you may decide that you want to learn to pray or you want to use prayer more. Prayer can be a way to get understanding and clarity if you open up to whatever "comes in" as you pray. Through prayer, you have a tool to give voice to your pain and then listen in the present to what messages are given to you after you offer your prayer. Do you pray for answers? For relief? Or do you pray for specific interventions or material goods? It is important to decide just what you are praying for. Prayer also stimulates production of serotonin (Newberg and Waldman 2010). You may find Psalm 91 helpful. The purpose of the psalm is protection, and it is particularly appropriate for those who are put in harm's way in the service of their country and its citizens, such as those who serve in the military and law enforcement, fire, and rescue personnel. For many, God's wings are "a mighty shield" and may even lend some protection from later PTSD.

Brussat and Brussat (2000) discuss many prescriptions for spiritual practice in their book *Spiritual Rx*. One prescription is to search for beauty; beauty is truly everywhere around you, but noticing it can be difficult when trauma and traumatic symptoms overshadow your ability to see. They also examine the prescription of faith, stating that "faith [is] not something you have but…something you are in—a relationship. It involves an awareness of and an attunement to God's presence in your everyday experiences" (81). When you have faith, you can choose and then remain true to a vision or an aspiration—e.g., the vision of yourself as healed from your traumatic past. In order to follow that vision, you need some level of trust (one of the five psychological needs) in yourself, in Providence, and in others. If you pray and have a conversational relationship with a Higher Power, you can ask for guidance in following that vision.

We have spoken of forgiveness in chapter 6. One aspect of a spiritual journey is to examine forgiveness in three contexts: forgiveness of self, allowing release from guilt and shame; forgiveness of others (to the extent that is possible); and forgiveness from God, which you may seek depending on your spiritual practices. Through your spiritual quest, if you choose that route to try to find meaning in what happened to you, you may look at what you want to do to forgive yourself and others or to seek God's forgiveness if you believe it is essential to your growth and recognize that forgiveness as real.

Another spiritual prescription involves keeping hope. The Brussats believe that hope can be learned and that it is the major ingredient of optimism.

What does the word "hope" mean to you? Do you have hope in your future—that you will be healed as much as you can be? Do you have hope now, in the present, in your ability to heal?

_____

_____

_____

Do you have any or all of the following three attitudes that may help you have hope of healing?

- patience—the ability to accept that healing takes time and often occurs on a time line other than your own

- courage to pursue healing without knowing what lies ahead, particularly if you still have memories that you have not faced

- persistence—the ability to keep going on with your healing, even after you finish this workbook

Another spiritual practice involves seeking joy or allowing yourself to have feelings of happiness and pleasure. You may discover that you find joy by doing for others as you seek meaning in your life.

When and where do you feel joy? How can you share joy with others or help others find joy?

_____

_____

_____

_____

According to the Brussats, "many people...define spirituality as the search for meaning and purpose...(that) involves both seeking and making" (2000, 172). Think of a time when you suddenly changed what you were going to do and as a result met someone you needed to meet or were presented with a new opportunity. There are many possible paths open to you at all times.

Is finding a purpose a difficult task for you? How do you show yourself that your life really does matter—to yourself, if not to others?

_____

_____

_____

_____

You alone know whether you view your God or Higher Power as anthropomorphic (having human qualities) or beyond human in attributes, and where you see God. You alone know if your connection to that Higher Power or God is personal or distant. Bourne (2001) notes that you may see God in

- natural beauty

- deep insights or truth

- creative inspiration

- love given or received

- premonitions

- miracles

- synchronicities (coincidences that are not coincidences)

- other visionary experiences

- challenges, tests, and traumatic experiences

EXERCISE: Ways to Improve My Spirituality

Bourne (2001) suggests a variety of ways to improve your spirituality. If you answer these questions, try not to do so merely with "yes" or "no," but write about when you use each way to improve your spirituality, if you do.

Do you pray as a way to communicate with your God or Higher Power? Do you pray to request something (e.g., forgiveness, healing, answers)?

_____

_____

Do you turn over your problems to your God or Higher Power for solutions?

_____

_____

Do you meditate in order to get in touch with deeper parts of yourself through quieting your mind or to reach a deeper level of connection with your God or Higher Power?

_____

_____

Do you read literature that is spiritual in nature? This might include the Bible or other works.

_____

_____

Do you meet with others in a spiritual fellowship, whether through church attendance, vision quests, workshops, Bible studies, mission trips, or other activities?

_____

_____

What type(s) of compassionate service do you do for others?

_____

_____

315

If you are seeking "a more optimistic and tolerant view of life" (Bourne 2001, 64), you may use some of the following suggestions and revelations to guide your quest:

1. Life is a school with the primary purpose of growth in consciousness and wisdom and the capacity to love.

2. Adversity and difficult situations are lessons in growth, sometimes even random, capricious acts of fate. In the larger scheme of things, everything happens for a purpose. (This may be difficult to accept but, if you have used your experiences to find your life purpose, you may have helped many others in many ways.) Through your experiences, you have hopefully learned compassion and empathy.

3. Your personal limitations (including disabilities and illnesses) can highlight the lessons you have the chance to learn in life and can be challenges to be used for growth.

4. Your life has a creative purpose and mission.

5. You have a higher source of support and guidance available to you if you ask.

6. You can contact your Higher Power directly through your personal experience.

7. The power of intention can promote what Bourne calls "miraculous consequences" if your intention is for the highest good.

8. Evil is the misuse of your creative power.

9. Love is stronger than fear and can overcome fear.

10. Death is a transition. Some part of your being transcends and survives beyond death.

Do you believe any of these principles? If so, which ones?

_____

_____

_____

Are there other statements or principles you can turn to that will help you on your healing path?

_____

_____

_____

What did you learn about yourself by completing these exercises about developing spirituality?

_____

_____

_____

Healing Rituals

When you feel guilt, shame, or grief, you may want to create a healing ritual to help yourself or to honor the person who died. A *healing ritual* is a structured activity designed to help release grief and pain. A ritual may help you find support from those around you as you learn to relate to the trauma in a new way. According to Williamson and Williamson (1994), rituals help fulfill needs for inner nourishment and meaning and are a way to experience both inner and outer transformation. They also are a means to enhance our spirituality and to bring about emotional healing after crisis and trauma. Rituals often spring from the symbols and images of everyday experiences. These symbols can give meaning, purpose, and energy to our lives. According to Catherall (1992), there are seven steps to a ritual. These steps are explored in the exercise that follows, which is intended to help you design your own ritual.

EXERCISE: **My Healing Ritual**

I want to do a ritual for _____ because _____.

1. Select a location to do the ritual. The location might be a grave, a mountaintop, a statue's base, or the Vietnam Veterans Memorial Wall.

    My location is _____.

2. Select something symbolic that stands for what you have suffered. What symbols might stand for your life before, during, and after the trauma? What did you lose because of the trauma—a home, innocence, your childhood, a loved one, certain possessions?

    My symbol is _____.

3. Select any props you might want to use in your ritual. Props help build the scene. You may want to use appropriate candles, stones, or pictures.

    My props include _____.

4. Decide if there is anyone else you want to include in the ritual who might give you support. This might be a friend, spouse, partner, child, or therapist.

    My companion is _____.

5. Think of what you want to say at the ritual. Do you want to give a eulogy to someone who has died? Do you want to say good-bye to someone or something? Do you have a poem, joke, anecdote, or song? For example, a memorial service was recently held at the first tee of a local golf course for a golfer who had died of cancer. It was a beautiful, warm day and those in attendance were asked to participate. Poetry, personal music, and stories were shared, and those who wanted to participated in a symbolic golf tournament in honor of him.

    My healing words are _____.

6. Choose a guide, leader, or assistant if you need one, and decide how that person can help you.

    My guide or help is _____.

    He or she will help me by _____.

7. Decide how you will bid farewell to people, feelings, events, or times of your life. You can use the ritual as a way to release your pain and hurt. Do you want to use the ritual to get rid of something—e.g., possessions that belonged to a perpetrator or drawings of abuse?

    I will be saying good-bye to _____.

Once you have put the ritual on paper, consider whether you want to actually do it. Can you make a commitment to do the ritual? When will you do it?

_____

If you like, write a bit about how completing this exercise helped you.

_____

_____

_____

The Ritual of the Phoenix Rising

Williamson and Williamson (1994) describe the ritual of the phoenix rising as an example of a healing ritual. The phoenix was a symbol of the Egyptian sun god and was believed to live for five hundred years. According to the myth, it then burned itself to ash on a pyre but did not die. Instead, it rose to live again in a state of youth. The phoenix can be a symbol of immortality and regeneration, as well as of transformation from what you are to what you want to become. You may use this ritual to shed things that are holding you back, such as survivor guilt, shame, worry, fear, lack of self-esteem, or indecision.

The ritual involves designing a personal phoenix medallion and creating your own affirmation to put on the medallion. The affirmation might say something like, "From the ashes of past traumas, I rise as a phoenix to a new freedom and sense of being." You also may choose your own personal symbols of freedom and transformation to use in this ritual. Williamson and Williamson (1994) suggest you take a black marking pen and write words that are personal symbols of freedom on the back of the medallion you have created. These words might include "faith," "self-love," "forgiveness," "patience," "praise," "strength," "truth," "spirituality," "redemption," "peace," or others.

JOURNAL EXERCISE: **My Phoenix Medallion**

Take a few minutes to decide on your own personal words and affirmations and write them in your journal. Now, close your eyes, and think about what your medallion will look like. (You also can make a real medallion from clay, cardboard, or other materials.) Draw a picture of the front and back of your medallion in your notebook or journal. Close your eyes and think some more before you write your healing words or affirmations on your medallion's back. You may draw a picture on its front as well. This medallion becomes a visual reminder of your commitment to growth. Put the medallion in a special place or carry it with you so that you can have access to it regularly. You may look at your medallion as often as you need, to remind you that you always have new opportunities to heal.

Regular Rituals

Sometimes participation in a regularly observed ritual unites you and others who have similar pasts or traumas and gives you a sense of group identification. Once a year, certain Quaker meetings are followed by a separation ritual for women who have lost a child. Women go to a designated tree and put an offering or gift on it for each child lost. The children may have died, been aborted, been miscarried, or been put up for adoption. These women share their grief and provide each other with support.

Another ritual occurred at 9:02 a.m. on April 19, 2001. At that time, in Oklahoma City, the names of each of the 168 victims of the Oklahoma City bombing were read as their empty chairs sat mournfully in the empty field that used to be the building in which they died. This ritual honored the victims and assured the survivors that their loved ones are remembered. When rituals such as these are repeated regularly, perhaps yearly, they can bring a sense of order through their familiarity and provide a safe way for the living to express their feelings both symbolically and directly.

An additional ritual might be created to help with forgiveness.

JOURNAL EXERCISE: **My Forgiveness Ritual**

Develop a ritual to help you let go of any unjust self-blame, shame, and guilt that you may still hold. This is a forgiveness ritual.

Connecting with Nature

Another way to seek meaning and purpose is to connect with nature. Gerry Eitner, creator of Communities of Peace and a Reiki master, has used and taught various methods to achieve advanced states of consciousness that shift and change old trauma-bound patterns, fears, and defenses. She has found that healing of trauma and related negative addictive behavior patterns can be done effectively in nature. Project Nature Connect, developed by educator and environmental psychologist Michael Cohen, provides safe, easy, and supportive experiences to restore the senses wounded by traumatic experiences. Through the use of these exercises, people who have been traumatized can become part of and build connections to the web of life—the supportive natural community. Project Nature Connect, in a series of interactions experienced in nature, restores these connections and senses to their natural state. The exercises emphasize natural attractions, positive feelings, and appreciation, building a framework for survivors to become connected to what is specifically positive and supportive for them. You can obtain more information about Project Nature Connect from the website http://www.projectnatureconnect.org.

The first two of the four following exercises for connecting with nature were designed by Michael Cohen (1977). The third was initially designed by Christina Brittain (2001) and has been modified by Gerry Eitner (personal communication). Eitner also modified the fourth from Project Nature Connect.

EXERCISE: **Gaining Permission**

This exercise begins to set the pattern to help you ask for and receive permission to interact with nature. You will also be able to begin distinguishing between what is naturally attractive and welcoming and what is not. As you complete this exercise, you will begin to notice differences in your interactions with other people as well as with nature.

1. Go to an attractive natural place like a wood, park, or backyard, or even to an indoor plant. The key factors are that the area should be natural, attractive, and safe.

2. You will find that something in this natural place will stand out and look very attractive, and you will be drawn to it.

3. Ask permission of that plant, tree, bush, or whatever to interact with it. This is generally done nonverbally and always respectfully.

4. Obtain its permission in some way. If you receive that permission, you will find yourself feeling acknowledged and connected. This will be a positive experience.

5. If you don't receive this permission, identify another attractive something, and obtain permission to interact with it.

6. Sense the connection; feel what gift this natural attraction has for you.

7. When you are finished with the experience, thank the natural attraction for interacting with you.

I tried this exercise when I

_____

_____

_____

The results of my trying this exercise in nature:

_____

_____

_____

EXERCISE: **Establishing Trust**

This closed-eye experience begins to establish your trust in the person you choose to lead you and in nature itself as you use your other senses.

1. Ask someone you like and trust and with whom you feel comfortable to be your nature guide. Go with that nature guide to an attractive natural place like a backyard, wood, or park.

2. Ask the area for permission to interact, as described above.

3. Take your guide's hand, close your eyes, and explore the area. Be open and receptive to gathering information through your other senses. Walk along and ask your guide to place your hand on natural things, like a tree, rock, or leaf. As you touch it, be receptive, noticing what you feel, smell, sense, or hear. Do you notice changes in temperature, hear more sensitively, feel more distinctly? Are you comfortable with the connections?

4. After interacting with each leaf, tree, rock, etc., thank it for sharing with you. Thank your guide for leading you.

I tried this exercise when I

_____

_____

_____

My experiences with this exercise:

_____

_____

_____

EXERCISE: **Sharing My Troubles with Nature**

Sometimes, when nothing feels safe, you still need to tell your troubles to someone or something. Nature can provide connection and comfort and a place where you can share (and look for) meaning.

1. Go to an attractive natural place like a backyard, park, or wood. A place with an indoor plant will do if needed.

2. Ask the place for permission to visit. Nature welcomes you when you see or feel something that attracts you. Sit down somewhere outside where you can easily see and interact with nature.

3. Now think about what is troubling you.

4. Tell the attractive part of nature what is troubling you.

5. Feel nature sharing your troubles; this sharing can make them easier to bear.

6. Continue to sit still and feel nature sharing your troubles with you.

7. When you feel your troubles getting lighter, express your appreciation to nature—e.g., pick up trash. Nature is always there to comfort you; do something to help nature.

As you share with nature, you may find that you see beauty around you and feel connected with something greater than yourself. Perhaps your Higher Power is some type of connection with nature. Allow yourself to take in whatever nature offers you.

I completed this exercise by

_____

_____

_____

What it taught me about letting go of my troubles and traumas:

_____

_____

_____

EXERCISE: **Affirming Positive Qualities**

1. Go to an attractive natural place like a backyard, park, or wood, or to an indoor plant.

2. Find something that is attractive to you and ask for permission to interact with it.

3. When you receive permission, identify what it is about the natural attraction that you like. (For instance, *I like that flower because it is pretty and graceful.*)

4. Recognize that you have those same (or similar) qualities and say to yourself, *I like myself because I am pretty and graceful.* Be sure to choose realistic qualities of both nature and, potentially, of yourself.

5. Continue the same process with other attractions.

I completed this exercise by

_____

_____

_____

What I learned through completing this exercise was

_____

_____

_____

How did it feel to you to try to connect with nature in this way? Remember to check out the Project Nature Connect website for more information about the program.

This chapter has looked at ways to find meaning in your life. Finding meaning for what you endured and survived can be a very difficult task. Keep these three attitudes in mind as you do so—keep your courage, try to be patient, and persist as you keep in mind that healing is possible.

If you are able to let go of those aspects of trauma that are not positive in your life, if you are optimistic, if you are a self-starter and are hardy, you will have a better chance to grow. We will discuss the concept of resilience in more detail in the final chapter of this workbook.

EXERCISE: **What I Learned from This Chapter**

What have you learned about yourself in this chapter? How have you let go of what happened to you? How have you grown? How do you reach out to others who are hurting? When and how do you show your appreciation of life? Have you bonded with other survivors? Have you joined any support groups or created a new group? How have you used your personal energy to survive?

_____

_____

_____

_____

12

Final Thoughts and Exercises

Now that you have worked through most or at least some of the exercises in this workbook, you have learned a great deal about trauma and about how trauma has transformed you. Hopefully you also have learned about yourself.

Trauma often transforms those who experience it. You may have heard this statement before, and you have read similar statements in this workbook. Your exposure to trauma has changed you in some way. You may have gone from a familiar everyday existence of comfort and predictability to an unfamiliar world of post-traumatic stress with its intrusions, avoidances, and physiological reactions. You may have experienced a lifetime of abuse and terror. As you have made a journey by completing the exercises in this workbook, you also may have changed and, hopefully, have learned to trust yourself and your intuitions more often or even most of the time. You may have been slogging along, putting one foot in front of the other, but you have kept on going. Now it is time to look at where you are today and where you hope to be tomorrow or the next day or the next.

Your Real Self

Masterson (1988) has proposed several characteristics that describe a real self. After each of the characteristics that are listed below, write a short description of how you meet this capacity now and what you might do to fulfill it even further.

I have the capacity to experience deeply a wide range of feelings, including joy and excitement, in a spontaneous way. I have the capacity to hope.

_____

_____

_____

I have the capacity to expect that I will get the things I need to survive.

I have the capacity to be assertive in expressing my wishes, dreams, and goals once I have identified them.

I have a good sense of self-esteem.

I am able to soothe my own feelings, even when they are painful, without wallowing in misery. If I need "poor me" time, I set a limit to how much time I spend in this way.

I am able to make and stick to commitments, in spite of obstacles and setbacks. I don't make commitments I am not able to keep.

I am able to be creative in seeking new ways to solve my problems.

_____

_____

_____

I am able to have personal relationships with others without being overcome by anxiety or, if anxiety comes up, I have the ability to self-soothe.

_____

_____

_____

I have the capacity to be alone with myself without feeling abandoned or despairing, without having to fill up my life with meaningless activity or bad relationships.

_____

_____

_____

I have a core self that persists through time and I am aware of that core and of who I am.

_____

_____

_____

I have the capacity to develop or maintain the other capacities listed above.

_____

_____

_____

Blessings

What are the blessings you now have in your life? Can you identify any? You may have more than you imagine. Do you have children, peace of mind, enough food on your plate at night, a job, physical relief, understanding of your symptoms, safety (in all its aspects or just in one or two aspects), prosperity, or other gifts? Do you have the respect of others for your survival and strong spirit? Do you have spirituality, the absence of fear, and an intimate relationship? All of these things and others are blessings.

In the space below, write down any blessings you can name.

_____

_____

_____

_____

_____

_____

_____

Health

Do you now consider yourself to be a healthy person? As a healthy person (or a person on the road to health), write your responses to the following statements (adapted from Caruso 1986).

I am aware of the trauma or traumas I experienced.

_____

_____

_____

I am aware of the feelings the trauma led to.

_____

_____

_____

I have a sense of my own identity as it is now, after the trauma, and how that identity has changed over time, even as I worked in this workbook.

_____

_____

_____

I know and trust the following feelings that working through the trauma has led me to:

_____

_____

_____

I have communicated about the trauma and my feelings with:

_____

_____

_____

I am empathetic with other victims and sensitive to them. I have showed this to others by:

_____

_____

_____

I recognize that the trauma or traumas impacted me in the following ways and hold myself in high regard because I have survived.

_____

_____

_____

I have kept good boundaries or learned to keep good boundaries in (behaviors, activities):

_____

_____

_____

I am now autonomous and do not need the approval of others to survive (list your specific traumas):

_____

_____

_____

I believe my perception of the traumas and their impacts is reality based upon objective information of:

_____

_____

_____

I am now willing to take the following risks and want to continue to grow:

_____

_____

_____

I am committed to life, and I show this commitment by:

_____

_____

_____

Life has meaning to me; I have hope that:

_____

_____

_____

I advocate for myself by:

_____

_____

_____

Coping with and Solving a Problem

As a trauma survivor, you may be faced with situations where you need to make a decision or solve a problem. In the past, if you felt helpless and out of control, you may not have tried to solve problems or make decisions on your own. Instead, you may have just let things happen around you, or continued to keep a victim role. Solving problems by *doing something*—by taking deliberate action—is a functional way of coping with a situation and eliminating some sources of stress for you. Developing realistic goals for solving a problem can make a crisis more manageable. Tedeschi and Calhoun (1995) describe the functions of coping with a problem as follows:

- a way to work through trauma

- a way to make a crisis manageable

- a way to reverse negative changes

- a way to appraise the degree of threat of a situation

- a way to use spiritual beliefs positively

- a way to learn through the experience of others

- a way to vent emotions

- a way to seek support when you need it

- a way to look at the impact of coping with your schemas

If you are able to cope successfully, you probably have:

- persistence, determination, confidence, flexibility, and tenacity

- the ability to connect emotionally with others

- the ability to accept your limitations when necessary

- an internal locus of control

- the perception you can do what you need to do (self-efficacy)

- optimism

- a problem-focused style

- hardiness (which involves commitments, a belief in your ability to influence life events, and the ability to respond to challenges brought about by the normal changes of life)

EXERCISE: How I Cope

How do you generally cope with a challenging situation, whether or not it involves a crisis? Check which of these apply to you, and give an example of when you use it.

☐ I don't view crises as insurmountable. An example of when I cope this way:

_____

☐ I deal with my feelings. I name them, accept them, and express them. An example of when I cope this way:

_____

☐ I adjust my attitude. An example of how I cope this way:

_____

☐ I make choices using a decision-making plan (like the one described just below). An example of when I cope by problem solving:

_____

☐ I accept my own imperfection and the mistakes I have made (and do make). An example of when I cope this way:

_____

☐ I take action, set goals, and move toward them. An example of when I cope this way:

_____

☐ I use language to build rapport and then translate the language spoken to an action plan. An example of when I cope this way:

_____

☐ I set realistic limits. An example of when I cope this way:

_____

☐ I remain calm and empathize with others. An example of when I cope this way:

_____

☐ I negotiate and compromise. An example of when I cope this way:

_____

☐ I distance myself from a situation without dissociating. An example of when I cope this way:

_____

☐ I seek social support, making contact and connections with others. An example of when I cope this way:

_____

☐ I educate myself and get information. An example of when I cope this way:

_____

☐ I use another method. An example of when I cope this way:

_____

Facing a Difficult Situation

Suppose you are going to go to your cousin's wedding and know that your father, who molested you, will be there. You have told your cousin you do not want to sit next to your father at the wedding. In fact, you really don't even want to go, but you and your cousin are very close emotionally. She does not know about the abuse (yet) and just wouldn't understand if you didn't come. You have not spoken to your father in three years—not since you wrote him a letter of confrontation. He wrote a simple letter back that said, "Let's be a family again." You need to develop a plan about how you'll react when you see him. How can you plan how you will react?

First, you might consider which emotions you think you will have and what you will do as they arise. What triggers will hit you upside your head? What can you do to calm yourself ahead of time? Then you could visualize yourself going to the wedding and then to the reception. Imagine that at the reception you have assigned seats and your father is across the table from you. What would you do? In short, imagine what might happen in the difficult situation and decide what resources you will need to cope with what might happen. This strategy is adapted from McKay and Rogers (2000). It is adaptable to any situation that resembles your prior trauma, when you have unexpected or even expected contact with your perpetrator, or if you have to deal with unsupportive others.

EXERCISE: **Coping with a Difficult Situation**

1. Fill in the blanks using the wedding situation described above.

    The triggers that I will have to deal with: _____

    _____

    I need cues around me to help me to cope. These might include my list of affirmations, a crystal, a stuffed toy, a small angel, or a miniature of my power shield. My cues:

    _____

    _____

    Aspects of timing I need to be able to cope (e.g., some time alone, time to go out of the room and throw things):

    _____

    _____

The coping strategy that will help me best is:

_____

_____

The relaxation strategies I will use to soothe and calm myself:

_____

_____

The self-talk that I can use:

_____

_____

2. Now, think of a problem that you are having or will have and apply the same strategy to yourself.

The situation I am facing: _____

_____

The triggers that I will have to deal with: _____

_____

I need cues around me to help me to cope. These might include my list of affirmations, a crystal, a stuffed toy, a small angel, or a miniature of my power shield. My cues:

_____

_____

Aspects of timing I need to be able to cope (e.g., some time alone, time to go out of the room and throw things):

_____

_____

The coping strategy that will help me best is:

_____

_____

The relaxation strategies I will use to soothe and calm myself:

_____

_____

The self-talk that I can use:

_____

_____

Formulating a Decision-Making Plan

Another strategy for coping with a tough situation is to use the following decision-making plan.

1. Describe the problem:

   - What is the problem situation?

   - What is wrong?

   - Why is it a problem now?

   - Who is responsible for the problem?

   - What circumstances are responsible for the problem?

   - What will happen if the problem is not solved?

   - How likely is it that what you believe will happen will happen? Circle the number that best describes it (1 = not likely; 10 = it will happen): 1   2   3   4   5   6   7   8   9   10

   - When did the problem start? What happened then? Who caused the problem?

   - Might the situation change, and what would it change into? What would happen then?

   - What needs to change if the problem is to be resolved?

- What are you thinking right now? How do you perceive the meaning of the problem?

- What are you feeling? What spontaneous internal physical responses are you aware of having (from the past as well as the present) that can give you information?

- What are you hearing? What sensory data from the present and triggered from the past are coming in? What intuitive sensations are you having?

- What are you doing? What actions are you taking or are you going to take, and what commitment to action are you willing to make?

- What do you want or intend to do? What are your core values now? What do you want to accomplish? What is motivating you to act?

- How does this problem relate to your earlier traumas? If so, which ones? What was the outcome of those traumas?

2. Understand the problem:

   - Have you asked yourself about the problem and why it is a problem?

   - Have you asked yourself what needs to happen?

   - Have you "sat" with the problem (that is, just spent some time with it without trying to resolve it)?

   - Have you considered if you want to avoid the problem? This may or may not be a feasible solution, but it may be an alternative to consider at this time.

3. Make a decision to solve the problem:

   - What five reasonable things could you to do resolve the problem for yourself?

      1. _____

      2. _____

      3. _____

      4. _____

      5. _____

- What are the pros and cons of each? (Use the space below for the first option, and write the pros and cons of the remaining options in your journal or notebook.)

Pros	Cons

Which of the five possible solutions seems to have the most pros for trying it?

4. It is up to you to decide if you will try your chosen strategy to help solve the problem. If you do, you may want to make a contract that

   - formulates a plan of action and sets a reasonable goal

   - considers alternatives, their likely costs, and their possible outcomes

5. Once you have tried your chosen strategy, look at its results. Ask yourself

   - What happened?

   - What about this strategy needs to change?

   - Is there another solution that also might work?

JOURNAL EXERCISE: **My Decision-Making Plan**

In your notebook or journal, you may use the description on the pages just above to formulate your own decision-making plan, use it to solve a problem you are having, and describe the results. Basically, the decision-making plan asks you to

1. State your problem.

2. Gather information.

3. Brainstorm about possible solutions.

4. Evaluate the pros and cons of each.

5. Decide which to use.

6. Do whatever you have decided to do.

Evaluate the strategy you chose and make any needed changes. Another simple problem-solving model developed by Peterson (1968) is to use the following prompts to describe the problem and its possible solutions.

My problem is _____.

The severity of my problem is _____.

The frequency with which the problem occurs is _____.

The problem bothers me because _____.

The last time this problem occurred was _____.

The changes I need to make are _____.

To improve the situation I must _____.

I would like _____ to happen because _____.

I can get help with the problem by _____.

If I decide not to make changes to solve the problem, then the impact will be:

_____

_____

Whatever problem-solving model you choose, remember not to try to solve problems without taking the time to look at a number of possibilities and consider the consequences for each. Making impulsive, radical changes can be unhealthy and can throw you into distress. Any plan will also be easier to follow if it is very specific.

Resilience

As you have done the work in this workbook, you have learned a great deal about yourself, what happened to you, and what can help you heal. One major characteristic of people who heal most is their ability to be resilient. Just what does it mean to be resilient?

Resilience is a dynamic process that emerges in response to aversive life circumstances (Masten and Wright 2010). It is the ability to maintain a mostly stable and healthy level of functioning following exposure to a trauma (Bonanno 2005). It is more than an absence of PTSD; it is a response pattern, with certain factors predisposing people toward resilience, including female gender, younger age, more education, flexibility, and goal-directed coping.

Resilience means having the ability to meet challenges and bounce back during or after difficult experiences. Developing resilience allows you to change the way you look at your suffering and makes it possible for you to seek the positives despite your pain. In essence, resilience means learning how to live well. French psychologist Boris Cyrulnik (2009), a World War II survivor who witnessed the deportation of his parents to a concentration camp, describes how victims of trauma show remarkable resilience. When we have survived the ordeal, life continues, but it is never the same, as one mother said years after her child was murdered.

Resilience differs from person to person. Everyone has some potential for resilience—to live through difficult things and learn from them. Resilience can be enhanced by strengths, skills, and resources from many areas: body, brain, personality, thoughts, feelings, flexibility, creativity, optimism, spirituality, humor, problem-solving skills, social skills, family, friends, values, beliefs, education, work, finances, sports, and more.

Post-traumatic growth refers to positive life changes in personal and social characteristics (social support, philosophy of life, and so on) following highly stressful events (Park 2009). These include developing closer relationships with significant others, becoming more confident and capable of coping with stress, appreciating life more, developing a deeper spiritual perspective, and becoming more compassionate following traumatic events.

EXERCISE: Assessing My Resilience

The following checklist contains numerous characteristics that combine to form resilience. Check off which of them you believe now describe you. The more you check, the more resilient you may be.

- ☐ I have a good self-concept.

- ☐ I have good self-esteem.

- ☐ I am sensitive to others' needs.

- ☐ I am generally cooperative with others.

- ☐ I am socially responsive.

- ☐ I have a good sense of humor.

- ☐ I am able to postpone getting my needs met (I can delay gratification).

- ☐ I am generally flexible.

- ☐ I can control my impulses when I need to do so.

- ☐ I believe in the future and plan for it.

- ☐ I have a good support system.

- ☐ I recognize that I have many opportunities in life available to me.

- ☐ I respect individual human beings.

- ☐ I respect appropriate authority.

- ☐ I am able to look for more than one solution to a problem.

- ☐ I am able to plan ahead.

- ☐ I have hobbies and interests beyond my traumas.

- ☐ I have a positive view of life and see life's joys (as well as its sorrows).

- ☐ I can problem-solve and have a strategy that I use.

- ☐ I have a sense of spirituality.

- ☐ I celebrate myself regularly.

☐ I celebrate others regularly.

☐ I believe that I have some level of control over myself and others.

☐ I would rather take action than wait for something to happen to me.

☐ I am able to find meaning even in bad things.

☐ I am someone others like and love.

☐ I am able to find someone to help me when I need it.

☐ I can ask questions in a creative way.

☐ I have a conscience that allows me to see my own goodness.

☐ I have a "knowing" about things that happen to and around me.

☐ I can disengage and separate from others if they are not good for me.

☐ I can attach to others and connect.

How many of these traits were you able to check? If you find that you still can check only a few, you may want to redo some of the exercises in this book. If you want to build your resilience, you need to monitor and observe how you interact in the world. See just when and how (or if) you use humor. When you are presented with a problem, try to come up with at least two solutions, and then weigh the pros and cons until you can make an appropriate choice between the solutions. You may want to try new hobbies or activities to broaden yourself. You also may want to seek out your spiritual side to a greater degree or become more connected with nature.

Developing a Sense of Humor and Finding the Positive

Have you ever wanted to choke the person who told you to "lighten up" or to "get a sense of humor"? Not so easy when the world seems to be closing in and your stress level is rising. But developing a sense of humor in the face of adversity can be done.

As with any other skill, developing a sense of humor takes some attention and practice. The following suggestions can help you focus on your sense of humor, defining what is amusing to you and deciding how you can use humor to cope. Earn your laugh and smile wrinkles by positive responses! In addition to helping you develop your sense of humor, this section provides suggestions on other ways to increase positive experiences.

KNOW WHAT MAKES YOU LAUGH

You may have lost touch with your playful side. Research has shown children laugh on average four hundred times a day, but adults laugh only a few times.

Think about the things that make you smile (e.g., TV comedies, the comics, jokes, morning coffee, a sunny day, etc.) and list them here:

_____

_____

_____

KNOW PEOPLE WHO CAN MAKE YOU LAUGH

Do people in your life fill you with joy or are they real downers? Which people are the negative influences in your life and which are the positive? List these people here (use extra paper if you need to):

Positive People	Negative People

Are you spending too much time with people who drain your energy? Are you letting others help you, or are you carrying the weight of the world on your shoulders? Look at your list of positive people and think of ways to develop these relationships. Spend more time with the people who add to your life and decrease the time with people who leave you feeling used up.

USE JOKES AND COLLECT THEM IN A HUMOR LOG

It doesn't matter if you are not a good joke-teller. It only matters if *you* find a joke to be funny. Jokes, anecdotes, and funny quotes are everywhere. Radio, TV, the Internet, and printed media are full of them. Bookstores have entire sections on comedy, so get out of the self-help section and find what's funny to you. Write down jokes or amusing stories in a humor notebook. You might even want to paste in your favorite fortune cookie predictions.

LAUGH AT LIFE

Never miss an opportunity to enjoy yourself. Remember the "someday we will laugh about this" philosophy and use it immediately. Look for the ironic, the ridiculous, and the absurd in situations that trigger you or lead to feelings of anxiety. Once you see things as not so awful, you can overcome them.

LAUGH AT YOURSELF

We all make mistakes. When you make a mistake, having the ability to laugh at yourself is as important as being able to laugh at life. This does not mean you need to be critical of yourself, but rather to see yourself in a more forgiving light, recognizing your humanness.

NEVER MISS AN OPPORTUNITY TO PLAY

Be spontaneous. Take a moment to read your humor log, tap along to your favorite song (or be really daring and sing), make love with your spouse or partner, call or write to a positive person on your list, or have ice cream or frozen tofu—especially if you just had a particularly difficult day.

SCHEDULE FUN TIME

Your fun time is just as important as your work schedule. Look at your calendar and make appointments with yourself and your positive people. Mark off your vacation time or plan days off in advance, so you don't book other appointments in those slots. Write all of your fun time activities in your calendar using bright gel pens, not in the blue or black you use to write in your business appointments and other obligations. When you look back over the previous month, are there several fun activities? Did you keep all of your fun appointments or did you skip them? Reevaluate what you scheduled and decide if you need to start simpler or change priorities. Fun time does not have to be long. Surely you can find time to take the kids to the park, go for a walk along a scenic trail, read a book, take a cooking class, see a movie, or just dance!

CELEBRATE SUCCESSES BIG AND SMALL

When was the last time you said "ta-da!" after you completed a goal? When life is stressful, even small accomplishments become big ones. Create a reward system for yourself. Don't wait for someone else to reward your good work or accomplishments; reward yourself. Sometimes just making it through a difficult day is reason enough. Set realistic goals and work toward them. Break the goal down into steps, so you can see your successes and celebrate each one. Use the following planning sheet as a guide.

EXERCISE: **Goal Planning Sheet**

Goal: _____

Planned completion date: _____

Step completed	Reward	Date

TREAT YOURSELF

If you enjoy it, do it! Use your fun time schedule to add enjoyable activities and people to your life. You may tend to feel guilty or self-indulgent when you celebrate yourself. But ultimately, you will be a better person if you treat yourself with care and compassion. Don't be afraid to have lunch with a friend after a promotion, soak in a tub after step aerobics, or stop for ice cream after completing a major report.

DON'T WAIT TO BE HAPPY; DO IT NOW!

This is part of celebrating life's successes. The sooner you say "ta-da," the better you will feel. If you bargain with yourself over your reward, you diminish your achievement. If you want to buy a new dress, don't tell yourself you will do it after you lose weight. Buy it in the size that fits and wear it as soon as you can.

SMILE, SMILE, SMILE

Seems simple enough, right? Yet you may not always practice this behavior. When tension builds, humans have a tendency to stiffen facial and other muscles and clench their jaws; tension then results in headaches and other ailments. Loosen up your tensed muscles by taking deep breaths and then smiling. It helps to use a mirror so you can see how you look as you become more relaxed. When talking to other people, smile at them. You will notice that they too will start smiling. This helps prevent or reduce discomfort during difficult discussions.

Practice all these activities over the next week or two. Then return to this page of the workbook and write down how your efforts have made you feel and how they have impacted your relationships with others.

How has working on your sense of humor felt? What changes has it made in your relationship?

More About Being Resilient

Amanda Lindhout, a freelance foreign correspondent and survivor of a violent childhood at the hands of an abusive stepfather, was in Somalia in 2008 (Brown 2015), and was kidnapped and held captive for more than a year. She spoke to the International Society for Traumatic Stress Studies in November 2013. She noted at that meeting that, in order to survive, she had to "learn to crawl out of this dark space" in her mind. Ms. Lindhout is an example of a resilient individual, bouncing back to some degree after what she endured; however, she has not escaped unscathed. She has found that telling her story is empowering. Researchers now are looking at whether or not there are biological brain markers or histories of various types of trauma, which may or may not show that some early hardship may actually prepare an individual for later experiences. However, biology does not appear to be the only factor leading to the presence or absence of resilience. In other words, it seems that "a genetic predisposition for resilience…only develops in a nurturing environment"(Brown 2015). The new field of epigenetics examines how genes can get turned on and off due to experience or environment. Researchers now, in this area as well as in others previously mentioned in this workbook, are seeing advantages to practices of mindfulness, yoga, and meditation. It appears that resilience may be a more normal response to a traumatic event than PTSD.

Looking at the Purpose of Your Life

Do you now have a purpose in life? Bourne defines life purpose as "something you need to do in order to feel whole, complete, and fulfilled in your life…that expresses a particular talent, gift, skill, or desire that you hold most dear…something that reaches beyond the limited needs and concerns of your own ego [and is] 'other-directed'…an important activity or service you could have come into this world to accomplish" (2001, 246).

EXERCISE: My Life Purpose

If you are sure of your life purpose, then write it here:

_____

_____

_____

If you are not sure, respond to the following questions and see where your answers lead you.

_____

_____

_____

How do you feel about the work you are doing? Is it fulfilling?

_____

_____

_____

Do you want to continue your education and, if so, in what area or areas?

_____

_____

_____

Do you have hobbies or interests you want to learn or follow? If so, what are they?

_____

_____

_____

If you were to write a motto for your life right now, what would it be? The motto of my life:

_____

_____

_____

If you could accomplish anything in your life, what would you hope to accomplish within the next year?

_____

_____

_____

The next five years?

_____

_____

_____

The next ten years?

_____

_____

_____

What values are most important to you and give you the most meaning? Do you value wealth? Material possessions? Good health? Close relationships? Family? Friends? Closeness with a Supreme Being?

_____

_____

_____

If you were to make a commitment to change one thing in your life that would make it easier for you to achieve your life purpose, what would it be?

_____

_____

_____

As Bourne (2001) notes, it is important to counter negative belief systems that might interfere with your trying to reach your dreams and goals. If you truly are on a path to achieve your life purpose, it is important to stick to the task and look for opportunities to achieve it whenever possible.

What are your reactions to completing this exercise?

_____

_____

JOURNAL EXERCISE: Drawings of Myself and My Life

Earlier in this book (chapter 1), you did the journal exercise "Drawings of Myself and My Life," in which you made a series of five drawings representing yourself and your life. Now that you have completed the exercises in this workbook, redo those drawings and see if your view of yourself and your world changed.

Psychological Wellness

The goal of working in this workbook has been to help you build psychological wellness. If you are psychologically well, you are able to maintain a healthy lifestyle that has balance in its physical (fitness, nutrition), social (relationships, support systems), emotional (self-worth, hardiness), vocational and educational (productivity), and spiritual (purpose, meaning, ethics, values) aspects.

In which of the five areas do you feel balanced? Unbalanced? Why?

_____

_____

_____

_____

How comfortable are you with yourself and your life?

_____

Do you like your present standard of living? _____

Do you like your home? _____

Do you like the pace of your life? _____

Are you satisfied with your employment? Your education?

_____

Are you clear with yourself as to who you are and what you are? _____

Do you have an inner sense of purpose for your life? _____

Do you keep the balance in all five areas of your life that we listed above?

_____

How do you balance between private and social time? Between personal and professional time? Between exercise and relaxation?

_____

_____

_____

Resourcefulness

A healthy person has learned to be resourceful and has a sense of coherence. Antonovsky (1987) defined *coherence* as personal beliefs that life (including stressor situations) is comprehensible, manageable, and meaningful, as well as structured and predictable. You know that bad things happen. In all likelihood, the rest of your life will not be trauma-free. However, the way you approach traumatic experiences may be changed by the work you have done in this workbook. You now may be able to approach new stressors and potential traumas (unless they are so incredibly overwhelming that there is no way to make sense of them) as challenges for which meaning is to be sought. If this is the case, you will be willing to invest your energy to work through those experiences, even if your energy is depleted. If so, hopefully you will be able to maintain some sense of balance, use action-oriented coping skills, realistically adapt the way you approach or avoid the new situation, and thrive as you become stronger than before.

Dunning (1997) has developed a list of thirteen characteristics that she calls the "Thirteen Cs of Salutogenesis." *Salutogenesis* means learned resourcefulness, or the ability to use stressful situations for self-direction and growth. This wellness model focuses on retaining control, even through traumatic events, and finding the benefits and meaning in what has happened to you. How many of these characteristics are you able to apply in stressful situations?

1. **Control:** a sense of autonomy and an ability to influence what happens around you in your environment

2. **Cohesion:** connecting or belonging with concerned others who care about you, your feelings, and your experiences

3. **Communication:** expressing positive self-discovery and growth with others through words and writings

4. **Challenge:** using stressor events as opportunities for growth and development and seeing hardships as something to overcome or change in some way (however small)

5. **Commitment:** remaining active in the pursuit of meaning

6. **Connection:** forming a bond of trust with others to help healing

7. **Clarification:** accepting that the event and its reasons for occurring go beyond your influence while still looking at what you can change or control

8. **Coherence:** making your trauma story logical and consistent with your past, present, and future

9. **Congruence:** seeing the event through the eyes of others; looking at external forces; accepting that every trauma you (or others) have experienced can lead to feelings of self-blame, responsibility, and failure; and doing the appropriate exercises to combat these feelings

353

10. **Commemoration:** developing ritualistic closures to events in order to memorialize them and to put them in the context of history

11. **Comfort or consolation:** developing feelings of relief and encouragement while accepting how things have changed

12. **Culture:** understanding how your cultural context and history impact your healing

13. **Closure:** achieving a sense that the traumatic event has truly ended, even though you will probably never be the same; understanding the differences between yourself now and yourself before the traumatic event

Are you a salutogenic person? Which of the Cs apply to you?

_____

_____

_____

In spite of it all, no matter how hard you work to deal with your trauma-based memories or how much you try to avoid the traumas that have befallen you, you remain a human being who has been through traumatic events. If you are fortunate enough to be someone who has walked through trauma toward healing and thrived or who has become an educator to help others on their healing paths, you have possibly found meaning in your life and have new goals.

EXERCISE: My Healing Alphabet

Take a few moments to develop your own healing alphabet based on all the work you have done. This exercise asks you to take each letter of the alphabet and come up with one to three words that describe you and your healing. For example:

A. accountability, achievement, anxiety

B. balanced, burned-out

C. compassionate, caring

D. dignified

...and so on.

A. _____

B. _____

C. _____

D. _____

E. _____

F. _____

G. _____

H. _____

I. _____

J. _____

K. _____

L. _____

M. _____

N. _____

O. _____

P. _____

Q. _____

R. _____

S. _____

T. _____

U. _____

V. _____

W. _____

X. _____

Y. _____

Z. _____

What do you see in the words you have chosen? Are there patterns to how you have healed?

_____

_____

_____

We want to thank you for making the commitment to heal and for doing all the hard work you have done in this workbook. Please remember that you can turn back to any of the exercises in this workbook at any time for a refresher.

To conclude, keep the following rules for being human in mind (Carter-Scott 1998):

1. You will receive a body. You may like it or hate it, but it is yours for the entire period of time you are here.

2. You will learn lessons. You are now enrolled in the full-time informal school called "life." Each school day will give you opportunities to learn lessons. You may like the lessons you have to learn or you may believe that your lessons don't really fit you and are stupid.

3. You will make no mistakes; rather, you will learn through your lessons. You will experiment and do trial-and-error learning. Some (if not much) of what you do will end in failure; this is part of the process called life.

4. Your lessons will repeat themselves until you learn them. Each lesson you are to learn will be presented to you (or will present itself to you) in various forms until you learn it.

5. As long as you are alive, you will have lessons to learn.

6. "There" is no better than "here." There is no geographical cure. If you move, your "there" will become a "here" and you will look for a new place to go.

7. What you love or hate in another person often is a mirror of you. When you love or hate something about another person, it reflects something you love or hate about yourself.

8. What you make of your life is up to you. You have the tools and resources, skills and information; how you use them depends on the choices you make. Remember, the choice is yours—to succeed, fight, or give up.

9. Your answers to your life's questions lie inside you. Look, listen, trust your own internal self and intuition to tell them to you.

10. You probably will forget these rules as you live life.

11. You can come back to these rules whenever you need or want to do so. Remember, *it can be done.*

Please keep in mind that healing requires time, effort, and commitment. If you are authentic in your healing journey, although some PTSD symptoms may never go away totally, your life's path will be more manageable. Just remember, as Reverend John Calvin Little, Mary Beth's father, ended every card, letter, and note to her, "It Can Be Done."

References

Adams, E. 1994. *Understanding the Trauma of Childhood Psycho-Sexual Abuse*. Bedford, MA: Mills & Sanderson.

Alderman, T. 1997. *The Scarred Soul: Understanding and Ending Self-Inflicted Violence*. Oakland, CA: New Harbinger Publications.

————. 2000. Helping those who hurt themselves. *Prevention Researcher* 7(4):5–8.

Amen, D. G. 2010. A well-seasoned mind: New scientific research shows these five spices are good for your brain. *AARP Magazine*, May/June, 18.

American Autoimmune Related Diseases Association. 2012. List of autoimmune and autoimmune-related diseases. www.aarda.org/research_display.php?ID=47. Accessed August 12, 2012.

American Hospital Association. 2011. More hospitals offering complementary and alternative medicine services. Press release, September 7. http://www.aha.org/press-center/2011?p=4.

American Psychiatric Association. 2013. *Diagnostic and Statistical Manual of Mental Disorders (DSM-5)*. 5th ed. Washington, DC: American Psychiatric Association.

Americans with Disabilities Act. 2010. *Title II Regulations Supplementary Information. 28 CFR Part 35*.

Antonovsky, A. 1987. *Unraveling the Mystery of Health: How People Manage Stress and Stay Well*. San Francisco: Jossey-Bass.

Astin, J. A. 1998. Why patients use alternative medicine: Results of a national study. *JAMA* 279: 1548–1553.

Astin, M. C., and B. Rothbaum. 2000. Exposure therapy for the treatment of post-traumatic stress disorder. *Clinical Quarterly* 9(4): 50, 52, 55.

Ayalon, O. 1992. *Rescue: Helping Children Cope with Stress*. Ellicott City, MD: Chevron Publishing.

Ayalon, O., and A. Flasher. 1993. *Chain Reaction*. London: Jessica Kingsley Publishers.

Baker, G. R., and M. Salston. 1993. *Management of Intrusion and Arousal Symptoms in PTSD*. San Diego, CA: Association for Traumatic Stress Specialists (International Association for Trauma Counselors).

Baker, W. B. 2004. *Healing Power of Horses: Lessons from the Lakota Indians*. Irvine, CA: BowTie Press.

Bandler, R. 1985. *Using Your Brain—for a Change*. Moab, UT: Real People Press.

Barnes, P. M., B. Bloom, and R. L. Nahin. 2008. Complementary and alternative medicine use among adults and children: United States, 2007. National Health Statistics Reports No. 12. http://www.cdc.gov/nchs /data/nhsr/nhsr012.pdf.

Barry, P. 2011. Prescription drug side effects: Medications can cause other conditions unrelated to the health problems they're prescribed to treat. *AARP Bulletin*, September 1, 14–16.

Beck, C. E., F. Gonzales, C. H. Sells, C. Jones, T. Reer, and Y. Y. Zhu. 2012. The effects of animal-assisted therapy on wounded warriors in an occupational therapy life skills program. *US Army Medical Department Journal*, April/June, 38–45.

Begley, S. 2011. No! The one word that can save your life. *Newsweek*, August 22 (29) 30–35.

Benson, H. 1975. *The Relaxation Response*. New York: William Morrow.

———. 1984. *Beyond the Relaxation Response*. New York: Berkeley Press.

Bills, C., N. Dodson, J. M. Stellman, S. Southwick, V. Sharma, R. Herbert, J. M. Moline, and C. L. Katz. 2009. Stories behind the symptoms: A qualitative analysis of the narratives of 9/11 rescue and recovery workers. *Psychiatric Quarterly* 80(3):173–189.

Bloom, S. 2000. Personal interview using trauma center protocol for the Sanctuary Program. In *Creating a Comprehensive Trauma Center: Choices and Challenges*, edited by M. B. Williams and L. A. Nurmi. New York: Plenum Publishing.

Bonanno, G. A. 2005. Clarifying and extending the construct of adult resilience. *American Psychologist* 60 (3): 265–267.

Boon, S., K. Steele, and O. Van der Hart. 2011. *Coping with Trauma-Related Dissociation: Skills Training for Patients and Therapists*. New York: W. W. Norton and Company.

Bourne, E. 2001. *Beyond Anxiety and Phobia: A Step-by-Step Guide to Lifetime Recovery*. Oakland, CA: New Harbinger Publications.

Bowthorpe, J. ed. 2014. *Stop the Thyroid Madness II: How Thyroid Experts Are Challenging Ineffective Treatments and Improving the Lives of Patients*. Dolores, CO: Laughing Grape Press.

Branscomb, L. 1990. *Becoming Whole: Dissociation and Me*. Decatur, GA: Lodestar Productions.

Breslau, N. 2012. Epidemiology of posttraumatic stress disorder in adults. In *The Oxford Handbook of Traumatic Stress Disorders*, edited by J. G. Beck and D. M. Sloan. New York: Oxford Press.

Briere, J. N., and C. Scott. 2015. *Principles of Trauma Therapy: A Guide to Symptoms, Evaluation, and Treatment*. 2nd ed. Los Angeles: Sage Publications.

Brittain, J. C. 2001. *Keepsake Stories*. Washougal, WA: Beyond the Bounds.

Brookman, M. 2001. *Simple Steps to Getting What You Want: A Process for Reuniting with Yourself*. Phoenix, AZ: Wallingford Publishing Company.

Brown, K. 2015. What makes a resilient mind. NOVA Next. PBS. http://www.pbs.org/wgbh/nova/next/body /mental-resilience/.

Bruhn, A. R. 1990. Cognitive-perceptual theory and the projective use of autobiographical memory. *Journal of Personality Assessment* 55(1–2):95–114.

Brussat, F., and M. A. Brussat. 2000. *Spiritual Rx: Prescriptions for Living a Meaningful Life*. New York: Hyperion.

Bunyan, J. 1965. *The Pilgrim's Progress*. Harmondsworth, UK: Penguin Books.

Burns, C.C. 1989. *The Feeling Good Handbook: Using the New Mood Therapy in Everyday Life*. New York: William Morrow.

Busuttil, W. 2002. The development of a 90-day residential program for the treatment of complex PTSD. In *Simple and Complex Post-traumatic Stress Disorder: Strategies for Comprehensive Treatment in Clinical Practice*, edited by M. B. Williams and J. F. Sommer. Binghamton, NY: Haworth Press.

Cantrell, B. C. 2009. *Souls Under Siege: The Effects of Multiple Troop Deployments and How to Weather the Storm*. Bellingham, WA: Hearts Toward Home International.

Capacchione, L. 2001. *Living with Feeling: The Art of Emotional Expression*. New York: Penguin Putnam.

Capps, R. 2013. Writing by service members and veterans: A medium to promote healing in self and others. In *Healing War Trauma: A Handbook of Creative Approaches*, edited by R. M. Scurfield and K. T. Platoni. New York: Routledge.

Carter-Scott, C. 1998. *If Life Is a Game, These Are the Rules: Ten Rules for Being Human As Introduced in Chicken Soup for the Soul*. New York: Broadway Books.

Caruso, B. 1986. *Healing: A Handbook for Adult Victims of Child Sexual Abuse*. St. Louis Park, MO: Beverly Caruso.

Catherall, D. 1992. *Back from the Brink: A Family Guide to Overcoming Traumatic Stress*. New York: Bantam.

Chadsey, J. 2014. How to keep from stressing over. A sermon delivered at the United Methodist Church in Warrenton, Virginia, November 16.

Chadsey, J., and J. Kim. 2014. Happiness can be learned through Christ. The habits of happiness, part 5. A sermon delivered at the United Methodist Church in Warrenton, Virginia, October 26.

Ciarrochi, J., and A. Bailey. 2008. *A CBT Practitioner's Guide to ACT: How to Bridge the Gap Between Cognitive Behavioral Therapy and Acceptance and Commitment Therapy*. Oakland, CA: New Harbinger Publications.

Cohen, B. M., M. Barnes, and A. B. Rankin. 1995. *Managing Traumatic Stress Through Art: Drawing from the Center*. Lutherville, MD: Sidran Press.

Cohen, M. J. 1977. *Reconnecting with Nature*. Corvallis, OR: Ecopress.

Cole, P. M., and F. W. Putnam. 1992. Effect of incest on self and social functioning: A developmental psycho-pathology perspective. *Journal of Consulting and Clinical Psychology* 60(2):174–184.

Colin, C. 2012. How dogs can help veterans overcome PTSD. *Smithsonian*, July–August. http://www.smithsonianmag.com/science-nature/How-Dogs-Can-Help-Veterans-Overcome-PTSD-160281185.html.

Collings, M. 2010. Reasons not to kill yourself. Available at http://www.ptsdafterchildbirth.blogspot.com/2010/11/reasons-not-to-kill-yourself-by-mari.html.

Comarow, A. 2008. Top hospitals embrace alternative medicine. *US News and World Report*, January 9. http://health.usnews.com/health-news/managing-your-healthcare/pain/articles/2008/01/09/embracing-alternative-care.

Conway, M. A., and C. W. Pleydell-Pearce. 2000. The construction of autobiographical memories in the self-memory system. *Psychological Review* 107(2):261–288.

Cooper, R. K. 2001. *The Other 90%: How to Unlock Your Vast Untapped Potential for Leadership and Life.* New York: Three Rivers Press.

Courtois, C. A. 1988. *Healing the Incest Wound: Adult Survivors in Trauma.* New York: W. W. Norton.

Covey, S. 1999. *The 7 Habits of Highly Effective People.* New York: Simon and Schuster.

Curro, E. 1987. Assessing the physiological and clinical characteristics of acute versus chronic pain. Introduction. *Dental Clinics of North America* 31(4):xiii–xxiii.

Cyrulnik, B. 2009. *Resilience: How Your Inner Strength Can Set You Free from the Past.* New York: Penguin.

Daniels, L. R. 2013. War-related traumatic nightmares as a call to action. In *Healing War Trauma: A Handbook of Creative Approaches,* edited by R. M. Scurfield and K. T. Platoni. New York: Routledge.

Daniels, L. R., and T. L. McGuire. 1998. Dreamcatchers: Healing traumatic nightmares using group dreamwork, sandplay, and other techniques of intervention. *Group* 22(4):205–227.

Davis, M., E. R. Eshelman, and M. McKay. 1995. *The Relaxation and Stress Reduction Workbook,* 4th ed. Oakland, CA: New Harbinger Publications.

DeAngelis, T. 2013. When the conflict comes home. *Monitor on Psychology* 44 (11): 62.

De la Monte, S. M., and J. R. Wands. 2008. Alzheimer's disease is type 3 diabetes–Evidence reviewed. *Journal of Diabetes Science and Technology* 2(6):1101–1113.

DeNicola, M. 2014. Nine common traits of happy people (that they don't talk about). *Collective Evolution,* June 28. http://www.collective-evolution.com/2014/06/28/8-common-traits-of-happy-people-that-they-dont-talk-about.

DiGrande, L., Y. Neria, R. M. Brackbill, P. Pulliam, and S. Galea. 2010. Long-term posttraumatic stress symptoms among 3,271 civilian survivors of the September 11, 2001, terrorist attacks on the World Trade Center. *American Journal of Epidemiology* 173(3):271–81.

Dolan, Y. 1991. *Resolving Sexual Abuse: Solution-Focused Therapy and Ericksonian Hypnosis for Adult Survivors.* New York: W. W. Norton.

Dunning, C. 1997. *The 13 Cs of Salutogenesis.* Tuscaloosa, AL: Traumatology Certification Training Program, University of Alabama.

Edwards, L., A. Heyman, and S. Swidan. 2011. Hypocortisolism: An evidence-based review. *Integrative Medicine: A Clinician's Journal* 10(4):30.

Ehlers, A., and D. M. Clark 2000. A cognitive model of posttraumatic stress disorder. *Behaviour Research and Therapy* 38 (4):319–345.

Eisenberg, D. M., R. C. Kessler, C. Foster, F. E. Norlock, D. R. Calkins, and T. L. Delbanco. 1993. Unconventional medicine in the United States. *New England Journal of Medicine* 328(4):246–252.

Ellis, A. 2001. *Feeling Better, Getting Better, Staying Better: Profound Self-Help Therapy for Your Emotions.* Atascadero, CA: Impact Publishers.

Engel, B. 1995. *Raising Your Sexual Self-Esteem.* New York: Fawcett Columbine.

Enright, R. D., and R. P. Fitzgibbons. 2000. *Helping Clients Forgive: An Empirical Guide for Resolving Anger and Restoring Hope.* Washington, DC: American Psychological Association.

Epstein, L. J. 2010. The surprising toll of sleep deprivation. *Newsweek*, June 28 and July 5, 75.

Fennell, P. A. 2001. *The Chronic Illness Workbook: Strategies and Solutions for Taking Back Your Life.* Oakland, CA: New Harbinger Publications.

Figley, C. R. 1989. *Helping Traumatized Families.* San Francisco: Jossey-Bass.

———. 1995. *Compassion Fatigue: Coping with Secondary Traumatic Stress Disorder in Those Who Treat the Traumatized.* New York: Brunner Mazel.

Figley, C. R., B. E. Bride, and N. Mazza, eds. 1997. *Death and Trauma: The Traumatology of Grieving.* Washington, DC: Taylor and Francis.

Friedman, M. J. 2000. *Post-traumatic Stress Disorder: The Latest Assessment and Treatment Strategies.* Kansas City, MO: Compact Clinicals.

Friedman, M. J., P. P. Schnurr, and A. McDonagh-Coyle. 1994. Post-traumatic stress disorder in the military veteran. *Psychiatric Clinics of North America* 17(2):265–277.

Gatchel, R. J., and D. C. Turk. 1996. *Psychological Approaches to Pain Management.* New York: Guilford Press.

Gershon, M. D. 1998. *The Second Brain: The Scientific Basis of Gut Instinct and a Groundbreaking Understanding of Nervous Disorders of the Stomach and Intestine.* New York: HarperCollins.

Gooneratne, N. 2008. Complementary and alternative medicine for sleep disturbances in older adults. *Clinics in Geriatric Medicine* 24(1):121–138.

Grand, L. C. 2000. *The Life Skills Presentation Guide.* New York: John Wiley and Sons.

Grant, M. 1997. *Pain Control with Eye Movement Desensitization and Reprocessing.* Wyong, New South Wales, Australia: Wyong Medical Centre.

Grossman, D. A. 1996. *On Killing: The Psychological Cost of Learning to Kill in War and Society.* New York: Little, Brown.

Hayes, S. C., D. Barnes-Holmes, and B. Roche, eds. 2001. *Relational Frame Theory: A Post-Skinnerian Account of Human Language and Cognition.* New York: Plenum Press.

Headquarters, Department of the Army. 2002. *Survival (FM 3–05.70).* Washington, DC: Department of the Army.

———. 2012. *Army 2020: Generating Health and Discipline in the Force Ahead of the Strategic Reset.* Washington, DC: Department of the Army.

Herman, J. L. 1992. *Trauma and Recovery.* New York: Basic Books.

Hoge, C. W. 2010. *Once a Warrior Always a Warrior: Navigating the Transition from Combat to Home.* Guilford, CT: Global Request Press.

Hölzel, B. K., J. Carmody, M. Vangel, C. Congleton, S. M. Yerramsetti, T. Gard, and S. W. Lazar. 2011. Mindfulness practice leads to increases in regional brain gray matter density. *Psychiatry Research*, 191(1): 36–43.

Ilardo, J. 1992. *Risk-Taking for Personal Growth: A Step-by-Step Workbook.* Oakland, CA: New Harbinger Publications.

Janoff-Bulman, R. 1992. *Shattered Assumptions: Towards a New Psychology of Trauma.* New York: Free Press.

Johnson, P. J., A. Ward, L. Knutson, and S. Sendelbach. 2012. Personal use of complementary and alternative medicine (CAM) by US health care workers. *Health Services Research* 47(1 Pt. 1):211–227.

Kabat-Zinn, J. 1994. *Wherever You Go, There You Are: Mindfulness Meditation in Everyday Life.* New York: Hyperion.

Kalantari, M., W. Yule, A. Dyregrov, H. Neshatdoost, and S. J. Ahmadi. 2012. Efficacy of writing for recovery on traumatic grief symptoms of Afghani refugee bereaved adolescents: A randomized control trial. *Omega* 65(2):139–150.

Kearney, D. J., C. McManus, C. A. Malte, M. Martinez, B. Fellemah, and T. L. Simpson. 2014. Loving-kindness meditation and broaden-and-build theory of positive emotions among veterans with post-traumatic stress disorder. *Medical Care* 52(12 Suppl 5):S32–38.

Knisely, J. S., S. B. Barker, and R. T. Barker. 2012. Research on benefits of canine-assisted therapy for adults in nonmilitary settings. *U.S. Army Medical Department Journal*, April–June, 30–37.

Kobasa, S. C. 1982. The hardy personality: Toward a social psychology of stress and health. In *Social Psychology of Health and Illness*, edited by J. Suls and G. Sanders. Hillsdale, NJ: Lawrence Erlbaum Associates.

Kohanov, L. 2003. Riding between the worlds: Expanding our potential through the way of the horse. Novato, CA: New World Library.

———. 2013. The messages behind emotions. Handout for Epona Workshops.

Krause, B. 2009. Seven essentials to a voc rehab win—part three. *Today in the Military.* November 12. http://www.military.com/opinion/0,15202,205644,00.html.

Kushner, H. S. 1981. *When Bad Things Happen to Good People.* New York: Avon.

Lang, P., J. 1979. A bio-informational theory of emotional imagery. *Psychophysiology* 16(6): 495–512.

Lavalle, J., and A. Heyman. 2013. Vitamins and minerals reference chart. IHR. http://www.metaboliccode.com.

Lavalle, J., and E. Hawkins. 2013a. Nutraceutical and nutrient reference chart. IHR. http://www.metaboliccode.com.

———. 2013b. Herbal supplements reference chart. IHR. http://metaboliccode.com.

LeDoux, J. 1997. Emotion, memory, and pain. *Pain Forum* 6(1): 36–37.

Leeds, J. 2010. *The Power of Sound: How to Be Healthy and Productive Using Music and Sound.* Rochester, VT: Healing Arts Press.

Leehan, J., and L. P. Wilson. 1985. *Grown-up Abused Children.* Springfield, IL: Charles C. Thomas.

Levine, J. 1997. Controlled trials of inositol in psychiatry. *European Neuropsychopharmacology* 7(2):147–155.

Levine, P. 1992. *The Body As Healer: Transforming Trauma and Anxiety.* Lyons, CO: P. Levine.

Levitin, D. J. 2006. *This Is Your Brain on Music: The Science of a Human Obsession.* New York: Dutton.

Lichtenthal, W. G., and D. G. Cruess. 2010. Effects of directed written disclosure on grief and distress symptoms among bereaved individuals. *Death Studies* 34(6):475–499.

Lighthall, A. 2012. Ten things you should know to help bring the OIF/OEF veteran all the way home. http://www.veteransheartgeorgia.org/ten-things-you-should-know-to-help-bring-the-oifoef-veteran-all-the-way-home/

Louden, J. 1997. *The Woman's Retreat Book: A Guide to Restoring, Rediscovering, and Reawakening Your True Self—in a Moment, an Hour, a Day, or a Weekend.* New York: HarperCollins.

Loue, S. 2008. *The Transformative Power of Metaphor in Therapy.* New York: Springer.

Marlantes, K. 2011. *What It Is Like to Go to War.* New York: Atlantic Monthly Press.

Masten, A. S., and M. O. Wright. 2010. Resilience over the lifespan: Developmental perspectives on resistance, recovery, and transformation. In *Handbook of Adult Resilience: Concepts, Methods, and Applications*, edited by J. W. Reich, A. J. Zautra, and J. S. Hall. New York: John Wiley.

Masterson, J. 1988. *The Search for the Real Self: Unmasking the Personality Disorders of Our Age.* New York: Free Press.

Matsakis, A. 1994a. *Post-traumatic Stress Disorder: A Clinician's Guide.* Oakland, CA: New Harbinger Publications.

———. 1994b. *Post-traumatic Stress Disorder: A Complete Treatment Guide.* Oakland, CA: New Harbinger Publications.

———. 1998. *Trust After Trauma: A Guide to Relationships for Survivors and Those Who Love Them.* Oakland, CA: New Harbinger Publications.

———. 1999. *Survivor Guilt: A Self-Help Guide.* Oakland, CA: New Harbinger Publications.

Mayer, E. A. 2000. The neurobiology of stress and gastrointestinal disease. *Gut* 47(6):861–869.

Mayo Clinic. 2015. Tai chi: A gentle way to fight stress. Foundation for Medical Education and Research. http://www.mayoclinic.org/healthy-living/stress-management/in-depth/tai-chi/art-20045184?pg-2.

McCann, I. L., and L. A. Pearlman. 1990. *Psychological Trauma and the Adult Survivor: Theory, Therapy, and Transformation.* New York: Brunner/Mazel.

———. 1992. Constructivist self-development theory: A theoretical framework for assessing and treating traumatized college students. *Journal of American College Health* 40(4):189–196.

McEwen, B. S. 1998. Protective and damaging effects of stress mediators. *New England Journal of Medicine* 338 (3):171–179.

McCrae, R. R. 1992. The five-factor model: Issues and applications. *Journal of Personality* 60(2):175–215.

McGraw, G. R. 2008. *Spirit of the Rising Hawk: How to Soar Through Life with Power, Purpose, Perspective, and Peace.* Culpeper, VA: Rising Hawk Foundation.

———. 2012a. God is sound. March 22, 2012, blog post on *The Fortress of Potential: Discovering the Power, Mystery, and Expansiveness of Life.* http://risinghawk.wordpress.com/2012/03/22/god-is-sound.

———. 2012b. God is sound, part 2. March 23, 2012, blog post on *The Fortress of Potential: Discovering the Power, Mystery, and Expansiveness of Life.* http://risinghawk.wordpress.com/2012/03/23/god-is-sound-part-ii.

McKay, M., and P. Rogers. 2000. *The Anger Control Workbook*. Oakland, CA: New Harbinger Publications.

McLaren, K. 2001. *Emotional Genius: Discovering the Deepest Language of the Soul*. Columbia, CA: Laughing Tree Press.

Meagher, I. 2007. *Moving a Nation to Care: Post-Traumatic Stress Disorder and America's Returning Troops*. Brooklyn, NY: Ig Publishing

Meichenbaum, D. 1994. *A Clinical Handbook/Practical Therapist Manual for Assessing and Treating Adults with Post-traumatic Stress Disorder*. Waterloo, Ontario, Canada: Institute Press.

Metropolitan Washington Council of Governments Health Care Coalition. 2001. Getting a good night's sleep. *Total Wellness: Becoming a Total Person* 9(4):1.

Michelon, P. 2012. *Max Your Memory: The Complete Visual Program*. London: Earling Kindersley.

Miller, S., D. Wackman, E. Nunnally, and P. Miller. 1989. *Connecting Skills Workbook*. Littleton, CO: Interpersonal Communication Programs.

Mills, J. T., and A. F. Yeager. 2012. Definitions of animals used in healthcare settings. *US Army Medical Department Journal*, April–June, 12–17.

Mizuki, C. 2013. Mindful Awareness practice to foster physical, emotional, and mental healing in service members and veterans. In *Healing War Trauma: A Handbook of Creative Approaches*, edited by R. M. Scurfield and K. T. Platoni. New York: Routledge.

Moore, A., and P. Malinowski. 2009. Meditation, mindfulness, and cognitive flexibility. *Consciousness and Cognition* 18(1):176–186.

Mundahl, P., D. Parks, D. Gray, and J. Fields. 1995. *The Women's Specialized Program Patient Workbook*. Brattleboro, VT: Brattleboro Retreat.

Muss, D. 1991. *The Trauma Trap*. London: Doubleday.

National Center for Complementary and Alternative Medicine (NCCAM). 2008. What is CAM? NCCAM Publication No. D347. Updated April 2010.

National Comorbidity Survey. 2005. NCS-R appendix tables: Table 1. Lifetime prevalence of DSM-IV/WMH-CIDI disorders by sex and cohort. Table 2. Twelve-month prevalence of DSM-IV/WMH-CIDI disorders by sex and cohort. http://www.hcp.med.harvard.edu/ncs/publications.php.

Neergaard, L. 2009. Nicotine hit could slow recovery from PTSD. *Des Moines Register*, Metro Edition, January 28, 11E.

Neff, K. D. 2003. Self-compassion: An alternative conceptualization of a healthy attitude toward oneself. *Self and Identity* 2(2):85–102.

———. 2009. Self-compassion. In *Handbook of Individual Differences in Social Behavior*, edited by M. R. Leary and R. H. Hoyle. New York: Guilford Press.

———. 2011. *Self-Compassion: Stop Beating Yourself Up and Leave Insecurity Behind*. New York: HarperCollins.

Neff, K. D., S. S. Rude, and K. Kirkpatrick. 2007. An examination of self-compassion in relation to positive psychological functioning and personality traits. *Journal of Research in Personality* 41(4):908–916.

Newberg, A., and M. W. Waldman. 2010. *How God Changes Your Brain: Breakthrough Findings from a Leading Neuroscientist*. New York: Ballantine.

Norris, J. K. 2011. The power of sound to heal. *Noetic Post* 3(1):1–2.

Park, C. L. 2009. Overview of theoretical perspectives. In *Medical Illness and Positive Life Change: Can Crisis Lead to Personal Transformation?*, edited by C. L. Park, S. C. Lechner, M. H. Antoni, and A. L. Stanton. Washington, DC: American Psychological Association.

Pearlman, L. A., and K. W. Saakvitne. 1995. *Trauma and the Therapist: Countertransference and Vicarious Traumatization in Psychotherapy with Incest Survivors*. New York: W. W. Norton.

Pennebaker, J. W., and R. S. Campbell. 2000. The effects of writing about traumatic experience. *Clinical Quarterly* 9(17): 19–21.

Pert, C. 1999. *Molecules of Emotion: The Science Behind Mind-Body Medicine*. New York: Simon and Schuster.

Peterson, D. 1968. *The Clinical Study of Social Behavior*. New York: Appleton Century and Crofts.

Power, E. 1992a. *Managing Ourselves: Building a Community of Caring*. Brentwood, TN: E. Power and Associates.

———. 1992b. *Managing Ourselves: God in Our Midst*. Brentwood, TN: E. Power and Associates.

Resick, P. A. 1994. Cognitive processing therapy (CPT) for rape-related PTSD and depression. *Clinical Quarterly* 4(3/4):1, 3–5.

Resick, P. A., and M. K. Schnicke. 1993. *Cognitive Processing Therapy for Rape Victims: A Treatment Manual*. Newbury, CA: Sage Publications.

Riggenbach, J. 2013. *The CBT Toolbox: A Workbook for Clients and Clinicians*. Eau Claire, WI: PESI Publishing and Media.

Robjant, K., and M. Fazel. 2010. The emerging evidence for narrative exposure therapy: A review. *Clinical Psychology Review* 30 (8): 1030–1039.

Rohn, J. 2014. Eight traits of healthy relationships. *Success*, February 14. http://www.success.com/article/rohn-8-traits-of-healthy-relationships.

Rosenbloom, D., and M. B. Williams. 2010. *Life After Trauma: A Workbook for Healing*. New York: Guilford Press.

Rosenthal, M. 2013. PTSD avoidance: Is it grounding your recovery to a halt? *Trauma! A PTSD Blog*. April 3. http://www.healthyplace.com/blogs/traumaptsdblog/2013/04/03/ptsd-avoidance-is-it-grounding-your-recovery-to-a-halt/.

———. 2015. *Heal Your PTSD: Dynamic Strategies That Work*. San Francisco: Red Wheel/Weiser.

Rothschild, B. 2000. *The Body Remembers: The Psychophysiology of Trauma and Trauma Treatment*. New York: W. W. Norton.

———. 2011a. *Eight Keys To Safe Trauma Recovery: Take-Charge Strategies to Empower Your Healing*. New York: W. W. Norton and Co.

———. 2011b. *Trauma Essentials: The Go-To Guide*. New York: W.W. Norton and Co.

Saindon, C. 2001. Good sleep hygiene. *Selfhelp Magazine*, February 14.

Schauer, M., F. Neuner, and T. Elbert. 2011. *Narrative Exposure Therapy: A Short Term Treatment for Traumatic Stress Disorders.* 2nd rev. ed. Cambridge, MA: Hogrefe Publishing.

Schiraldi, G. R. 1999. *Building Self-Esteem: A 125-Day Program.* Ellicott City, MD: Chevron Publishing Company.

———. 2000. *The Post-traumatic Stress Disorder Sourcebook: A Guide to Healing, Recovery, and Growth.* Los Angeles: Lowell House.

———. 2011. *The Resilient Warrior: Before, During, and After War.* Ashburn, VA: Resilience Training International.

Scurfield, R. M. 1994. War-related trauma: An integrative experiential, cognitive, and spiritual approach. In *Handbook of Post-traumatic Therapy*, edited by M. B. Williams and J. F. Sommer. Westport, CT: Greenwood Press.

———. 2011. 40 lessons unlearned about war and its impact: From Vietnam to Iraq. http://www.patriotoutreach.org/40_lessons.html.

Selye, H. 1936. A syndrome produced by diverse nocuous agents. *Nature* 138: 32–46.

Shapiro, F. 1995. *Eye Movement Desensitization and Reprocessing.* New York: Guilford Press.

Shomon, M. J. 2002. *Living Well with Autoimmune Disease: What Your Doctor Doesn't Tell You… That You Need to Know.* New York: HarperCollins.

Siegel, R. D. 2010. *The Mindfulness Solution: Everyday Practices for Everyday Problems.* New York: Guilford Press.

Simpson, K. R. 2011. *Overcoming Adrenal Fatigue: How to Restore Hormonal Balance and Feel Renewed, Energized, and Stress Free.* Oakland, CA: New Harbinger Publications.

Smyth, L. D. 1999. *Clients' Manual for the Cognitive-Behavioral Treatment of Anxiety Disorders.* Havre de Grace, MD: Red Toad Company.

Solomon, R. 2001. Dynamics of fear. Unpublished manuscript.

Southwick, S. M., and D. S. Charney. 2012. *Resilience: The Science of Mastering Life's Greatest Challenges.* New York: Cambridge University Press.

Spring, D. 1993. *Shattered Images: The Phenomenological Language of Sexual Trauma.* Chicago: Magnolia Street Publications.

Stien, P. T., and J. Kendall. 2004. *Psychological Trauma and the Developing Brain.* Binghamton, NY: The Hayworth Maltreatment and Trauma Press.

Sugar, J. A., and J. D. Ford. 2012. Peritraumatic reactions and posttraumatic stress disorder in psychiatrically impaired youth. *Journal of Traumatic Stress* 25(1):41–49.

Suyemoto, K. L., and X. Kountz. 2000. Self-mutilation. *Prevention Researcher* 7(4):1–4.

Taylor, P., ed. 2011. *The Military-Civilian Gap: War and Sacrifice in the Post-9/11 Era.* Washington, DC: Pew Social and Demographic Trends.

Tedeschi, R. G., and L. G. Calhoun. 1995. *Trauma and Transformation: Growing in the Aftermath of Suffering.* Thousand Oaks, CA: Sage Publications.

Tedeschi, R. G., C. L. Park, and L. G. Calhoun, eds. 1998. *Post-traumatic Growth: Positive Changes in the Aftermath of Crisis*. Mahweh, NJ: Lawrence Erlbaum Associates.

Tennen, H., and G. Affleck. 1998. Personality and transformation in the face of adversity. In *Post-traumatic Growth: Positive Changes in the Aftermath of Crisis*, edited by R. G. Tedeschi, C. L. Park, and L. G. Calhoun. Mahweh, NJ: Lawrence Erlbaum Associates.

Terr, L. 1994. *Unchained Memories: True Stories of Traumatic Memories Lost and Found*. New York: Basic Books.

Thompson, B. 2012. Experiential avoidance and its relevance to PTSD. *Portland Psychotherapy* (blog). October 19. http://www.portlandpsychotherapyclinic.com/training/blog/experiential-avoidance-and-its-relevance-ptsd.

Thompson, M. 2015. Unlocking the secrets of PTSD. *Time Magazine*, April 6. 185(12): 40–43.

Tick, E. 2005. *War and the Soul: Healing Our Nation's Veterans from Post-traumatic Stress Disorder*. Wheaton, IL: Quest Books.

Tompkins, M. A. 2014. Using CBT to challenge beliefs and promote curiosity during exposure therapy. *New Harbinger Blog for Professionals*, November 25. https://www.newharbinger.com/blog/using-cbt-challenge-beliefs-and-promote-curiosity-during-exposure-therapy.

Trautman, K., and R. Connors. 1994. *Understanding Self-Injury: A Workbook for Adults*. Pittsburgh, PA: Pittsburgh Action Against Rape.

Turunen, T. 2014. Trauma recovery after a school shooting: The role of theory-based psychosocial care and attachment to facilitating recovery. Academic dissertation. Tampere, Finland: Juvenes Print.

US Army WRAIR Land Combat Study Team. 2006. 10 tough facts about combat and what leaders can do to mitigate risk and build resilience. Washington, DC: Walter Reed Army Institute of Research.

US Department of Veterans Affairs. 2015. Health study for a new generation of US veterans. http://www.publichealth.va.gov/epidemiology/studies/new-generation/.

Van der Kolk, B. A. 1988. The biological response to psychic trauma. In *Post-traumatic Therapy and Victims of Violence*, edited by F. Ochberg. New York: Brunner/Mazel.

———. 1996. The complexity of adaptation to trauma: Self-regulation, stimulus discrimination, and characterological development. In *Traumatic Stress: The Effects of Overwhelming Experience on Mind, Body, and Society*, edited by B. A. Van der Kolk, A. C. McFarlane, and L. Weisaeth. New York: Guilford Press.

———. 1999. The body keeps the score: Memory and the evolving psychobiology of posttraumatic stress. In *Essential Papers on Post-traumatic Stress Disorder*, edited by M. Horowitz. New York: New York University Press.

———. 2014. *The Body Keeps the Score: Brain, Mind, and Body in the Healing of Trauma*. New York: Viking.

Van der Oord, S., S. Lucassen, A. A. Van Emmerik, and P. M. Emmelkamp. 2010. Treatment of post-traumatic stress disorder in children using cognitive behavioural writing therapy. *Clinical Psychology and Psychotherapy* 17(3): 240–249.

Virginia State CISM Team Members. 1998. *Telecommunication Stress Workshop*. Critical Incident Stress Management Annual Training, Virginia Beach, VA, June.

Weathers, F. W., B. T. Litz, T. M. Keane, P. A. Palmieri, B. P. Marx, and P. P. Schnurr. 2013. The PTSD checklist for DSM-5 (PCL-5). Scale available from the National Center for PTSD at http://www.ptsd.va.gov.

Weekes, C. 1986. *More Help for Your Nerves*. New York: Bantam Doubleday Dell Publishing Group.

White, M. 2013. Narrative therapy. http://www.massey.ac.nz/~alock/virtual/narrativ.htm.

Williams, M. B. 2012. Slogging the bog of war to return to the world of work. A workshop. Warrenton, VA: M. B. Williams.

Williamson, G., and D. Williamson. 1994. *Transformative Rituals: Celebrations for Personal Growth*. Deerfield Beach, FL: Health Communications.

Wilson, J. P., M. J. Friedman, and J. D. Lindy. 2001. *Treating Psychological Trauma and PTSD*. New York: Guilford Press.

Wise, S., and E. Nash. 2013. Metaphor as heroic mediator: Imagination, creative arts therapy, and group process as agents of healing with veterans. In *Healing War Trauma: A Handbook of Creative Approaches*, edited by R. M. Scurfield and K. T. Platoni. New York: Routledge.

Woll, P. 2009. *Resilience 101: Understanding and Optimizing Your Stress System After Deployment: Workbook for Veterans and Service Members*. Chicago: Human Priorities.

Wormeli, R. 2009. *Metaphor and Analogies: Power Tools for Teaching Any Subject*. Portland, ME: Stenhouse Publishers.

Yeager, A. F., and J. Irwin, J. 2011. Rehabilitative canine interactions at the Walter Reed National Military Medical Center. *US Army Medical Department Journal*, April–June, 57–60.

Yount, R. A., M. D. Olmert, and M. R. Lee. 2012. Service dog training program for treatment of posttraumatic stress in service members. *US Army Medical Department Journal*, April–June, 63–69.

Yule, W., A. Dyregrov, F. Neuner, J. W. Pennebaker, M. Raundalen, and A. van Emmerik. 2005. *Writing for Recovery: A Manual for Structured Writing After Disaster and War*. Bergen, Norway: Children and War Foundation.

Yule, W., A. Dyregrov, M. Raundalen, and P. Smith. 2013. Children and war: The work of the Children and War Foundation. *European Journal of Psychotraumatology* 4:18424.

Zampelli, S. O. 2000. *From Sabotage to Success: How to Overcome Self-Defeating Behavior and Reach Your True Potential*. Oakland, CA: New Harbinger Publications.

Mary Beth Williams, PhD, LCSW, CTS, is an author, researcher, lecturer, and trainer in the area of trauma. In addition, she treats trauma survivors in private practice at the Trauma Recovery Education and Counseling Center in Warrenton, VA. Williams is former president of the Association of Traumatic Stress Specialists. She is a trainer for US Customs and Border Protection, cofounder of the proposed 501(c)(3) US Vet Source, and author of many articles, chapters, and books about trauma disorders.

Soili Poijula, PhD, is a clinical psychologist, licensed psychotherapist, and director at Oy Synolon Ltd., a center for trauma psychology in Finland, where she has done pioneering work as a developer of post-trauma psychotherapy.

FROM OUR PUBLISHER—

As the publisher at New Harbinger and a clinical psychologist since 1978, I know that emotional problems are best helped with evidence-based therapies. These are the treatments derived from scientific research (randomized controlled trials) that show what works. Whether these treatments are delivered by trained clinicians or found in a self-help book, they are designed to provide you with proven strategies to overcome your problem.

Therapies that aren't evidence-based—whether offered by clinicians or in books—are much less likely to help. In fact, therapies that aren't guided by science may not help you at all. That's why this New Harbinger book is based on scientific evidence that the treatment can relieve emotional pain.

This is important: if this book isn't enough, and you need the help of a skilled therapist, use the following resources to find a clinician trained in the evidence-based protocols appropriate for your problem. And if you need more support—a community that understands what you're going through and can show you ways to cope—resources for that are provided below, as well.

Real help is available for the problems you have been struggling with. The skills you can learn from evidence-based therapies will change your life.

Matthew McKay, PhD
Publisher, New Harbinger Publications

If you need a therapist, the following organization can help you find a therapist trained in cognitive behavioral therapy (CBT).

The Association for Behavioral & Cognitive Therapies (ABCT) Find-a-Therapist service offers a list of therapists schooled in CBT techniques. Therapists listed are licensed professionals who have met the membership requirements of ABCT and who have chosen to appear in the directory.
Please visit www.abct.org and click on *Find a Therapist*.

For additional support for patients, family, and friends, please contact the following:

Anxiety and Depression Association of America (ADAA) **Visit www.adaa.org**

National Center for PTSD **Visit www.ptsd.va.gov**

National Suicide Prevention Lifeline
**Call 24 hours a day 1-800-273-TALK (8255)
or visit www.suicidepreventionlifeline.org**

For more new harbinger books, visit www.newharbinger.com

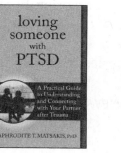
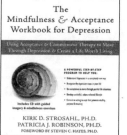

Register your **new harbinger** titles for additional benefits!

When you register your **new harbinger** title—purchased in any format, from any source—you get access to benefits like the following:

- Downloadable accessories like printable worksheets and extra content
- Instructional videos and audio files
- Information about updates, corrections, and new editions

Not every title has accessories, but we're adding new material all the time.

Access free accessories in 3 easy steps:

1. Sign in at NewHarbinger.com (or **register** to create an account).

2. Click on **register a book**. Search for your title and click the **register** button when it appears.

3. Click on the **book cover or title** to go to its details page. Click on **accessories** to view and access files.

That's all there is to it!

If you need help, visit:

NewHarbinger.com/accessories

new harbinger
CELEBRATING
40 YEARS